PLEAS D0277179 K

QUICKER READING

by

HARRY BAYLEY, B.A., M.Ed.

Principal, Leyland Motors Limited
Day Continuation School

LONDON

SIR ISAAC PITMAN & SONS, LTD.

First Published 1957
Reprinted 1959, 1961

SIR ISAAC PITMAN & SONS, Ltd.
PITMAN HOUSE, PARKER STREET, KINGSWAY, LONDON, W.C.2
THE PITMAN PRESS, BATH
PITMAN HOUSE, BOUVERIE STREET, CARLTON, MELBOURNE
22-25 BECKETT'S BUILDINGS, PRESIDENT STREET, JOHANNESBURG

ASSOCIATED COMPANIES
PITMAN MEDICAL PUBLISHING COMPANY, Ltd.
39 PARKER STREET, LONDON, W.C.2

PITMAN PUBLISHING CORPORATION
2 WEST 45TH STREET, NEW YORK

SIR ISAAC PITMAN & SONS (CANADA), Ltd.
(INCORPORATING THE COMMERCIAL TEXT BOOK COMPANY)
PITMAN HOUSE, 381-383 CHURCH STREET, TORONTO

The author gratefully acknowledges permission to reproduce the following material—

Exercises 2, 20 and 40, from *The Case Book of Sherlock Holmes*, by permission of John Murray (Publishers) Ltd., and of the executors of the late Sir Arthur Conan Doyle.

Exercises 31 to 36 inclusive and 39, by courtesy of the Controller of Her Majesty's Stationery Office.

All other exercises are reproduced by permission of *The Manchester Guardian*, the author concerned, or both.

PRINTED IN GT. BRITAIN BY BELL AND BAIN, LTD., GLASGOW

F2-(B.599)

PREFACE

DURING the last fifteen years, large numbers of people in the United States have been trained to read at twice and even three times their original speed without losing any of the comprehension of the material which they are reading, and in some cases with a slight improvement in comprehension.

The techniques which have been so successful in America have been used in this country with similar results. This course at Leyland Motors Limited has enabled executives to read at more than double their original speed, and to acquire a further reading technique which has enabled them to deal with their everyday reading in a very much shorter time. The course has been successful with executives of many other companies, with students in Technical Colleges, with Police Officers and a French version has been used in Paris recently.

Quicker reading techniques have been developed because of the increasing amount of written material which the executive, the professional man and woman and the student find that they have to read and absorb. They are a modification of and improvement on the good reading ability which such people already have and all good readers can, with practice, effect such an improvement in their reading speed and ability as to make the necessary time and effort well worth while.

This course is based on one which was primarily designed to improve the reading speed of executives, but it has been found to be capable of a wider application. It has been successful with men of twenty-five and men over sixty, with University graduates and with men who left school at fourteen, and monthly tests over a year following the course have shown that there is no falling away from the high levels reached, and that people, once they have improved their reading ability and incorporated this new technique into their everyday life, retain their high speeds for as long as they are regular readers.

TABLE OF CONTENTS

WHY QUICKER READING?

As the tempo of modern life increases, and as the range of man's knowledge is extended, one of the most irritating aspects of the professional man's working life is the amount of written material which he must read. It may be in the form of letters, government circulars or text-books and scientific and technical journals which must be read if he is to keep abreast with the latest developments in his own line.

That this proves a most irksome burden is shown by the way such journals and government pamphlets accumulate on the desk of the busy man. Such accumulations can only lead to neglect of this written matter and such neglect is harmful to efficiency.

In this country and in America, methods have been sought to ease this burden, and three possible solutions have been proposed. The first is to reduce the amount of written material to be read by persuading the authors to present their materials in a more understandable form, by expressing their ideas more clearly, avoiding set phrases and reducing unnecessary verbiage. Sir Ernest Gower has been an able exponent of this solution, and in his book *Plain Words* he says—" Only the right words can convey the right meaning; the golden rule is to pick these words and to use them only."

This is indeed a counsel of perfection, but it has had little effect on the literary outpourings of civil servants to whom it was particularly addressed. Another exponent of this idea was George Bernard Shaw, who reduced his answers to correspondence to a minimum by simply writing " Yes " or " No " on a postcard; generally it was " No "; but he had few followers in this, for business custom and the ordinary rules of polite society are both opposed to such rude brevity.

The second solution to the problem of the large amount of reading matter which faces the professional man is to have the material simplified and presented in an abbreviated form. The continued success of *Readers' Digest* and of the many other Digests is a good example of the successful application of this method, and some attempts have been made to use this technique in connexion with technical literature. There is on sale in this country at least one magazine which performs this service for production engineers by giving abbreviated reports of innovations in the production engineering field. But the mass of written material which we have to face does not lend itself particularly to the " Digest " technique, for much of it is personal and ephemeral and of only temporary value. In addition it is not always possible to reduce a difficult and complex idea to a simple and abbreviated form without losing a good deal of the meaning. With the best will in the world it is impossible to express Einstein's Theory of Relativity in simple English so that it can be clearly understood by all.

We must digest our own reading and the only way we can do this more efficiently is to learn to read better and quicker. The word *better* is vital here, for it must be clearly understood that when the quicker reading technique is used correctly, the amount of the material which is remembered after one reading is at least as much, and generally more, than that remembered after a slow reading. This third solution, although it is something of a novelty in this country, has been widely adopted in America, where the techniques of quicker reading have been developed over the last twenty years and are now firmly established as being of great value to the busy executive, the professional man and woman, and the student.

Almost all the American business organizations which run courses in supervisory training at any level incorporate a course in quicker reading, and in the larger cities Reading Clinics have been established. Here the whole range of reading ability from the backward to the high speed reader is dealt with, usually in a building specially designed for the purpose, and which is staffed with teachers, an oculist, a psychologist and a psychiatric social worker.

Mr. Percy Wilson, Her Majesty's Chief Inspector of Schools, after a recent visit to the United States said—

" Some reading clinics in America certainly overemphasize the idea of speed alone, and they seem to have little difficulty in doubling or trebling most people's reading rate. But most of the clinics are not satisfied to stop at that. They want not only speed but understanding."—*The Listener*, 10th March, 1955.

The techniques employed in America are tried and tested and their success has been established beyond doubt, and the present writer makes no claim to originality on this score. The methods used in this book are those which have been successfully employed in America for the last twenty years. It is the *aim* of the course which is different, and this has led to the use of material of a different quality, for in many American test pieces the vocabulary is simple and the ideas are straightforward and well connected.

This is not the case with the reading material which faces the average executive at Leyland Motors Limited, for whom this course was originally designed. He is not faced with a pile of almost completely monosyllabic stories to read, but a large amount of material where, not only is the vocabulary difficult, but the ideas are complex, occasionally somewhat disjointed and often not clearly expressed.

The aim of this course is to enable you to read at double your normal reading speed the kind of material which you are likely to find on your desk any morning, be it correspondence, a government circular or an article in the technical press. As a result of this, it follows that the material used in this course is far more complex and involves a much larger vocabulary than that employed by the normal American " quicker reading " course.

In the selection of material a close approximation to the same level of difficulty (or a little higher) as the executive's daily reading has been aimed at, and some attempt has been made to group material in order of increasing difficulty.

In order that comprehension might be adequately tested, material about which the average executive in a motor engineering firm might have prior knowledge has had to be rejected, and this has, of course, increased the difficulty of most of the test pieces as compared with the executive's daily reading, which is generally about some topic with whose background he is familiar.

The grouping of the material in order of difficulty results in a somewhat variable rate of increase in speed and reading ability. The idea is that the student should be speeded up on relatively easy material and then be changed to progressively more difficult material without any loss of speed or comprehension. It has been found that with the average reader, a fifty per cent increase in speed can be expected during the course of the first few lessons, and that there is continuous improvement as long as the same type of material is used. When the reading speed has been at least doubled, more difficult material is introduced and there is generally a slight falling off in speed. After some practice, this is recovered, and this is the pattern for the rest of the course; a high speed is reached and then maintained in spite of a considerable increase in the difficulty of the material.

That quicker reading is within the reach of the average good reader has been proved in America over the last twenty years, and experiments in this country by the author and others have done nothing to cast doubt on the validity of the results quoted by the American pioneers in the teaching of the quicker reading technique.

WHAT IS YOUR READING SPEED?

BEFORE we can measure any improvement, we must find out what your reading speed is now. The following two passages will establish this. You should read them at your normal speed and then answer the questions at the end.

It is most important that you have an accurate record of the time it takes you to do this and a stop watch is the best means of checking your time. If you haven't one and cannot easily get one, you can do it with an ordinary watch with a second hand. If you are using an ordinary watch, a note should be made at the side of the paper of the time at which the passage is to be started. The reading should start when the second hand is at zero, and a note be made of the time of finishing. This may seem rather an elaborate procedure, but if these times are not noted then an error of a minute is often made. Split second accuracy of timing is not essential, and times can be rounded to the nearest five seconds in order to calculate the speed in words per minute. The improvement in reading speeds will be quite obvious although the timing may be somewhat rough.

So if you have everything ready you can go ahead with the following test piece, but don't forget to start your stop watch or make a note of the time on your ordinary watch.

EXERCISE 1

Welcoming the Return of the Sun by K. Westcott Jones

[START TIMING] The phenomenon of the Midnight Sun above the Arctic Circle is familiar to thousands of visitors from lower latitudes every summer. The opposite effect when the sun is near its maximum southerly declination during the winter months is rarely observed by foreigners in North Norway. Nevertheless a population of 400,000 persons living in advanced conditions in Norway's three northernmost counties of Nordland, Troms, and

Finmark is plunged into darkness from the end of November to mid-January.

This dark period, relieved only by a pale glow of Arctic twilight for an hour or so around noon if the sky is clear, is known as "Mörketiden." It includes a state of mind among many adults described vaguely as "dark fright." More than half the persons aged 50 or over suffer from this mental condition during the depths of winter. It causes depression, nerves, inability to sleep at the normal time, yet renders patients virtually comatose once they have fallen asleep, when it may take several hours to awaken them.

The return of the sun is therefore extremely welcome to both Laplanders and Norwegians. In order to observe some of the celebrations which take place at the time of the year's first sunrise, I made a January voyage by coastal steamer from Bergen to twenty-six towns and settlements in the Norwegian Arctic as far as Kirkenes near the Soviet frontier.

Although calculations show that the disc of the sun cannot be visible until after 23rd January, in the region of North Cape its oblique rays below the horizon cause a surprisingly powerful twilight which heralds its return at least a fortnight beforehand. This light glows in the sky for as long as eight hours, and the strange effect is called "Tussmörke."

Most Laplanders are nomadic, but live in tent communities during the winter on the Finmark plateau or the desolate Varanger-Halvöy. Each family lives in its own tent, surrounded by branded reindeer which always stay close at hand. On the day that the full disc of the sun becomes visible for the first time after Mörketiden, the heads of the families announce the Sun Day celebration. This takes the form of general prayer during the period the sun is unobscured, but it is not sun worship. The Lapps (or Same, as they prefer to be called) are entirely Christian. After the thanksgiving prayers, families gather in their tents to drink black coffee and eat smoked reindeer meat. If any alcoholic drinks have been stocked by the men, they go from tent to tent offering a small sip, but supplies are unobtainable on the high plateau and any liquor acquired during visits to the coastal township the previous summer is invariably exhausted before the Sun Day feast.

The Same are in no way concerned with the fixed date of sunrise, but reserve their celebrations until they can see the disc cloudlessly revealed. As a result, numerous festivals take place on different days across the North of Norway, while the few Laplanders who may be visiting coastal towns follow their customs on seeing the sun for the first time, praying in the street if occasion arises.

Norwegians celebrate the return of the sun in definite ways. They, too, await cloudless vision, even though it may take a week after the known reappearance of the sun above the horizon. A holiday is declared in the town sighting it, and schools close. At Vardö, in Finmark, guns are fired from the fort to announce the Sun Day. The general custom all over the North is to take " Sol Kaffe " (Sun Coffee) at the homes of friends, which practice resembles the Scottish Hogmanay celebrations. Some small townships stage dances and offer coffee and cakes at the community hall, but in most cases the revelry is carried out in private houses.

Vardö, facing east into the Arctic Ocean, was first to sight the sun this year and celebrated Sun Day on 25th January. Vadsö, some fifty miles south-east of Vardö, followed with a festival the next day. I was fortunate in seeing the year's first sunrise at Masöy, in seventy-one degrees North, on 27th January, when it presented an unforgettable spectacle, bathing the top promontory of Europe with rich light for the first time for sixty-nine days.

Laplanders outside Karasjok on the Finmark plateau had their first glimpse of the sun and called a Sun Feast on 28th January. Reports indicate that several Same who were journeying across the plateau in a snowmobile from Kautokeino left the vehicle to pray in the snow shortly before they were due in Karasjok.

Although the sun is now well above the horizon each day and advancing as fast as twenty-five minutes every twenty-four hours to the condition whereby the Arctic enjoys constant light, several places on the North-West coast have yet to see it, owing to obstructing mountains or persistent cloud. Tromsö, a town of twelve thousand people, described as the " Paris of the Arctic," does not keep " Sun Coffee " celebrations, but all school children in the town were given a holiday on 30th January when the sun broke clear of cloud and shone on the harbour for more than an hour.

Surprisingly, a few mountain-girt villages in Southern Norway are unable to obtain a glimpse of the sun until March, and one Telemark village called Rjukan does not celebrate until early

April. An attempt was made to reflect the sun into Rjukan's deep valley by a mirror erected on the top of a mountain, but the artificial celebrations lacked fervour in spite of the efforts of Sam Eyde, the mirror's builder, and the Rjukan Festival in April has become the latest but most widely attended in Norway. [STOP TIMING]

Put your reading time here.........................

Now answer these questions which will test how much of the passage you have retained. For each statement there is only one correct answer. Tick the alternative which you think is correct, and when you have done this mark your answers right or wrong.

1. The dark period causes people over fifty—
   (a) To be very cheerful and happy.
   (b) To carry on their work as normal.
   (c) To leave the district.
   (d) To go to bed until it is over.
   (e) To suffer from depression.
2. The day the celebration is held is—
   (a) The day the sun's light is first seen again.
   (b) The day the full circle of the sun is clearly seen.
   (c) The day when the sun should appear above the horizon.
   (d) The first clear day after February first.
   (e) The second Sunday in February.
3. In Lapland the sun's return is celebrated by—
   (a) A day's holiday for the school children.
   (b) An outburst of drunkenness.
   (c) Prayers and a family gathering.
   (d) The firing off of pistols and revolvers.
   (e) A sledge ride.
4. In Norway the celebration consists of—
   (a) Heavy drinking of spirits.
   (b) A carnival through the streets of the town.
   (c) A day's holiday for everybody.
   (d) A public celebration in the evening.
   (e) A holiday from school and coffee drinking.
5. Some towns do not see the sun until March because—
   (a) They face north.
   (b) They are high on a plateau.
   (c) They face due east.

(*d*) They are covered by fog in the winter.

(*e*) They are at the bottom of deep valleys.

The correct answers are at the foot of page 18. You can find your speed of reading by dividing the number of words by the number of seconds you took and multiplying the answer by sixty or alternatively by looking in the following table. This passage has 940 words.

Time	Speed	Time	Speed
2.00	470	4.00	235
2.10	432	4.10	225
2.20	402	4.20	217
2.30	376	4.30	209
2.40	352	4.40	202
2.50	333	4.50	194
3.00	313	5.00	188
3.10	296	5.10	181
3.20	282	5.20	176
3.30	268	5.30	171
3.40	256	5.40	166
3.50	245	5.50	161
4.00	235	6.00	157

Speed........................ Comprehension........................

You have got the idea now of how we are going to test your speed and comprehension throughout this book, and it is quite possible that you read at slightly less than your normal speed because you were unfamiliar with the set-up, or you may have got most of the answers wrong for the same reason.

The following passage is one of a series of three taken from the same book of short stories by the same author which you will read as you work through the book so that you can compare your speed on material of identical difficulty. For the level of difficulty of the vocabulary and content are bound to be very similar. In order to compare these speeds you should get a good score on the comprehension tests in them all, for that is the only proof that you have understood what you are reading. If you got less than three out of five correct on the previous exercise, read a little more slowly, for that is not good enough.

Read this at your normal comfortable speed and time it.

EXERCISE 2

Extract from " The Adventure of the Illustrious Client "
by Sir Arthur Conan Doyle

[START TIMING]   I was living in my own rooms in Queen Anne Street at the time, but I was round at Baker Street before the time named.   Sharp to the half-hour, Colonel Sir James Damery was announced.   It is hardly necessary to describe him, for many will remember that large, bluff, honest personality, that broad, clean-shaven face, above all, that pleasant, mellow voice.   Frankness shone from his grey Irish eyes, and good humour played round his mobile, smiling lips.   His lucent tophat, his dark frockcoat, indeed, every detail, from the pearl pin in the black satin cravat to the lavender spats over the varnished shoes, spoke of the meticulous care in dress for which he was famous.   The big, masterful aristocrat dominated the little room.

" Of course, I was prepared to find Dr. Watson," he remarked, with a courteous bow.   " His collaboration may be very necessary, for we are dealing on this occasion, Mr. Holmes, with a man to whom violence is familiar and who will, literally, stick at nothing. I should say that there is no more dangerous man in Europe."

" I have had several opponents to whom that flattering term has been applied," said Holmes, with a smile.   " Don't you smoke?   Then you will excuse me if I light my pipe.   If your man is more dangerous than the late Professor Moriarty, or than the living Colonel Sebastian Moran, then he is indeed worth meeting. May I ask his name? "

" Have you ever heard of Baron Gruner? "

" You mean the Austrian murderer? "

Colonel Damery threw up his kid-gloved hands with a laugh.

" There is no getting past you, Mr. Holmes!   Wonderful!   So you have already sized him up as murderer? "

" It is my business to follow the details of Continental crime. Who could possibly have read what happened at Prague and have any doubts as to the man's guilt!   It was purely a technical legal point and the suspicious death of a witness that saved him!   I am as sure that he killed his wife when the so-called ' accident ' happened in the Splügen Pass as if I had seen him do it.   I knew, also, that he had come to England, and had a presentiment that sooner or later he would find me some work to do.   Well, what has Baron

Gruner been up to? I presume it is not this old tragedy which has come up again? "

" No, it is more serious than that. To revenge crime is important, but to prevent it is more so. It is a terrible thing, Mr. Holmes, to see a dreadful event, an atrocious situation, preparing itself before your eyes, to clearly understand whither it will lead and yet to be utterly unable to avert it. Can a human being be placed in a more trying position? "

" Perhaps not."

" Then you will sympathize with the client in whose interests I am acting."

" I did not understand that you were merely an intermediary. Who is the principal? "

" Mr. Holmes, I must beg you not to press that question. It is important that I should be able to assure him that his honoured name has been in no way dragged into the matter. His motives are, to the last degree, honourable and chivalrous, but he prefers to remain unknown. I need not say that your fees will be assured and that you will be given a perfectly free hand. Surely the actual name of your client is immaterial? "

" I am sorry," said Holmes. " I am accustomed to have mystery at one end of my cases, but to have it at both ends is too confusing. I fear, Sir James, that I must decline to act."

Our visitor was greatly disturbed. His large, sensitive face was darkened with emotion and disappointment.

" You hardly realize the effect of your own action, Mr. Holmes," said he. " You place me in a most serious dilemma, for I am perfectly certain that you would be proud to take over the case if I could give you the facts, and yet a promise forbids me from revealing them all. May I, at least, lay all that I can before you? "

" By all means, so long as it is understood that I commit myself to nothing."

" That is understood. In the first place, you have no doubt heard of General de Merville? "

" De Merville of Khyber fame? Yes, I have heard of him."

" He has a daughter, Violet de Merville, young, rich, beautiful, accomplished, a wonder-woman in every way. It is this daughter, this lovely, innocent girl, whom we are endeavouring to save from the clutches of a fiend."

" Baron Gruner has some hold over her, then? "

" The strongest of all holds where a woman is concerned—the hold of love. The fellow is, as you may have heard, extraordinarily handsome, with a most fascinating manner, a gentle voice, and that air of romance and mystery which means so much to a woman. He is said to have the whole sex at his mercy and to have made ample use of the fact."

" But how came such a man to meet a lady of the standing of Miss Violet de Merville? "

" It was on a Mediterranean yachting voyage. The company, though select, paid their own passages. No doubt the promoters hardly realized the Baron's true character until it was too late. The villain attached himself to the lady, and with such effect that he has completely and absolutely won her heart. To say that she loves him hardly expresses it. She dotes upon him, she is obsessed by him. Outside of him there is nothing on earth. She will not hear one word against him. Everything has been done to cure her of her madness, but in vain. To sum up, she proposes to marry him next month. As she is of age and has a will of iron, it is hard to know how to prevent her."

" Does she know about the Austrian episode? "

" The cunning devil has told her every unsavoury public scandal of his past life, but always in such a way as to make himself out to be an innocent martyr. She absolutely accepts his version and will listen to no other."

" Dear me! But surely you have inadvertently let out the name of your client? It is no doubt General de Merville."

Our visitor fidgeted in his chair.

" I could deceive you by saying so, Mr. Holmes, but it would not be true. De Merville is a broken man. The strong soldier has been utterly demoralized by this incident. He has lost the nerve which never failed him on the battlefield and has become a weak, doddering old man, utterly incapable of contending with a brilliant, forceful rascal like this Austrian. My client, however, is an old friend, one who has known the General intimately for many years and taken a paternal interest in this young girl since she wore short frocks. He cannot see this tragedy consummated without some attempt to stop it. There is nothing in which Scotland Yard can act. It was his own suggestion that you should be called in, but it was, as I have said, on the express stipulation that he should not be personally involved in the matter. I have no doubt, Mr. Holmes, with your great powers you could easily trace my client back through me, but I must ask you, as a point of honour, to refrain from doing so, and not to break in upon his incognito."

Holmes gave a whimsical smile.

" I think I may safely promise that," said he. " I may add that your problem interests me, and that I shall be prepared to look into it. How shall I keep in touch with you? "

" The Carlton Club will find me. But, in case of emergency, there is a private telephone call, ' XX.31 '."

Holmes noted it down and sat, still smiling, with the open memorandum-book upon his knee.

" The Baron's present address, please? "

" Vernon Lodge, near Kingston. It is a large house. He has been fortunate in some rather shady speculations and is a rich man, which, naturally, makes him a more dangerous antagonist."

" Is he at home at present? "

" Yes."

" Apart from what you have told me, can you give me any further information about the man? "

" He has expensive tastes. He is a horse fancier. For a short time he played polo at Hurlingham, but then this Prague affair got noised about and he had to leave. He collects books and pictures. He is a man with a considerable artistic side to his nature. He is, I believe, a recognized authority upon Chinese pottery, and has written a book upon the subject."

" A complex mind," said Holmes. " All great criminals have that. My old friend Charlie Peace was a violin virtuoso. Wainwright was no mean artist. I could quote many more. Well, Sir James, you will inform your client that I am turning my mind upon Baron Gruner. I can say no more. I have some sources of information of my own, and I dare say we may find some means of opening the matter up." [STOP TIMING]

Put your reading time here........................

1. Sir James Damery was—
   (*a*) A dark and swarthy foreigner.
   (*b*) A bluff honest Scotsman.

B

(*c*) A broad fair Scandinavian type.

(*d*) A big masterful aristocrat.

(*e*) A small fair Englishman.

2. He welcomed Watson's presence because—

   (*a*) Two heads are better than one.

   (*b*) They were dealing with a very dangerous man.

   (*c*) His medical knowledge would be useful.

   (*d*) He was an old acquaintance.

   (*e*) He had no confidence in Holmes alone.

3. Baron Gruner was—

   (*a*) A French Apache.

   (*b*) A dangerous American confidence trickster.

   (*c*) A foreign criminal of unknown origin.

   (*d*) The leader of a gang of anarchists.

   (*e*) A murderer from Austria.

4. He had not been convicted for the murder because—

   (*a*) He was innocent.

   (*b*) He had disposed of an important witness.

   (*c*) There were no witnesses to the crime.

   (*d*) He had bribed the judge.

   (*e*) The jury had failed to agree.

5. Holmes was commissioned—

   (*a*) To prevent Gruner committing another crime.

   (*b*) To have Gruner convicted of a previous crime.

   (*c*) To find out all about Gruner.

   (*d*) To help the police break up Gruner's gang.

   (*e*) To make Gruner leave the country.

6. At first Holmes would not act because—

   (*a*) He was afraid of Gruner.

   (*b*) He wanted to know who his client really was.

   (*c*) He was too busy with other cases.

   (*d*) He thought the case dull and uninteresting.

   (*e*) He thought Gruner had done no wrong.

7. Violet de Merville loved Gruner because—

   (*a*) He had an irresistible attraction for women.

   (*b*) He was such an upright character.

   (*c*) They had so many interests in common.

   (*d*) She was attracted by his criminal record.

   (*e*) He had hypnotized her.

8. They had met—

    (*a*) On an Atlantic liner.
    (*b*) During a winter sports holiday in Switzerland.
    (*c*) Whilst climbing in the Austrian Alps.
    (*d*) On a Mediterranean cruise.
    (*e*) At the Ascot race meeting.
  9. Gruner had told Miss de Merville—
    (*a*) Nothing of his past.
    (*b*) The complete truth about his past.
    (*c*) A completely biased version of his past.
    (*d*) A little about his past.
    (*e*) That he would turn over a new leaf.
10. Holmes' client was—
    (*a*) General de Merville.
    (*b*) A friend of General de Merville.
    (*c*) Sir James Damery.
    (*d*) Doctor Watson's best friend.
    (*e*) Revealed in the course of this extract.
11. The Baron lived—
    (*a*) In a hotel in Bloomsbury.
    (*b*) In a small house in the West End.
    (*c*) At a hotel near Hyde Park.
    (*d*) In an apartment at Surbiton.
    (*e*) In a large house at Kingston.
12. The Baron was a man—
    (*a*) Of very narrow tastes.
    (*b*) Who was interested in all kinds of sports.
    (*c*) Who was widely respected at Hurlingham.
    (*d*) Of no artistic tastes.
    (*e*) Of very wide interests.
The correct answers are at the foot of page 18.

See how many answers you have right and then work out your speed of reading and put it, and your comprehension score, in the space below. This passage has 1,500 words.

Time	Speed	Time	Speed
3.00	500	3.50	392
3.10	473	4.00	375
3.20	450	4.10	360
3.30	428	4.20	346
3.40	408	4.30	333

Time	Speed	Time	Speed
4.40	321	6.30	231
4.50	310	6.40	225
5.00	300	6.50	219
5.10	290	7.00	214
5.20	282	7.10	209
5.30	273	7.20	205
5.40	264	7.30	200
5.50	257	7.40	196
6.00	250	7.50	191
6.10	243	8.00	188
6.20	236		

Speed........................   Comprehension........................

Now you know your reading speed on two passages. It may be higher than the normal 200 words a minute or it may be lower. That is not important, for whatever it is you will be able to double it and maintain the same comprehension score or even improve on it. You will not be able to do this without hard and sustained effort, there is no magic about the systems advocated in this book, and if you feel that the advantages will not be worth the effort you should stop now.

You have now established your reading speed and are in a position to start to improve it. In the following chapters you will find a series of lessons which it is suggested should be done in stages, and there are supplementary exercises at the back.

You cannot expect to change the reading habit of a lifetime in the short time which it will take you to read these exercises each day, but you will be able to change them if you use the techniques which are suggested with all the reading that you do, not only during the time you are taking the course, but all the time.

At first you will have to make a conscious effort to do this and may find it rather trying and wish that you could go back to the jog-trot methods which you have used for so long. Within a few weeks, however, the new technique will become as automatic as your present method is now; there will be no conscious striving to improve, for the improvement will have become consolidated, and high speed reading will be your normal method.

THE READING PROCESS

BEFORE the question of how to improve reading technique can be considered, some knowledge of the reading process is essential, for high speed reading is merely the logical development of good reading.

Reading is a combined physical and mental activity, and during reading there is co-ordination between the muscles of the eye and the brain of a most complex nature. At the physical level the eye acts as a lens which is responsive to the light reflections of an object. A picture of that object, towards which the eye is directed, is reflected on to the retina, in the same way that the lens of a camera reflects an image on to a film. But the pictures provided by the eye are not recorded automatically, the brain selects what is desired, and retains some sights, whilst rejecting others.

The eye provides the picture and is, for most, the physical instrument of reading. It is necessary to be sure that the eye is working well before any reading improvement programme is undertaken, and if spectacles are worn, their efficiency should be checked.

The eye provides the picture, but the brain gives that picture meaning. In the same way, when the eye takes in a word, which is a symbol (possibly of an object) the brain gives that word meaning. The same word may have several different meanings, and in that case, the brain sorts out the correct one, having regard to the context.

When reading a line of print, the eye moves from left to right, not in a regular flow, but jerkily, stopping here and there, for very small intervals of time. This movement may be seen if a mirror is arranged so that the eyes of the reader may be clearly observed. At first, the only thing to be noticed is the large eye movement from right to left from the end of one line to the beginning of the next, but, after a time, it is possible to see the movements in between. Such eye movements have been accurately recorded on

17

cinema film and a comparison of the stops and the text being read has enabled their purpose to be definitely established.

It is accepted that reading only takes place whilst the eye is stopped, and as soon as possible, the eye moves on to the next stopping place. This is usually farther along the line, but there may be a backward movement if the text has not been perfectly understood. The number of stops which the eye makes for each line of print is linked with the reading ability of the reader and the difficulty of the subject matter. Whatever material is used, the slow reader makes many more eye stops or fixations, as they are called, than the efficient reader does, and this is the main reason why it takes him so much longer. In addition, he goes back fairly frequently to read again what he has not perfectly understood. Such backward movements are called regressions. The following diagram illustrates the eye movements of the slow reader—

s   s   s   s   s   s   s   s   s

Almost everyone, with training, can read better and faster.

It is clear that the slow reader stops his eyes at every word and then goes back to read some of them over again. The efficient reader's eye movement diagram shows that he adopts a different method—

s   s   s   s

Almost everyone, with training, can read better and faster.

The number of stops, or fixations, has been reduced and there are no backward movements or regressions at all. There is a tendency away from reading word by word and towards taking in a phrase at a time. The high speed reader carries this tendency even farther and can take in such a line in not more than two glances, and his eye movements for the same line could be diagrammatically illustrated thus—

s   s

Almost everyone, with training, can read better and faster.

Answers to Exercise 1—1 (*e*), 2 (*b*), 3 (*c*), 4 (*e*), 5 (*e*).

Answers to Exercise 2—1 (*d*), 2 (*b*), 3 (*e*), 4 (*b*), 5 (*a*), 6 (*b*), 7 (*a*), 8 (*d*), 9 (*c*), 10 (*b*), 11 (*e*), 12 (*e*).

It should be remembered that watching the eye movements of an individual will only indicate what type of reader he is on that kind of material. Many fixations and regressions are the mark of the poor reader, and few fixations and no regressions the mark of the good reader.

An individual has little conscious control over his eye movements, although he can usually decrease the number of regressions which he makes, therefore he cannot improve his reading merely by reducing the number of fixations. It is his capacity to understand the material, judged by himself, which controls the number of stops. When he improves his reading ability generally, that will reduce the number of fixations.

It is only by raising the general level of reading ability and improving by other methods the eye span, that is the amount that can be taken in and understood at one glance, that reading ability may be improved by positive methods, for the other improvements which may be made are results of the breaking down of faulty reading habits which have been built up and maintained throughout a person's reading career. This may have lasted for a considerable period of time and such habits are not going to be wiped out in a day or a week.

The eradication of bad habits of any kind needs hard work and perseverance and, above all, a strong will to root them out. It is so with bad reading habits, but the busy executive has a very strong motive to get rid of them, and provided he is prepared to make the necessary effort during and after the course, he is bound to succeed.

The part played by the eye in reading is important, but not essential, for Braille has shown that reading can be carried on without sight. The vital part in reading is played by the brain, which enables the meaning to be discovered, and, if desired, retained. The speed at which we understand what we are reading is much lower than that at which we can see the words, and here again, old habits and old saws impede the desire to improve technique, for everybody has been told at some time to read more slowly and carefully in order to get better understanding. Excellent advice for the beginner, but an impediment to the efficient. Experience with quicker reading techniques has proved that the average reader reads at a speed far below his best, and that it is quite possible for him to double his reading speed and still understand what he reads. Comprehension is the name given to the process by which we understand what we are reading, and increasing the speed of comprehension is the aim of the quicker reader.

Comprehension

Comprehension is entirely a mental process, the nature of which is not clearly understood, but the connexion between fast and efficient reading and good comprehension was noted by the pioneer enquirers into the nature of the reading process. They noted, too, an occasional tendency amongst children to attempt to read faster than their comprehension would allow, and their reaction to that was to tell the children to read slowly and carefully, a precept which is of no value to the adult reader whose powers of comprehension are much superior to those of a child.

It is quite possible, of course, for adults to read so fast that their comprehension begins to fade, but the speed at which this happens is far in excess of their ordinary reading speed. During the first course at Leyland Motors, one of the students, who began the course with a reading speed of 350 words per minute, read a passage at more than 1,000 words per minute, but with very poor comprehension. He had gone beyond his ability to take in the meaning. He dropped his speed and was able to read similar passages at 750 words per minute with satisfactory comprehension.

It is clear that speed of comprehension varies in accordance with the reader's estimate of the difficulty of the material, that the normal detective story with a strong plot and a small number of characters can be understood more quickly than a Government White Paper, but whatever type of matter is read, speed can usually be improved without loss of understanding.

That this should be so, is so contrary to general opinion that some further explanation must be attempted. When people read at their normal speed, at a comfortable jog trot of about 200 words per minute, or less if the material is thought to be very difficult, they are well within their mental capacity and have mental energy to spare. This often provides distractions which may take the form of semi day-dreams about a word which has associations for them, or of worries about whether they have understood what they are reading, causing them to regress, to turn back, and often to lose the thread of the argument.

The high speed reader is not troubled by such distractions. All his mental energy is devoted to acquiring the meaning of the passage as quickly as possible, and it is noticeable that he is less likely to be diverted by outside influences. He is, in fact, absorbed in his job, and has no attention to spare for anything else. His understanding is almost at full stretch, and, provided that he does not go beyond this, he will have as good a mastery of what he has read quickly as if he had taken twice the time.

To claim that he will have as good an understanding as with a slow reading is quite different from claiming that he will have perfect comprehension. The only valid measure of the extent to which a passage has been understood is the correct answering of questions based on the passage or the re-writing of the most important points of the passage. Because of difficulties of marking, the first measure is the one generally adopted, and again in order to make the marking uniform, the question is usually asked in the form of a statement which has to be completed by the testee selecting one response out of five. This is the kind of test of comprehension which is used in this course and its reliability and validity are accepted.

Experiments have shown that the normal comprehension score on tests of this type, however slowly the passage has been read, is about sixty to seventy per cent, if no re-reading of the passage is allowed. These are the conditions under which the quicker reading test pieces are given and a sixty to seventy per cent score on the comprehension tests is regarded as satisfactory. It is at this level that the comprehension tests which form an integral part of any quicker reading course are aimed. The number of questions which may be asked about any passage depends, to a large extent, on the content of the passage. If a simple narrative is being read, then all that needs to be remembered is the main outline of the plot, but if a detailed account of an unfamiliar process is being read, many more detailed questions are required in order to discover how much has been understood.

The first type of passage is not extensively used in this course which has been designed with the reading of executives in mind, and the level of difficulty of the passages used is high. As the main aim of the course is to speed up the reading and comprehension of executives, reading for pleasure has been left out of account.

In the selection of passages, care has been taken to choose none in which a prior knowledge of the subject matter would be expected from an executive of a large engineering firm, as such prior knowledge would invalidate any comprehension test, for the reader might be able to answer the questions without reading the passage at all. So varied are the interests of individuals, however, that there are likely to be passages of a general nature with the contents of which some individuals may be familiar. These cannot be used by them as tests of comprehension.

Reading Speed

The idea of measuring reading efficiency by the time taken to read a passage and understand its contents has been accepted for many years. It is customary to speak of children as being quick or slow readers according to whether they are efficient or not. In most pursuits, speed is used as a criterion of efficiency provided that a reasonable standard of performance is maintained, and this is the basis of many of the pay schemes in industry. For time is money and the time of the busy executive is worth more than that of most other workers.

Quicker reading is work-study applied to reading and the chief measuring instrument is the stop watch and the comprehension test. The early pioneers of the reading process assessed reading speeds as the number of words read per second, which had the disadvantage of either bringing in many awkward fractions, or making the measure a rather vague one if the figures were rounded to the nearest word. Nowadays, the usual measure is the average number of words read in a minute, and this is the measure which has been adopted for this course.

Once again it must be pointed out that a reading speed without a reasonable level of comprehension has no validity, but it must be accepted that the first efforts at quicker reading may result in comprehension scores slightly below the sixty to seventy per cent level for the occasional student, and he should not be discouraged by this. The reason for this is that he is trying consciously to improve a technique which has long become automatic, he is giving thought to a thing about which he has not had to think for a long time, and the result may be a temporary weakness in understanding what is written which is shown by relatively poor scores on the comprehension tests.

Although the reader may be keen on improving his technique, it is difficult for him to break the easy going habits of a lifetime, and there may be an unconscious reluctance to speed up in some cases, a natural desire to take things easy. This resistance to improvement is generally soon broken down, and speed and comprehension increase together.

Every test piece is this book should be accurately timed, and a stop watch is the best instrument for this purpose.

THE remainder of this book is devoted to improving your reading speed as measured on the first two test pieces whilst maintaining your comprehension at the sixty to seventy per cent level. You should read the book and do the exercises over a period of several days, doing not more than two or three sections per day, and remember that you cannot change the habits of a lifetime in a short period of a few days. You must practise the methods suggested here in all your reading throughout the training period, so that they will become automatic and you will replace your present inefficient technique by a new and efficient method.

HOW TO IMPROVE

THE essential thing for improvement is confidence in your ability to improve and a realization that the work involved, and it will be hard work, will be worth the trouble because of the benefit which quicker reading will be to you. You have read of the improvement shown by people of widely varying types and you may be sure that you can do the same, provided that your present standard of reading is already high enough for you to have read the initial test pieces and completed a reasonable number of correct questions on the comprehension tests.

Forget all about " Reading Slowly and Carefully " and accept the idea that you can with training read twice as fast, just as so many other people have done.

Make sure that you are comfortably seated and have adequate light. Concentrate on the job in hand, don't smoke or make any unnecessary movements whilst you are reading.

Head Movements

One of the most common movements is to move the head from side to side as you read a line. There is no need for this, as your eyes will swivel over a much wider angle than is needed for them to read a line. If you are not sure that you can stop moving your head voluntarily, hold it in your hands and make a conscious effort to speed up and you will find that you can read the following exercises a little faster than you did the first ones.

EXERCISE 3

The " Planing Hull " in Dinghy Sailing by Philip Hays

[START TIMING] Since 1939 the number of racing dinghies in Great Britain has multiplied, it has been estimated, between five and six times. A yachting magazine has pointed out that for the 1939 season the Yacht Racing Association, as it then was, listed

126 racing fixtures; for the coming season the Royal Yachting Association list totals 1,334. These figures help to illustrate the development, amounting almost to a revolution, which has overtaken small-boat sailing since the war.

At its worst, dinghy-racing is rarely dull. At its best—and it is often at its best—it provides as much interest for those taking part in it as riding in the Grand National or going down the Cresta Run. There can be few sports which give competitors so many rewarding moments; and even fewer which are open to so many people, at such low cost.

The development of the planing hull is probably the main reason for the growth of the sport. Planing is the word used to describe the phenomenon involved in sailing on the water instead of through it. Given a wind of sufficient strength—in many cases, ten or twelve knots will do—a racing dinghy can be persuaded to rise those few inches which make all the difference to its performance. From then on it will behave like a runaway, and keeping it under control will need most of the strength and ingenuity of the helmsman and his crew; or of the helmswoman and her crew, since every class nowadays has its feminine experts.

With the larger dinghies (18 ft or thereabouts) the maximum speed will be around sixteen to eighteen knots. Anyone seeing for the first time a comparatively small sailing craft going at this speed will probably wonder if he can believe his eyes.

Frequent capsizes are the price that is paid for this sort of speed. In a race on the Thames last autumn for the Merlin-Rocket class, on an occasion when a strong and gusty wind got up soon after the start, 40 out of the 50 competitors capsized. In general, capsizing is to the small-boat sailor what the occasional fall is to a hunting man; it is not so much a measure of his competence but of his preference for being a thruster, for " pressing on regardless." The modern dinghy can normally be righted by its occupants without outside help, and its buoyancy bags enable it to be sailed on while bailing is in progress. Races have been won by boats which have capsized not once, but twice.

Planing can only be achieved when the boat is sailing " off " the wind; that is, with the wind on the beam or aft of it. This in itself has altered the principle by which races were mainly won or lost. For many years races had mainly been won—in the larger yacht racing classes they still are—by performance on the wind, with the competitors close-hauled to a wind coming from ahead. After a race had been in effect decided by the windward leg of the course, the downwind legs were frequently a procession, restful but unexciting. They provided opportunities for producing sandwiches and coffee.

Nowadays, so long as there is a good breeze—and it is not often that the British climate fails to supply one—every moment of a race offers opportunities to the hardworking helmsman and crew to improve their position. Close-hauled sailing in a big criss-crossing fleet of boats calls for immense skill. A reaching leg, with the wind on the beam, may see a boat go ahead in a series of breathless surges. With the wind astern, working the spinnaker will give helmsman and crew few dull moments.

Trailers

The growth of interest in sailing small boats has been accompanied by the growth of the trailer movement. Thanks to his trailer, the enthusiastic sailor can be racing one week-end at an open meeting near Bristol, the next at Hunstanton, the next on a Birmingham reservoir. (On the next he may even contemplate visiting his home club on the Solent, to be greeted like a prodigal son.) Part of his annual holiday may be spent at one of the classic regatta weeks—Cowes or the Clyde, Poole or Burnham-on-Crouch. Another part will almost certainly be spent at his class championship week in still another part of the country. If, like a considerable number of leading helmsmen, he owns two or three boats of different classes, his opportunities are doubled or trebled.

At all these meetings the local helmsman has the opportunity to rub shoulders with visiting rivals who may have sailed in the Olympics or be approaching that status. There is constant interchange of ideas and improvement in standards.

One minor revolution has gone almost unnoticed. Five years ago it was still possible to regard small-boat sailing as a sport for which " any old clothes " would do. It is now generally appreciated that to keep going until the end at the top of the performance a helmsman and his crew will be all the better for being dry and warm, rather than being spray-soaked and numbed with cold. So clothes are chosen for quality, and the manufacturers have not neglected their appearance; an open dinghy meeting is a bright and colourful scene. How much of the attractiveness and colour is due to the influence of the increasing number of young women sailors is an interesting speculation. [STOP TIMING]

Put your reading time here.......................

1. The number of racing dinghies has—
   (a) More than doubled since 1945.
   (b) Been trebled since 1940.
   (c) Increased four times since 1935.
   (d) Increased between five and six times since 1939.
   (e) Increased between eight and ten times since 1935.

2. Dinghy-racing is—
   (a) Expensive but exciting.
   (b) Cheap but not very thrilling.
   (c) Reasonably cheap and most exciting.
   (d) Fairly expensive and occasionally thrilling.
   (e) Very expensive and very thrilling.

3. The maximum speed with a large dinghy is—
   (a) Between six and eight knots.
   (b) Between eight and ten knots.
   (c) Between ten and twelve knots.
   (d) Between twelve and fourteen knots.
   (e) More than fourteen knots.

4. Races are now decided more by the boat's performance—
   (a) When sailing against the wind.
   (b) When sailing with the wind astern.
   (c) When sailing with the wind on the beam.
   (d) At all times.

5. Dinghy sailors usually—
   (a) Sail in their home waters.
   (b) Wear old clothes.
   (c) Take their boats about the country.
   (d) Are men only.
   (e) Rarely capsize.

The correct answers are at the foot of page 30.

This exercise has 900 words and you can work out your speed from the following table.

Time	Speed	Time	Speed
2.00	450	3.20	270
2.10	415	3.30	255
2.20	385	3.40	245
2.30	360	3.50	235
2.40	337	4.00	225
2.50	318	4.10	216
3.00	300	4.20	209
3.10	284	4.30	200
3.20	270		

Speed........................   Comprehension........................

Now try the next exercise and remember to keep your head still.

EXERCISE 4

Dead Falls by Stephen Bone

[START TIMING] Our car, covered with dust from half the provinces of Sweden, ran on through the summer night. It was hardly dark enough for headlights and we could see the fields below us where the hay was drying on long fences; the wooden farmhouses, each with its group of barns and stables, dairies and byres; and the curves of the great river—the Indalsälv—wanly reflecting the pale sky. As always in Northern Sweden the horizon was serrated by the pointed tops of innumerable fir trees, but the great sub-arctic forest through which we had been travelling all day had at last drawn back a little and the cultivated valley floor was two or three miles wide.

On the edges of this farmland, where it began to slope upwards to the wooded hills, there were some old whitewashed churches, but in the middle of the valley there was none, for in the days of Swedish church building this farmland had been covered with water and a long sinuous lake extended where the peasants now cut their hay. The lake had filled the valley since long before history, but after the early hours of 7th June, 1796, it filled the valley no longer. We would stop a little further on and visit Döda Fallet—the Dead Falls—in order to understand more clearly what had happened on that memorable night.

The dusty road and the big river travelled down the valley in company; whenever we looked to the right there was the gleam of water a mile away and a few hundred feet below. We rounded a corner and saw a parking place and a shuttered refreshment hut. A single yellow light shone from the window of a small restaurant where, in spite of the late hour, they were still busy washing up. Paper wrappings and picnic rubbish were entangled in the roadside bushes.

Long flights of steps descended precipitately through pines and birches to a confusion of rocks, smoothed and scoured and worn into potholes by the water which had once thundered over them, for we were standing on the rocky ridge which used to dam back the waters of the Indalsälv and over these rocks they once tumbled in a huge white confusion, sweeping on down into the narrow gorge which now holds nothing but a dark, stagnant pool.

This great waterfall must have been a wonderful spectacle, but the people who lived up the valley all hated it. Many of them worked as lumbermen, but if they tried to float timber downstream the logs arrived torn and smashed and useless. Many were fishermen, but no salmon could jump such an obstacle. The people were poorer than their downstream neighbours and they blamed the fall.

There had been talk of doing something about it. The natural dam was not all rock; some was sand and gravel deposited by a glacier long vanished, but even so it could hardly be shifted by the spadework of a few peasants. However, there was one ingenious man named Huss and nicknamed " Wild." He saw that a small but impetuous river could be diverted so that it would erode the gravelly part of the dam. " Wild " Huss diverted it so that it cut a deepening gulley in the soft soil.

When June comes in Northern Sweden the rivers are brimming with snow water from the mountains. In June, 1796, the Indalsälv was in full flood. " Wild " Huss had weakened the barrier, and on the night between 6th and 7th June it collapsed. The lake emptied, the great waterfall fell silent, and a huge mass of water hurled itself down the sleeping valley. It was as if someone had emptied Windermere in a few hours. Incredible as it seems, no one appears to have been killed, but even " Wild " Huss must have been appalled at what he had done.

The logs could now come down and the salmon could go up,

c

and there was the old bed of the lake to be cultivated. Those who benefited from the change were at least as numerous as those who had lost houses and cattle, and the author of this catastrophic alteration became popular when his awestruck neighbours had recovered from their shock.

As we stood on the odd rocks in the middle of the Dead Falls I reflected that practical men dislike waterfalls to-day as then. No. They dislike them more now than they did then, for waterfalls to-day are not only obstacles to river navigation; they are seen as vast sources of power not properly utilized. "Running to waste," says the hydraulic engineer sourly as he thinks in terms of kilowatts, and soon the rocky chasm will be dry and dusty and the thundering white water will flow decorously down iron pipes to the power station.

Swedes seem to find this dead waterfall of great interest. We can show them plenty. There are the Falls of Clyde, the Falls of Morar, and the falls on the River Spean—dead or nearly dead. There are the dry boulders marking the place where spray once rose from Earlstoun Linn, wetting the rowan trees by Allengibbon Bridge. There is the grudging trickle that comes down the great ravine at Foyers, a trickle so small that on the arrival of tourists, the local inhabitants are said to supplement it with bucketfuls and "pail their ineffectual Foyers," as an Edwardian traveller once said.

Even in Sweden with its vast river system and its small population some concern is now felt, and it is hoped that a little of this wild beauty may yet be saved from the demands of electrified railways, lighting, heating, radios, refrigerators, telephones, vacuum cleaners, electric irons, cookers, immersion heaters for hot water, clever little razors, and all this gadgety collection that binds us firmly together with bits of copper wire.

" They'll keep Stora Sjofallet up in Lapland," said my Swedish friend. " It's a big tourist attraction, but that's the only one I really feel sure about."

" Perhaps High Force will survive for a bit," I said: " they charge admission there, and so they do at Devil's Bridge, but if the charabancs fall below twenty a day, I expect those waterfalls will be put into pipes like so many others."

Answers to Exercise 3—1 (*d*), 2 (*c*), 3 (*e*), 4 (*d*), 5 (*c*).

" And we'll get more English tourists in Lapland," said he.
" Come on, we'll never reach Sundsvall to-night." [Stop Timing]
Put your reading time here.........................

1. This passage is about—
    (*a*) The biggest waterfall in Sweden.
    (*b*) A waterfall which is used for electric power.
    (*c*) A picnic by a waterfall.
    (*d*) A waterfall which is now dry.
    (*e*) Methods of draining lakes.

2. The author at the time was—
    (*a*) Ski-ing in Norway.
    (*b*) On a tour of Sweden.
    (*c*) On a tour of Norway.
    (*d*) On a tour of Lapland.
    (*e*) On the way home from Lapland.

3. " Wild " Huss—
    (*a*) Diverted the waterfall to make electric power.
    (*b*) Drew off water for irrigation.
    (*c*) Built a dam and made a waterfall.
    (*d*) Caused a flood to annoy his neighbours.
    (*e*) Diverted a stream and eroded the dam.

4. The waterfall is now—
    (*a*) The site of a statue to " Wild " Huss.
    (*b*) A popular place for a picnic.
    (*c*) Only visited by lumberjacks.
    (*d*) One of the show places of the district.
    (*e*) The home of a hydro-electric engineer.

5. When the dam collapsed—
    (*a*) Thousands of people were hurt.
    (*b*) Hundreds of people were killed.
    (*c*) Some people were drowned.
    (*d*) Many people were hurt.
    (*e*) There was no loss of life.

You will find the correct answers at the foot of page 34.

This passage has 1,090 words and you can work out your speed
from the following table.

Time	Speed	Time	Speed
2.30	445	3.50	284
2.40	409	4.00	272
2.50	384	4.10	260
3.00	363	4.20	251
3.10	342	4.30	242
3.20	327	4.40	233
3.30	311	4.50	225
3.40	297	5.00	218
3.50	284		

Speed........................   Comprehension........................

Now that you have stopped moving your head, you should have shown an increase of speed.

ARE YOU A SILENT READER?

You will no doubt answer " Yes " to the question at the top of this page, but if your present reading speed is less than 400 words a minute, you answer " No."

When you were taught to read, your ability was checked by reading aloud, and a link has been established between the written word and the sound of it which is difficult to break, but which is one of the main causes of slow reading.

You have all seen very slow readers in the bus or public library who actually say each word out loud as they read it, the next stage being moving the lips but not making any sound. I hope you don't do that, but I am sure that if your reading speed is below 400 words a minute that you are putting in sound between the eyes and the meaning.

Instead of seeing the word or words and recognizing their meaning immediately, as you do with a road sign, you are interposing an unnecessary stage. This means that your reading cannot exceed the speed at which you can talk to yourself. Which may be why the average reading speed of adults is 200 words per minute.

You must try and reduce this tendency to sound, although it is only in your mind, so *think of it* when you do the next exercise.

EXERCISE 5

Greyfriars For Ever by Alan Shadwick

[START TIMING] " Hello, Hello, Hello ";

Now surely I know that voice? It rings a bell—a school bell. Hark how it comes echoing down the corridor of the years as I open this book in a shop in the Charing Cross Road. Is that you, Bob Cherry, and is it possible that you are still at school—you who were a boy when I was a boy, and how long before that, from all accounts? I see that it is possible, for you were still at Greyfriars in 1948 when Mr. Frank Richards put out this novel.

But the stentorian cry that used to thrill me as the sound of trumpets now grates a little on my middle-aged ear. Put a sock in it, Cherry, while I recall the lineaments of that land of lost content where I never thought to come again.

For I was a Greyfriars boy. Indeed Mr. Frank Richards surely created his school specially for such as me. He was a great educational benefactor who put his school fees as low as twopence a week. It was not much to pay to pass, if only after a spiritual fashion, straight from the streets of Lancashire to the lanes of Kent. The swaying tram might be grinding slowly but exceedingly surely towards a red brick school which was turning black in a district ironically called Greenacres, but with the twopenny magazine open on the knee (when it might have been more profitable to be glancing at a French vocabulary) one was wafted on a fragrant air to that brighter world " down South," as Mr. Priestley's Jess Oakroyd used to put it with such eloquent economy.

It seemed a world in which the winters were cleaner and colder, the summers hotter, and the autumns crisper than we knew them in the rude North. A jam tart in the Greyfriars tuckshop was not the same thing as a jam tart on the counter of a shop in Oldham. The latter comestible (one slips into the Greyfriars lingo) was somehow mixed up with mill girls at dinner time, or with high teas in the gaslight, but jam tarts and doughnuts at Greyfriars evoked the flash of white flannels and the merry sound of bat against ball, bicycle rides through lanes, incredibly leafy, and even picnics by the sea. For if I remember rightly, we had all this and the ocean too. There was never a dull moment. How could there be, with Bob Cherry swaggering up and down the passages making that fearful row, and Harry Wharton continually punting a footer about in the quad, with all that bumping of Billy Bunter and ragging of Mr. Quelch, all those booby traps and apple-pie beds? It was an active life. With the exception of a few cads, Greyfriars fellows were not the sort to frowst over a study fire on a half holiday. Now in the uproar of the Charing Cross Road, I feel the impact of that staggering morale. It is not quite forty years on, but those fellows show no sign of weakening. Flicking through the pages I find Bob Cherry suffering an unjust sentence

---

Answers to Exercise 4—1 (*d*), 2 (*b*), 3 (*e*), 4 (*b*), 5 (*e*).

of expulsion. Naturally, Cherry is innocent, " I'd rather be sacked than tell lies," he says again, " A fellow can't cheek his pater." It is enough to make an old boy of the school take off his hat and stand for a few moments in silence, even in a London bookshop. Now the young Lord Mauleverer emerges, like a noble peak amid the stormier elements. As usual, he is resting his aristocratic limbs in a deep armchair, and to hear him talk you would think it was the smoking room in a club in St. James's. " Mind shuttin' up, Skinner? " he drawls. " You rather get on a fellow's nerves, if you don't mind me mentioning it." Not at all, Mauly, we don't mind a bit. We like to hear you runnin' on like that, and saying " Yaas." This languid posturing puts us in mind of the Scarlet Pimpernel, cool as a cucumber in a tight corner, or Sir Francis Drake finishing his game of bowls and thrashing the Spaniards as well. It is the beautiful sang-froid of old England, horribly dated but bearing the charm of all period pieces.

But when Billy Bunter hurls a rolled-up newspaper and it catches Lord Mauleverer " under a noble ear " and the young nobleman cries out " Oh gad! What the dooce! " it is too much for me. It is altogether too much if I am to believe that he is still fifteen years of age. Nevertheless, I will buy this book, for there is one voice in it that does not ring false under the arches of the years. It is odd that the most grotesque character at Greyfriars should remain the most convincing. I'll have the book for Billy Bunter's sake. He was always hard up, hungry, and hopeful.

Nothing has happened in the intervening years to cast a doubt on the likelihood of that situation. Summers are not so golden after all, and there is something to be said for frowsing over the fire on a beastly day. There is also something to be said for decent jam tarts. Besides, what library is complete without a place for England's fat boy? [STOP TIMING]

Put your reading time here........................

1. The author states—
   (a) He went to school at Greyfriars.
   (b) Attended another school in the North.
   (c) Was educated by Frank Richards.
   (d) He didn't like Greyfriars.
   (e) He went to Greyfriars on the tram.

2. The author believes—
   (*a*) That food in the South is best.
   (*b*) That Oldham food is dirty.
   (*c*) That ordinary food seems better in schoolboy's stories.
   (*d*) That life at Greyfriars was dull.
   (*e*) That his schooldays were better than Bob Cherry's.

3. The author—
   (*a*) Hates Bob Cherry and Harry Wharton.
   (*b*) Finds the tales of Greyfriars annoying now.
   (*c*) Remembers his childhood with sadness.
   (*d*) Has fond memories of Cherry and Wharton.
   (*e*) Thinks Cherry and Wharton ridiculous.

4. The only character who still seems true to life is
   ....

5. The author found the book about Greyfriars in—
   (*a*) Oldham.
   (*b*) Charing Cross Road.
   (*c*) Tottenham Court Road.
   (*d*) The school library.
   (*e*) A railway bookstall.

The correct answers are at the bottom of page 38.

This has 750 words and you can find your speed from the following table.

Time	Speed	Time	Speed
1.30	500	2.30	300
1.40	449	2.40	281
1.50	410	2.50	265
2.00	375	3.00	250
2.10	346	3.10	237
2.20	322	3.20	225
2.30	300	3.30	214

Speed......................   Comprehension......................

Did you notice that you were putting sound in between the words and the meaning? I expect that you did.

There is no easy way to reduce it. It is a matter of practice and the following exercises are for this purpose.

EXERCISE 6

The Technician by Donald Howorth

[START TIMING] We had reached that stage of the flight when we no longer had any interest in our fellow-passengers, nor in the magazines, nor in sighting ships on the tinfoil Atlantic.

The engineer officer awoke me with a blow on the shoulder. "How're you doing, kid?" he said. The voice and the awakening punch were familiar from somewhere remote. Then there was the face, glowing as though a lamp were lit inside, that on each morning of the first months of the Air Force had watched my awakening from the next bed. In those days, having roused me, he would lean back again on his bolster and smoke his pipe, watching with tranquil blue eyes the man who moved about the room; and when I stirred, he would make a gesture of derisive approval with the pipe stem and announce the day, the date, and the year. It happened every morning. He was then an old man, 27 or 28, with the Christian name of Cartwright (so called, we understood, after his maternal grandfather, who had invented a self-opening umbrella), and before he joined up he ran his own garage somewhere in Birmingham.

"There are a lot of sharks in our business," he would say. "You wouldn't last five minutes, kid."

He was clever. He mended the sprung sole of my boot with only the bent nails that came out of it. He made the lock on the door of our room work. And one day, without practice, he reassembled a ·303 Browning. None of us had really seen the parts before then. A corporal regularly pulled the thing to bits for us, but he was very sad, and we either dozed or read the " Daily Mirror." This day the armaments officer sneaked in.

"Yah pipple very sharp," he said. " Understand this sort of thing without paying attention. You, cadet, would you be good enough to reassemble it for us?"

Cartwright looked at the parts as though he were in two minds whether to recommend a new one instead. Then he slowly began to put it together, turning each part over in his hand, understanding them, establishing a sort of communion with them as a man does with wine. " There you are, Sir, as good as new."

He said afterwards that the parts put themselves together for him. " Things always do as I want them. For you they don't.

As soon as you touch a thing, springs fly out all over the room. Now me, I'm the same way with people. It's a hoodoo; stay with me long enough and you'll be a goner."

He told me of a childhood companion flung off a roundabout which he had pushed too hard, of an aunt burned out of her home by the firework he dropped, of a workman who one day fell from a scaffold high on the garage wall because he did not know Cartwright had emptied concrete from a bucket and overbalanced when he lifted it. His whole life, calmly reviewed through tobacco smoke, unrolled like the scenario of a heartless Mack Sennett.

It was obviously senseless to have accepted his offer to teach me to swim, but it promised an escape from the humiliation of the official method. A sergeant would draw us across the surface with a long pole to assure us, as he said, that " Water is buoyant." But he was prone to play to the gallery, and when his brief verbal wit ran out he would dabble us about at the end of the pole like a man cleaning a brush; this was always well received. So I took up Cartwright's offer (his grandfather had been Warwickshire's champion swimmer), and one day we went to the baths alone. He showed me on the banking how to cup my hands and lift my head to breathe; then, without warning, he nudged me in at the deep end. I remember the crash as though the glass roof had shattered, the leaping fronds of water, chlorine bitter in the throat, the contorted tiles below, lights bouncing momentarily across the surface. I saw him fill his pipe; and again I saw him light it (it immediately glowed, of course, like a brazier). I wondered whether they would let him have a last smoke before they hanged him; and in the serenity of the thought I began to move forward through the water towards the pipe.

" Not bad for a beginner," he said, " but you'll have to cultivate a smoother stroke."

" I might have drowned."

" I thought you were going to at one time, kid, but that's life— sink or swim." He prodded his pipe. " You won't have to yell like you did; you've got to grow up sometime."

I survived our remaining months together with only minor injuries. It was his flying instructor whom he maimed, a precise young man who might have gone far. Their Tiger Moth,

---

Answers to Exercise 5—1 (*c*), 2 (*c*), 3 (*d*), 4 Billy Bunter, 5 (*b*).

approaching the runway a little wide, was seen to side-slip and shatter on the earth. " He won't walk again," Cartwright said in hospital. " Don't know what went wrong with him. He was driving. I was just sitting there enjoying the ozone, hands off, feet off. He'd have gone slap into No. 1 hangar if I hadn't given the rudder bar a gentle prod."

When he recovered he was dropped from the course and sent off to a flight engineers school. That was the last I saw of him until this day twelve years later returning from New York. He was wearing the ribbon of the D.F.M. on his civil airline uniform.

" Got that for keeping all the separate pieces airborne," he said. " Only three of us got out of that packet. They were remustered into another crew which also ' let out unlucky.' Civil aviation was surer!—though I've been in a couple of picnics since I joined this mob."

I did not learn exactly what the " picnics " were because he had to get back to the cockpit. " Can't manage without me, kid. I'm the king-pin of this outfit."

Shortly afterwards the warning to fasten belts was illuminated, but it was only a precaution against turbulence as we crossed the Scottish coast, and we cruised in to a smooth landing at Prestwick.

I had intended to go on to London, but I found on inquiry that there was a train from Glasgow which would get me to my destination almost as soon as the later one from London and with less trouble. It was a fine morning, and I always like to have a look at Sauchiehall Street. [STOP TIMING]

Put your reading time here.......................

1. The author had first met the engineer—
    (*a*) When they were both at the same school.
    (*b*) When they joined the army together.
    (*c*) In the Fleet Air Arm.
    (*d*) On a visit to America.
    (*e*) When they were both in the R.A.F.
2. Cartwright was particularly good at—
    (*a*) Anything connected with machinery.
    (*b*) Getting his own way with people.
    (*c*) Flying an aeroplane.
    (*d*) Radar and television.
    (*e*) Annoying his instructors.

3. He regarded himself as—
    (a) A clever man with many friends.
    (b) A stupid man whose friends did well.
    (c) A clever man without any friends.
    (d) A stupid man whose friends did badly.
    (e) A clever man whose friends did badly.
4. Cartwright was taken off flying duties because—
    (a) Of a plane crash.
    (b) His failure to pass examinations.
    (c) He annoyed the instructors so much.
    (d) Nobody liked him.
    (e) He was bored with the course.
5. The author's real reason for taking the train was—
    (a) He wanted to look around Glasgow.
    (b) He was bored with the flight.
    (c) Cartwright was on the plane.
    (d) He thought it would be quicker.
    (e) He didn't like flying.

The correct answers are at the foot of page 42.

This passage has 1,000 words and you can find your speed from the following table.

Time	Speed	Time	Speed
2.00	500	3.20	300
2.10	461	3.30	286
2.20	429	3.40	273
2.30	400	3.50	261
2.40	375	4.00	250
2.50	353	4.10	240
3.00	330	4.20	231
3.10	315	4.30	222
3.20	300		

Speed........................   Comprehension........................

Remember reduced vocalization means increased speed.

ON TALKING TO YOURSELF

THE theory that you are putting sound in between the word and the meaning has now been proved to you by your own experience. Everyone, even the most efficient reader, does it to some extent. There is no question of cutting it out altogether. But you must reduce it, for it is holding you back. When you do it you are not presenting the material to your brain at the speed at which it can be absorbed. The result is that you have, as it were, mental energy to spare and this takes one of two forms. Either you go off into a sort of day dream based on some pleasant recollection aroused by what you are reading, perhaps the name of some foreign town which you have visited, or you begin to doubt whether you are understanding what you are reading, and go back again to make sure. Perhaps a name which has been mentioned earlier in the passage is repeated towards the end, and you begin to worry about what was said about the person in the beginning, so you go back to find out. When you do this you lose the thread of the whole passage. You must make a conscious effort to reduce this talking to yourself when you attempt the next two exercises.

EXERCISE 7

Tied Petrol Stations by A Garage Proprietor

[START TIMING] The recent announcement by one of the major oil companies that it intends to build some 250 petrol stations must have caused many motorists to wonder what is happening in the field of petrol distribution and retailing.

Before the war, the large oil companies were content to sell their petrols through privately owned stations, offering a range of different brands; the range available at one site depending mainly on the number of pumps installed. Since the war, following the practice adopted in America and many other parts of the world,

41

the major oil companies have each sought to obtain sole representation at a petrol retailing site.

The interest in petrol retailing shown by the producers has resulted in a much-needed improvement in appearance and service provided by many privately owned petrol stations. The producer has assisted the retailer with specialized advice, with staff training schemes, and, above all, by the provision of capital to provide a clean, attractive station, which instead of being an eyesore, in many cases has become an asset to the neighbourhood. It is true that the oil companies have not been willing to provide capital, in some cases running into many thousands of pounds, without binding trading agreements and/or mortgages on the properties. The majority of such agreements are perfectly fair business arrangements from which both sides stand to gain.

From the point of view of the motoring public, it would appear to matter little who runs the petrol stations, provided they are efficient, but it is to be hoped that local authorities will stand firm and prevent the erection of excessive numbers of new ones. Whereas before the war the products of three or more companies might be sold from two petrol stations in one locality, now since the companies each wish to have their own " solus site " at least three are required. Local authorities are, in consequence, continually being faced with planning applications for the erection of new stations which all too frequently are put forward with little regard to the real needs of the consumer.

Quite apart from the effect of an increased number of stations on the general amenities of an area, the point may soon be reached where the available petrol business is spread among too many retail outlets with the result that none can function on an economically sound basis, particularly if each tries to provide a seven-day-a-week, round-the-clock service. Naturally, the company-owned sites are in a better position to withstand such competition, and inevitably, it will be the small man who is driven out of business. It is surely in the interests of all to avoid redundancy. At the moment it seems that this factor is only considered as a last resort.

The present action of the oil companies does not meet with the approval-of large sections of the motor trade, particularly of the

Answers to Exercise 6—1 (*e*), 2 (*a*), 3 (*e*), 4 (*a*), 5 (*c*).

small man who plays such a large part in the sale and service of motor vehicles all over the country. Too frequently to be ignored, disturbing reports are heard of traders who strive to remain independent being refused supplies of particular brands of motor fuels on that account. It is probable that oil company-owned filling stations will be leased to establish members of the motor trade on much the same lines as a public house is leased by a brewer. Operating policy is likely to be closely defined, and present information suggests that the owner will drive a hard bargain. It seems unlikely that the oil companies will attempt to run stations themselves, since experience in this connexion in America was not encouraging.

For the moment, at least, the motorist can sit back and watch the keen competition between petrol suppliers and retailers develop. It is to be hoped that it may result in a reduction in price, but it is not in anybody's real interest that it should lead to a wave of cut-throat competition. Until the Government makes a substantial reduction in the very high petrol duty of 2s. 6d. a gallon, there is little incentive for the oil companies to make appreciable reductions in price, and it must be borne in mind that the retail price of petrol (excluding tax) is but little more than twice what it was in 1938. This compares well with other basic commodities. Nevertheless, there is reason to believe that while most car owners want clean, prompt, and generally efficient service they do not look for free matches, keyrings, dusters, sponges, or similar articles. [STOP TIMING]

Put your reading time here........................

1. Before the war—
    (a) Petrol stations only sold one brand of petrol.
    (b) Petrol stations were few and far between.
    (c) Petrol stations only sold three brands of petrol.
    (d) Petrol stations sold two brands of petrol.
    (e) Petrol stations sold as many brands as they had pumps.
2. The petrol companies have—
    (a) Encouraged people to improve their service.
    (b) Lent money to improve amenities at petrol stations.
    (c) Built many new stations.
    (d) Bought many petrol stations.
    (e) Carried on as before the war.

3. The companies require new stations because—
    (*a*) More petrol is being sold than ever before.
    (*b*) They all want a solus site.
    (*c*) The number of stations is insufficient.
    (*d*) The supply of petrol is inadequate.
    (*e*) Building has been restricted until now.
4. This is seen as a threat to—
    (*a*) The small business.
    (*b*) The smaller oil firms.
    (*c*) The employees of the oil firms.
    (*d*) Public transport.
    (*e*) The independent garage.
5. Petrol prices cannot be much reduced because—
    (*a*) Freight charges are very high.
    (*b*) It is only twice its pre-war price.
    (*c*) Profits are very low.
    (*d*) Of the tax on petrol.
    (*e*) Of international price agreements.

The correct answers are at the foot of page 46.

This passage has 750 words, and you can find your speed from the following table.

Time	Speed	Time	Speed
1.30	500	2.20	322
1.40	449	2.30	300
1.50	410	2.40	281
2.00	375	2.50	265
2.10	346	3.00	250
2.20	322		

Speed........................   Comprehension........................

You may be finding that your speed is not going up regularly, but in fits and starts. There is nothing to be surprised at in this, for it would be impossible to find a set of exercises which were perfectly graded for all people. Variation is also introduced by yourself, for your performance will vary to some extent according to your state of mind. What we are concerned about is the general tendency to improve.

The next exercise is a little longer but bear in mind that you are trying to read faster by reducing the amount of inner speech.

You don't have to cut out vocalization completely before you can make real progress. All you have to do is to reduce it.

There are many degrees of this fault ranging from the very slow reader who has to speak the word he reads, to the high speed efficient reader who hardly ever uses inner speech. You are some-where in between, perhaps nearer the first than the last at the moment, but as you move towards greater efficiency you will vocalize less and less.

EXERCISE 8

Looking for Lions from a Correspondent

[START TIMING] I can honestly tell my grandchildren that I have taken part in a lion-hunt, though unless I yield to temptation I shall have to add that the real hero of the expedition was a motor car. And I shall also have to add that. But truth has many aspects and some can fairly be left to the end of a narrative.

Nairobi is full of interesting stories about lions, some of them quite possibly true. Shortly before we arrived (they told us) a lion chased a buck on to the main road from Nairobi to the airport, killed it, and sat in the middle of the road to eat his dinner. Nobody was particularly anxious to tell the lion to hurry up, and this lion liked a leisurely meal. Cars arrived in both directions, saw the lion, and stopped. Soon there were long lines of cars and lorries. Their drivers hooted angrily but the lion ignored them. After hold-ing up traffic for the best part of an hour he shook his mane, waved his tail in a condescending fashion, and moved off to have a nap.

I had two objectives in my personal lion-hunt. I wanted (a) to meet a lion at a reasonably polite distance—and (b) to find a discarded lion's claw to take home as a trophy. One can buy a lion's claw in Nairobi but they are mostly set in gold and cost rather a lot of money. I thought it would be cheaper as well as more enterprising to go and look for a claw myself.

With three companions I set off in an A.50, hoping that this would be respectable enough to meet with the local lion's approval. The "Visitor's Guide to Nairobi," published by the East African Tourist Travel Association, is quite firm about this.

"It is not uncommon (it says) to see a fine, maned lion looking with disgust at some old car, and then preening dignity and approval at the more expensive modern limousines."

D

The A.50 was nearly new, and I hoped it would come up to the lion's standard.

One seeks lions in the Royal Nairobi National Park, which is a stretch of country some hundreds of square miles in extent where lions and a host of other really wild animals wander freely. The park begins within a few miles of Nairobi and one can drive in it at will (or at least, wherever, the car can be persuaded to go). A car is essential, one is permitted to enter the game reserve only in a car, and warned not to get out of it. The " Visitor's Guide " explains, " The animals . . . have grown accustomed to the sight of shiny, smelly motor cars, almost to the point of treating them with disdain, and never, apparently, aware that they contain people."

The roads in the game reserve are not exactly roads as the Ministry of Transport would classify them in England; if we had C, D, and E roads coming after B roads on English maps, some of the game reserve roads might perhaps qualify for E. But by African standards they were familiar enough, and the Austin had nothing to worry about for the first few miles. The dust, of course, was appalling, and the springs were tested by dry ruts, but they were no worse than one would expect on a rather poor farm track in England. The lions were elusive but we met six giraffes, a magnificent herd of zebra, and several groups of most graceful, gazelle-like animals.

Then we met some baboons. We stopped the car to have a closer look at them, and in a moment they were all over us, climbing on the bonnet, jumping on the roof, and pawing at the windows. Fortunately, we shut the windows quickly. The baboons looked attractive and playful, but they are given a bad character—a paw through an open window can inflict a nasty injury. The only way to get rid of them was to drive on, and when the car started to move they hopped off readily enough. It was soon after leaving them that the thought occurred to me; what happens if we break a back axle?

What happens indeed? One of our party was a Kenya resident, and he told us a cheerful story of a man who was with his wife in the game reserve when their car broke down some miles from the outside world. After trying (and failing) to get it started, he

---

Answers to Exercise 7—1 (*e*), 2 (*b*), 3 (*b*), 4 (*a*), 5 (*d*).

decided that the only thing to do was to walk through the reserve for help. Leaving his wife shut safely in the car he set off, and had a bad two hours, but he emerged uneaten. The ending was encouraging, but none of us was particularly eager to volunteer to go on foot for help. Happily, the car still sounded healthy.

Still we had met no lions. It was about four o'clock in the afternoon and we decided it was probably too early and too hot. Lions like the cool of the evening and in the next hour or so would probably appear. We followed a signpost marked " Hippo Pool " and in a mile or two came among some trees with a river a few yards away. We met a native ranger who said that at this spot it was safe to leave the car. Confidence is a strange human commodity. There seemed no particular reason why this little glade should be safer than anywhere else, but we all accepted it as perfectly safe. And it was. We made our way to the river and were rewarded by seeing the nostril of a hippo showing just above the water, when one looked very hard, and a large and particularly ugly crocodile resting on a flat rock—safely on the far side of the river.

Time was getting on and we renewed our lion-hunt. We carefully studied a herd of zebra to see if they were moving in any particular direction, reasoning that the zebra were more alert to the presence of lions than we were. We thought that the herd did show some signs of restlessness, and very slowly we drove on the general line in which they were moving.

The next problem was technical: there was no road. The country was fairly flat, scrub-covered grass, but once off the road there was not even a track for a car. And the fairly long grass might easily conceal small ravines, several feet deep. But lion hunting is exhilarating, and I doubt if any of us really thought of the outrageous demands we were making on the car. We just followed the herd of zebra across the scrub.

The Austin jolted and grumbled a little, but took hillocks and a tussock very gallantly in bottom gear. We were finally stopped by a quite unmistakable ravine, about a dozen feet across and six feet or so in depth—not even the Austin could take it. It was lined with low bushes, beyond which the zebra were going out of sight. There was nothing to be done but to go back.

So, ingloriously, our lion-hunt ended. As we bumped and jolted our way back to the nearest track, we met another car coming towards us. We met it again about half an hour later and were disgusted to be told that about two minutes after we had left, no fewer than eight lions walked out of the bushes that had stopped us. " They lay on the ground like kittens and rolled over," the driver of the lucky car said.

We agreed that if we had seen no lions, at least we could say fairly truthfully that the lions in the bushes had had a good look at us. And it is something to have been looked at by eight lions, if not perhaps very heroic. But then the real hero of the hunt was the uncomplaining Austin. [STOP TIMING]

Put your reading time here........................

1. This incident happened—
   (a) In Sierra Leone near Freetown.
   (b) In the Kruger National Park.
   (c) In India near Nullahbad.
   (d) In Kenya near Nairobi.
   (e) In Rhodesia near Salisbury.

2. Lion claws—
   (a) Are easily found.
   (b) Are expensive to buy unmounted.
   (c) Are difficult to find.
   (d) Are never found.
   (e) Are unsuitable as a trophy.

3. In the National Park—
   (a) People can walk about safely.
   (b) There are no places where people may walk.
   (c) It is essential to be well armed.
   (d) The animals will even attack cars.
   (e) People should generally stay in their cars.

4. In order to find lions—
   (a) The author walked near the Hippo Pool.
   (b) He tried to hire a native tracker.
   (c) He followed a herd of zebra.
   (d) He asked a native ranger.
   (e) He took along a deer as bait.

5. The author saw—
   (a) Baboons, giraffes and lions.
   (b) Zebra, deer and lions.
   (c) Eight lions rolling on the ground.

(d) Zebra, deer and giraffes, baboons and hippo.

(e) Zebra, deer and giraffes and lions.

6. What make of car was used ?........................

The correct answers are at the bottom of page 50.

This passage has 1,270 words and you can find your speed from the following table.

Time	Speed	Time	Speed
2.00	635	3.30	363
2.10	585	3.40	346
2.20	545	3.50	332
2.30	508	4.00	317
2.40	476	4.10	305
2.50	444	4.20	293
3.00	423	4.30	282
3.10	401	4.40	272
3.20	381	4.50	263
3.30	363	5.00	254

Speed........................   Comprehension........................

* * *

YOU MUST PRACTISE YOUR NEW READING TECHNIQUE ON ALL YOUR READING FOR YOU CANNOT CHANGE THE HABITS OF A LIFETIME MERELY BY COMPLETING THE EXERCISES IN THIS BOOK

NEVER LOOK BACK

ONE of the results of the slow and inefficient reading which excessive vocalization causes is a lack of confidence in your ability to absorb what you are reading. This may reach such a state that you have an almost irresistible tendency to go back and read over again some passage which you are not sure that you have understood.

You must fight this tendency, and it will help you if you take a sheet of plain paper and move it down the page as you read so that it covers what you have already read and makes it impossible for you to look back.

You could buy a machine which would do this for you, but if you get a sheet of paper or a ruler and cover the lines as you read the next exercise you can do without a machine.

The mechanical help is useful but it is more important that you should make up your mind now that you are not going to look back.

EXERCISE 9

The Tremor by Charles Greaves

[START TIMING] I have read lately that the scientists have now discovered that the universe is not governed by immutable laws; there are " wobblings." Well, it is the same with married life. Take the case of Ernest Pinder and his wife. Ernest came here from Accrington way shortly after the 1914-18 war, he having got a job in Simpson's dyehouse. He found lodgings and, shortly afterwards, attended the local chapel one Sunday evening. He liked the choir and, being a moderate tenor himself, asked to join it. Ernest made his first appearance on the following Sunday morning, little knowing that destiny was working her wiles. For,

---

Answers to Exercise 8—1 (*d*), 2 (*c*), 3 (*e*), 4 (*c*), 5 (*d*), 6 Austin.

facing him among the contraltos was the generous figure of
Myrtle Winterbottom. The Winterbottoms were, and always had
been, a highly respectable family, especially on the distaff side.
No Winterbottom ever skimped her corners. Not one had been
known to visit the frozen-meat end of the butcher's; only the
prime English for them.

In time Ernest was introduced to Myrtle. They got on well
together and began walking out. Eventually Ernest was honoured
by being invited to Sunday tea. As he sat at the table he observed
that the Winterbottoms were nourished on good solid fare and
plenty of it and that he was the smallest figure in the room.
Afterwards Mrs. Winterbottom took him aside and inquired about
himself. She then told him that of her four daughters Myrtle
was her pet. She almost monopolized Ernest all the evening,
except for the half-hour when the family markedly withdrew and
left Myrtle and himself in the parlour. As he left the house
Ernest felt pretty much the same as when he left the
dentist's after having a tooth out. All the same he determined
so to discipline himself that he would be worthy of such a
family.

He succeeded and presently married Myrtle. They went to
Prestatyn for the honeymoon and fell in love with the place. On
their return they occupied a small new house in Chrysanthemum
Avenue, which was new itself at the time and ablaze with salmon-
coloured brick. Myrtle turned out to be a good manager. Of
all the curtains in the avenue hers were the soberest and best-
laundered. She had two sets, unlike those people whose windows
were covered with newspaper for a whole day while a swift
washing and drying took place. Also she conformed to Mrs.
Beeton's dictum of having a place for everything and everything
in its place. Her pans were cleaned immediately after use and
replaced among the alignment on the shelf, the colossus at one
end and the one for boiling an egg at the other. She sieved her
washing up water, with the result that her sink was never blocked.
Magazines and newspapers were either burned or placed in a
rack, according to whether they were done with or not; Myrtle
never had hillocks beneath her chair cushions. Ernest cleaned
the downstairs windows, in and out, twice a week; he broke up
the coal and filled the scuttle. He cleaned his boots in an outhouse
at the bottom of the garden. He thwacked the carpets over the

clothes line and trained himself to wallpapering and distempering. Occasionally in the evening they tried a duet together, but mostly Ernest smoked a pipe while Myrtle sewed or knitted in the opposite chair. At ten o'clock they both went to bed.

The years slipped by and their only regret was that they had no children. In their leisure time they always went out together; round the fields in summer, on their periodic visits to relatives, and to chapel on Sunday. They both agreed when they were married to put aside a certain amount every week, and they never missed. Each wakes week they went to Prestatyn; not only that but to the same lodgings in Prestatyn. Ernest for that week mingled a few packets of cigarettes with his pipe-smoking and his game of bowls with Myrtle looking on from one of the seats round the green, as she did at home in the park. Their lives ran smoothly. They seemed destined to be the perfect couple.

And then it happened. Early one evening the neighbours heard voices. As near as possible and from concealed vantage-points ears were cupped. There was no doubt about it, the Pinders were having a row; more than a row. It was a real up-and-downer. They were shouting at the top of their voices. They told each other exactly what they thought.

For several days after the two were scarcely seen outdoors. When at last they did emerge, instead of being shamefaced they looked happier. Since then Ernest goes to a football match when he likes. There are times when he misses choir practice. Myrtle joined the chapel theatre group and accepted a part. She bought another set of curtains—gay chintz. She periodically visits a hairdresser and keeps the grey in her hair concealed.

So it goes on. But what roused the curiosity of the neighbourhood was the reason for the quarrel. They both kept quiet about it until Ernest confessed to a crony.

"Myrtle were bred out if t' family had only knowed it. But they piled it on how prim and proper her'd been browt up so I trained misel' to be t'same, and Ah did that weel that she had to keep on wi' it to live up to me. It lasted a long time, and then it began to get on her nerves and her started giving me t' rough end of her tongue. It went wuss and wuss, and Ah could see it'd end in a bust up. And that's what it did."

"But what touched it off, like?" the crony asked.

" It were me," Ernest said. " Ever sin we'd bin wed Ah were sort of o'Doctor Jekyll and Mesthur Hyde. Her catched me pinching raisins in t' pantry." [Stop Timing]

Put your reading time here........................

1. Ernest first met Myrtle—
    (*a*) In Accrington.
    (*b*) At Simpson's dyehouse.
    (*c*) At his lodgings.
    (*d*) At the choir meeting.
    (*e*) At the butchers.

2. Ernest thought that the Winterbottoms—
    (*a*) Were his social equals.
    (*b*) Were slightly above him socially.
    (*c*) Were below him socially.
    (*d*) Were much above him socially.
    (*e*) Were not easy to get on with.

3. Their home was—
    (*a*) Fairly clean and reasonably comfortable.
    (*b*) Clean and uncomfortable.
    (*c*) Not very clean but very comfortable.
    (*d*) Very clean and comfortable.
    (*e*) Very clean but very uncomfortable.

4. For their holidays they always went to........................

5. This story is about—
    (*a*) A Yorkshire couple who are married but eventually separate.
    (*b*) A Lancashire couple who take years to understand each other.
    (*c*) A Yorkshire couple who are always quarrelling.
    (*d*) A Lancashire couple who never quarrel.
    (*e*) A Lancashire couple who couldn't live up to their ideals.

The correct answers are at the foot of page 56.

This passage has 1,000 words and you can find your speed from the following table.

Time	Speed	Time	Speed
1.40	600	2.40	375
1.50	545	2.50	353
2.00	500	3.00	330
2.10	461	3.10	315
2.20	429	3.20	300
2.30	400	3.30	286
2.40	375		

Speed...................... Comprehension......................

I hope that you resisted the temptation to vocalize that bit of dialect.

Note—You were not able to look back very far then and if you move your paper a little more quickly down the page you will force yourself to read faster.

Try this with the next exercise.

EXERCISE 10

Home from Peking by John Clews

[START TIMING] The last lap of our journey inside Siberia began, as did the others, in the early morning and we left Omsk Airport with the rising sun behind us and slightly to starboard. Our final contact with Asia was during a short stop at Sverdlovsk, the industrial centre on the eastern slopes of the low range of hills forming the central mass of the Urals, the natural dividing lines between Asia and Europe. Our next stop was at Kazan, on the Volga. As we passed over the broad river we could see its muddy waters swelling in flood everywhere, covering the newly ploughed fields for some distance on either side, right up to the bottoms of the gardens of the mud-walled thatched cottages in the near-by settlements.

From Kazan we went on to Moscow. In the whole 4,000 mile journey from Irkutsk we had stayed in the same republic, the Russian S.F.S.R., the largest of the sixteen making up the U.S.S.R. We travelled by an eighteen-seater Illyitch plane of the Soviet line " Aeroflot " and used a sister machine for the flight to Prague. These planes are some thirty to forty miles an hour faster than the ubiquitous Dakota, but I was told by an airman who has often flown them that they handled badly in rough weather, which would explain why they are grounded so often under conditions that would not be considered too bad here. On the Soviet planes we used, the safety regulations were not so strict as they are in the West. Safety belts were not provided and there was no stewardess. At every stop a Red Cross girl was among the first on board to see if she was needed.

Moscow has been described so often that there is little fresh to add. I saw some magnificent buildings and wonderfully wide streets, almost too wide for pedestrians, but for the strict traffic rules. The Metro as I saw it was all it claimed to be. I will never forget my two visits to the Bolshoi Theatre, celebrating its hundred and seventy-fifth anniversary this year. The first time I saw the beautiful Soviet ballet-cum-opera *The Fountain of Bakhtchisarai* by Asafiev, with its wonderfully savage Tartar dances; the star of the evening was the young ballerina Strutchkova, reputedly rivalling the great Ulanova herself. My second visit was to Borodin's opera *Prince Igor*, the Polovtsian dances from it have largely been made popular here by the Huddersfield Choir recording, but even a Yorkshireman would admit that it gives no idea of the spirit with which it was imbued at the Bolshoi Theatre. Little wonder an encore was demanded. Surprisingly enough even this theatre was not free of that bane, the claque.

We were taken a tour of the sights of Moscow, the Kremlin, Lenin's Tomb, St. Basil's Cathedral, the Dynamo Sports Stadium, and so on; all fine buildings. A huge new university block is being built on the outskirts which will eclipse even the London University buildings. Yet, in spite of the numbers of flats going up, Moscow is still a very overcrowded city and I saw many shanty-like dwelling houses which would have been condemned and pulled down here long ago. These contrasted greatly with the fine modern public buildings and office blocks that were shown to us. In places even the highway leading from the Airport into the city needed repairing, and once more I was thankful for the Pobieda's suspension.

On the last section of the homeward journey my Scottish colleague, Kerr Fraser of Glasgow University, and I travelled alone. We were seen off by our Komsomol hosts, who had looked after us very well and efficiently the whole time. Nothing had been too much trouble and they even sent a multilingual representative from Moscow to await our arrival in Irkutsk. The Customs examination at Moscow Airport was very thorough and all our notes and papers were taken into a near-by office for inspection. It was pleasant to see how carefully the porters handled our luggage. Moscow Airport is served only by the Soviet planes, even on the lines with the Eastern European countries, and we embarked once more on an Illyitch, together with a returning delegation of French women. Our interpreter told us that one was " a heroine of the French people." " Oh, yes," we replied. " You mean she was in the Maquis during the war?" "No, no," he answered in a surprised voice. "She's a Fighter for Peace, of course." Thus do concepts of the same words differ.

We stayed in Prague and left the next morning by a familiar Dakota of the Czechoslovak Airlines (C.S.A.), then still running a joint service with B.E.A. to London. The Czechoslovak crew lacked a stewardess, as usual, but there was really little need for one on this run, since the passenger traffic with the West had been virtually nothing for a long time, except for the occasional delegation and officials. That passenger traffic was not expected by C.S.A. was obvious from the planes on which I travelled, which had all but a dozen seats removed and the space filled with cargo.

As we said goodbye to our Czech colleagues I reflected that after five years of visiting Eastern Europe the situation was now such that these farewells were for me permanent ones. We in the National Union of Students have always believed in personal contact between all ordinary people and students of all countries as one of the best practical means of preserving real peace. We have long been striving to get exchanges between ordinary British students and those from the Communist countries as private individuals doing as they please and going where they will—as they can do in Western Europe—and not just attending political rallies disguised as Festivals and Congresses. A limited exchange has been possible and we are awaiting a visit of a Soviet student delegation in the rather vague future, together with a Chinese visit tentatively scheduled for the autumn. But these are on a very small scale and usually affect only the more important students, not the rank and file. From this last visit and others I know that most people on both sides of the Curtain have appallingly little

---

Answers to Exercise 9—1 (*d*), 2 (*d*), 3 (*e*), 4 Prestatyn, 5 (*e*).

knowledge about the true situations in each other's countries. The youth and students I have met in the countries I have visited want to see for themselves how we live and receive our own people freely in their homes. The barriers to such exchanges are erected by those indeterminable beings Higher Up.

So for the last time I left Prague and flew homewards above the fleecy clouds dappling the woods and fields of Bohemia with the morning sunlight of a spring day. Four hours later we touched down at Northolt. [STOP TIMING]

Put your reading time here............................

1. This extract describes—
    (a) The beginning of a journey to Northern Siberia.
    (b) A journey from Siberia.
    (c) A tour of Russia.
    (d) A tour of Russia and the European countries.
    (e) A plane journey.

2. The Russian Illyitch plane—
    (a) Is more stable in bad weather than the Dakota.
    (b) Has more powerful engines than the Viscount.
    (c) Is grounded more often than the Dakota.
    (d) Is always run with a steward.
    (e) Is very common in Western Europe.

3. In Moscow—
    (a) The streets were narrow and dirty.
    (b) There were no new buildings.
    (c) The opera was second rate.
    (d) The roads were uniformly good.
    (e) The opera and ballet were excellent.

4. Moscow Airport—
    (a) Deals with planes of all nations.
    (b) Deals with Soviet planes only.
    (c) Deals with Soviet planes and Eastern European planes.
    (d) Deals mainly with military planes.
    (e) Is noted for the speed of the Customs examination.

5. The National Union of Students—
    (a) Does not believe in student exchange.
    (b) Believes that student exchange should be limited to the best students.

(c) Believes that only delegations of students should visit other countries.

(d) Believes that there should be no visits of delegations.

(e) Believes that there should be as much student exchange as possible.

The correct answers are at the bottom of page 60.

This passage has 1,150 words and you can find your speed from the following table.

Time	Speed	Time	Speed
1.30	766	2.50	406
1.40	688	3.00	383
1.50	628	3.10	363
2.00	575	3.20	345
2.10	530	3.30	329
2.20	494	3.40	314
2.30	460	3.50	300
2.40	431	4.00	287
2.50	406		

Speed........................   Comprehension........................

A WARNING ABOUT VOCALIZATION

YOU have been attacking vocalization for some time now and are getting the upper hand of it. You may be so preoccupied with watching how much you talk to yourself that you are neglecting the main purpose of your reading, which is to extract the information from the passage. The result of this means that you are getting low comprehension scores. If you are doing this, then you should relax. You know all about how much you vocalize and you can see that it is holding you back. You have accepted the idea, now let it work without your personal supervision. Stop watching what you are doing in your mind and concentrate on reading, and will probably find that you have got over the hurdle at last and can read much faster and still answer the questions.

Try this as you read the next two exercises.

EXERCISE 11

Ale Between The Acts by John Batten

[START TIMING] The eight-year-old in the brown woollen pixie hood, sitting next to Mum and Dad in the semi-circular front row of chairs, crunched potato crisps from a crackly greaseproof bag. The rest of the dance hall was thinly filled with an audience mostly in its teens, equal numbers of boys and girls, and a few grown-ups. A barman walked round the four rows of chairs selling threepenny programmes, and several more grown-ups, regulars, came in with glasses of beer. A woman brought a glass of orangeade for a teen-age daughter.

Then through the double doors of the hall, beyond which could be seen white napkins covering snacks on a bar counter, came a procession of richly costumed men and women, eight of them, walking briskly, taking sly looks at their audience as they passed the rows of chairs, their buckle-shoed feet making no sound on the thick carpet covering the glossy dance floor. They filed behind two tall wooden screens hand-painted to represent timber and plaster walls.

The barman-programme seller went to the light switch by the door. One by one the garish dance hall lights in their saucer-shaped yellow and brown plastic shades, suspended mushroom-wise from the ceiling on chromium-plated stems, went out. A young man with thick black hair stepped forward and switched on the portable floodlights standing before the screens. The blue and white chequered ball of crystal glass hanging from the centre of the room glistened and sparkled in the reflected light.

From behind the screens the players stepped on to the stage which had been fashioned from portable bar fittings covered with a rug. Behind, a square black clock with chromium hands had stopped at half past two. A French grandmother in black gown and drooping black picture-hat spoke words which took the audience back three hundred years. She was surrounded by her clamouring family. Molière's *Tartuffe* had begun. The play had come to the pub.

As the play unfolded in the semi-darkness and the audience grasped its purport, cigarettes went out, hands ceased to reach for glasses on the round tables scattered among the chairs. The little girl in the front row neatly folded her paper bag as she finished her crisps and sat entranced with the strange words, the zeal of the players, the flashing eyes, and the grand gestures and unaccustomed clothing.

Presently the landlady herself came in. Jim, the barman, could well take care of the two or three customers in the saloon for whom the play was not the thing. For her part she preferred comedy. She sat at the back of the hall and listened with the rest.

Now there was laughter as the audience warmed to the actors, so close to them, so real in their endeavours, though divided in time by three centuries, their foppish finery of ruffles, bows, and buckles as unlike anything most of them had seen as a ten-shilling joint of beef. They sighed with the lovers, resented the urbane stupidity of Orgon and his high-handed treatment of his pretty daughter, and laughed, while not so sure of their laughter, at Tartuffe himself.

In the two ten-minutes intervals a few went to the bar, to

Answers to Exercise 10—1 (*b*), 2 (*c*), 3 (*e*), 4 (*b*), 5 (*e*).

which the landlady returned, and had their glasses of beer, but most stayed in their seats, blinking in the dance hall lights, re-reading their programmes, chattering, and waiting impatiently for the players to finish their sandwiches and drinks and to return to the floor before them.

To a stranger the landlady reported that most of the audience was unknown to her. " No, they're not my regulars," she said, " only a few. That one over there, in the cap and with the purple scarf, with his wife, he's one. And some in the middle row. Of course if it was Saturday night, now, it would be different. But there'd be a dance on, you see, so they couldn't have the hall."

Molière clowned lightly on through the evening, until at a quarter to ten all ended well. The little girl was sleepy but pleased; the regular in the cap, smiling, had time for another beer, his wife for her glass of stout. And the players? They were content too, for supper was ready, and the motor-coach outside would soon speed them to their homes. [STOP TIMING]

Put your reading time here........................

1. This is an account of—
   (a) A Shakespearean play in a public house.
   (b) A Spanish play in a Dance Hall.
   (c) A school play.
   (d) A French play in a public house.
   (e) A French play in a Dance Hall.

2. The hall was—
   (a) Quite full.
   (b) Three quarters full.
   (c) Half empty.
   (d) More than half empty.
   (e) Quite empty.

3. The play—
   (a) Was not successful.
   (b) Was partially successful.
   (c) Did not arouse much interest in the audience.
   (d) Held the audience well.
   (e) Interested most of the audience.

4. The audience—
   (a) Contained few regular customers.

E

    (*b*) Was half regulars and half strangers.

    (*c*) Was all regulars.

    (*d*) Was all strangers.

    (*e*) Contained no regular customers.

5. During the two intervals—

    (*a*) All the audience went for refreshments.

    (*b*) Most of the audience went out.

    (*c*) All the audience remained in their seats.

    (*d*) Most of the audience remained in their seats.

    (*e*) Half the audience went out.

The correct answers are at the bottom of page 64.

This passage has 750 words and you can find your speed from the following table.

Time	Speed	Time	Speed
1.00	750	2.00	375
1.10	640	2.10	345
1.20	564	2.20	322
1.30	500	2.30	300
1.40	449	2.40	281
1.50	410	2.50	265
2.00	375	3.00	250

Speed......................   Comprehension......................

That was a short one, the next is longer but you should be able to read it at the same speed if not faster.

EXERCISE 12

The Dutch in Indonesia by Lois Mitchison

[START TIMING] A few weeks ago a market woman refused to sell me any of the pile of fruit she had in front of her. I protested loudly—and in English. A bystander hastily intervened. I got my oranges and the explanation. It was a boycott of the Dutch, not of foreigners generally. Indonesia welcomed other foreigners, the bystander assured me, but I should know that the Dutch . . . and he started on the long list of reasons why the Indonesians and the Dutch so much dislike each other. It was not a very effective boycott; but again and again I met Indonesians melting into sudden friendliness when they found that I was English and not Dutch and explaining bitterly and emotionally what the Dutch had done to them when Indonesia was a Netherlands Colony and what the Dutch still did to sabotage the new state. That was why, according to an Indonesian Foreign Office official, relations are, " very, very bad."

It was odd that relations should be so bad. It is a political truism that the British have never before been so well liked in India; the Americans are popular in the Philippines; even in Vietnam, after eight years of war, there is a certain mutual tolerance and a recognition among the Vietnamese of the great French qualities. Yet Jakarta, with muddy canals down the centre of its main streets, swarms of bicycles, and high-pitched red-tiled roofs over gabled buildings, is no less a Dutch city than Bombay is English or Saigon French. The Indonesian cultured man breakfasts off a rich sandwich of powdered chocolate, processed cheese, thin sliced raw beef, and boiled eggs, just as surely as his Indian contemporary eats scrambled egg, toast and marmalade, or a Vietnamese coffee and croissants. An Indonesian lady who adds white " lingerie touches," a locket, and a modesty vest to her blouse is as influenced by her colonial background as the Saigonese staggering on high spike-heeled sandals or the North Indian girl with the warm, woolly British vest under her sari.

An Indonesian middle class house is furnished in heavy panelled darkness oddly inappropriate to Jakarta's hot, damp climate. A Dutch legacy, too, I was told by some of the foreign business men, is much of the Indonesian bureaucracy with its maddening insistence on photographs, on forms filled out six times, and the absolute necessity of official knowledge of one's mother's maiden name and one's grandfather's place of birth.

The Indonesian Foreign Office official to whom I talked said that President Sukarno had a room in his palace full of pictures of " Dutch cruelties " during the two " police actions " against Indonesian Nationalists in 1947 and 1949.

He and others spoke of the " treachery " of the second police action which broke the United Nations truce line, and of the atrocities committed by a minority of Dutch Army officers. There was also talk of Dutch manners which used often to be exclusive and arrogant (the perennial difficulty of the " Whites only " club comes up again in Jakarta); and of the Dutch imprisonment of Indonesian political leaders in the malaria-ridden New Guinea

exile camp. But British manners in India, so neutral observers
tell me, were often worse, and we imprisoned Indian politicians
too. Yet Indonesians say, not only to the English but to Americans
and visiting Indians like Madame Pandit, " if only we had been
colonized by the British." They talk of the better educational
system the British encouraged in India; the most often quoted
figure here is that when the Dutch left, Indonesia only had 1,000
doctors to a population of 80,000,000. Under Dutch rule, people
say, there was no chance for those Indonesians who had been
educated in Holland or in the two universities in the then Dutch
East Indies to rise to senior positions. And the Dutch are blamed
for Indonesia's present desperate shortage of professional men
and trained administrators.

Like many Indians, Indonesians find their feelings towards the
Dutch fascinating to analyse and discuss. Holland, I was told,
is a small country without imagination or genius. But the man
who told me this had a calendar reproduction of one of the
better-known Dutch seventeenth-century portraits hanging on his
study wall behind him. One of the material disadvantages of
being colonized by Holland, the Indonesians find, is that Dutch
is not a useful language, and it was taught in every school in the
Dutch East Indies. India, Burma, Ceylon, Japan, Australia, the
Philippines, Malaya, even China—all Indonesia's neighbours—
speak English. So the Indonesians have dropped Dutch from
most school curricula.

But the first reason which most Indonesians give for their
present bad relations with the Dutch is that the Netherlands still
holds West Irian, or New Guinea. The Dutch say the Indonesians
have neither the money nor the men to develop New Guinea;
they would make unstable neighbours for Australia; the New
Guinea natives are different ethnically from the Malay Indonesians.
Why should they hand over to another less efficient colonial
Power? The Indonesians say the Dutch have done very little to
develop New Guinea anyway (a view which may be contrasted
with the special articles from Hollandia published in the
Manchester Guardian in October). They say that all Indonesia
was to have been given freedom, and West Irian is an integral part
of Indonesia. This appeal to Indonesian nationalism over West

---

Answers to Exercise 11—1 (*d*), 2 (*d*), 3 (*d*), 4 (*a*), 5 (*d*).

Irian may well have begun two years ago as an attempt to divert public attention from the economic difficulties and political instability of the Government; and some foreigners say that it is still a Government-sponsored movement. But all the Opposition politicians in Indonesia now seem to feel as strongly as the Government—and trade unions, women's organizations, and opposition newspapers, all of which have criticized the Government on other issues—have never suggested that the Dutch should be allowed to keep West Irian.

There are still about three thousand Dutch officials employed by the Indonesian Government. These officials are essential to the New State. Some of them are government technicians, and about a thousand are still in key posts, often as " advisers " to senior Indonesian officials. In a few instances the Indonesian Government has tried to replace them by English, German, or Yugoslav experts, but Dutch is still much the easiest language for most Indonesians, and the old Dutch civil servants have an irreplaceable knowledge of the country and the bureaucratic machinery. Indonesians vaguely accuse these officials of " disloyalty." There are, they say, a few cases of actual sabotage (although they will produce no concrete evidence of this)—and more of the Dutch denigrating the Indonesian Government.

The Indonesians also complain that Dutch business still controls their economy. The biggest banks, the most effective import and export houses, much of the rubber and oil of Indonesia is Dutch. There are few experienced business men in Indonesia, and few economic experts, as the country's economic difficulties witness; but the Indonesian would like to replace all foreign firms by Indonesian firms. No foreigner who the Indonesian Government thinks could be replaced by an Indonesian is allowed to send savings out of the country; the big majority of import and export licences must go to Indonesian firms—to be re-sold at a profit very often to foreigners.

Over other people's quarrels it is very easy to remember the proverbs about cutting off one's nose to spite one's face, and letting the dead bury the dead. Holland needs the money she still gets from Indonesia and the employment given to her nationals there. She cannot afford to fight a war over West Irian, but then neither can Indonesia, which also needs Dutch business experience and Dutch officials. But this co-operation that both sides need so badly is almost impossible in an atmosphere so poisoned by dislike and suspicion. [STOP TIMING]

Put your reading time here.........................

1. In Indonesia—
   (a) There is bad feeling against all foreigners.
   (b) People like the Dutch but dislike other foreigners.
   (c) Only the English are popular.
   (d) The people dislike the Dutch but like other foreigners.
   (e) The people welcome all foreigners.

2. At breakfast—
   (a) The cultured Indonesian has a native breakfast.
   (b) The cultured Indonesian has an English breakfast.
   (c) The cultured Indonesian has a Dutch breakfast.
   (d) The cultured Indonesian has a little fruit and a drink.
   (e) The cultured Indonesian has a few raisins and some wine.

3. The Indonesians think—
   (a) That India was better treated by the English.
   (b) That the Dutch and English were similar as colonizers.
   (c) That the Dutch were superior to the English as colonizers.

4. The Indonesians think—
   (a) That the Dutch are doing a good job in New Guinea.
   (b) That they should control New Guinea.
   (c) That UNO should take over New Guinea.

5. The Indonesians—
   (a) Have replaced all Dutch civil servants by natives.
   (b) Have allowed all Dutch civil servants to remain.
   (c) Are trying to recruit more Dutch civil servants.
   (d) Have only retained the essential Dutch civil servants.
   (e) Have every confidence in the Dutch civil servants.

6. Co-operation between Dutch and Indonesians is—
   (a) Unlikely and undesirable.
   (b) Possible but unlikely.
   (c) Neither likely nor desirable.
   (d) Against the best interests of Indonesia.
   (e) Unlikely but desirable.

The correct answers to the questions are at the foot of page 68.

This passage has 1,300 words and you can work out your speed from the following table.

Time	Speed	Time	Speed
2.00	650	3.30	372
2.10	599	3.40	354
2.20	558	3.50	340
2.30	520	4.00	325
2.40	487	4.10	312
2.50	459	4.20	300
3.00	433	4.30	289
3.10	410	4.40	278
3.20	390	4.50	269
3.30	372	5.00	260

Speed........................ Comprehension........................

BREAKING THE SOUND BARRIER

LET us go over again what you have been doing up to now. You have increased your reading speed by stopping all unnecessary movements and by reducing the sound barrier which you used to put between the word and its meaning. You have stopped the time-wasting habit of going back to read again something you have already read.

If you have gained poor comprehension scores in some of the tests, don't worry. You have been bringing an automatic method into the open and changing it, but your changes should be fairly well established now and you can expect your comprehension scores to increase and then remain steady.

The extent to which you have been successful in reducing vocalization is reflected by your increase of speed, but you must keep on making efforts, for you have not yet reached your ceiling on this type of material unless you are reading at 700 to 800 words per minute. There is still plenty of headroom, so bear that in mind with the next two exercises.

EXERCISE 13

A Sea of Glory by Stephen Parkinson

[START TIMING] As long as he could remember Mr. Gurney had been an Unauthorized Person. He knew Cardinal Wolsey defined man's state as one of hope blossoming into honours and coming within a near miss of greatness before being blighted by an envious frost, but he never saw his own career in such a light. No, Mr. Gurney modestly identified himself with the great unwashed of all ages and rubbed along in a drooling rhythm of uneventfulness. If one day he felt Olympian and full of promise, next day he knew he was passé if not putrid. His friends, on the

---

Answers to Exercise 12—1 (*d*), 2 (*c*), 3 (*a*), 4 (*b*), 5 (*d*), 6 (*e*).

other hand, saw no difference. To them his state was one of constant mediocrity. It was quite comfortable to be an Unauthorized Person barred from privileged places by lines as arbitrary as the 38th parallel. Mr. Gurney would not have wanted to be a Tudor cardinal and in the twentieth century he did not even envy executives in nationalized industries.

Twenty years ago in the untested optimism of youth he believed that life should have a capital L. He was ever casting about for experience—vivid, pulsating, divine experience that would give him the key to men and matter. But the obsession grew less urgent. He matured. His stars were set in their course and he felt that to have them otherwise might give him ideas.

Once he saw greatness at close quarters. A neighbour became Mayor of the town. Each day a large limousine rolled down the road and its appearance with its magnificent flunkeys transformed little Mr. Higgs into His Worship. Instead of talking to him over the hedge about greenfly and composts, Mr. Gurney in the momentous year raised his hat to the First Citizen, giving him full honour as an Authorized Person.

All went well until he and Mrs. Gurney received a handsome card with an embossed coat of arms inviting them to the Town Hall. Mrs. Gurney had a new dress and Mr. Gurney levered himself gently into his dinner jacket. It was an occasion and they could not help being impressed when a major-domo rapped on the floor with a wand and cried: " Pray silence for His Worship the Mayor."

They noticed that it did something to Mr. Higgs too. The scuttling worried little man was benign. He had poise and a measured tread as he moved among his guests conferring recognition. The scarlet fur-trimmed robe made him bigger; the gold chain somehow suggested that he had a chest. Nothing would have induced Mr. Gurney to dig him in his civic ribs and suggest that his front lawn was getting unkempt through neglect.

Going home on the last bus Mr. Gurney felt that his good wife was not with him in spite of the nearness of her ample form. She had a faraway look, and in fact she was thinking how dignified she could be if she were always assured of deference. When Mr. Gurney asked if she had enjoyed herself she gazed at him stonily. There was a hint of unsympathetic appraisal in the gaze. Without knowing Mr. Gurney grew alarmed.

As they sipped their cocoa Mrs. Gurney said, "They never did anything about that loose paving stone in Sandy Lane after you complained, did they? If you stood for the Council you would be able to make them fix it."

Mr. Gurney was thunderstruck. More than that he felt hurt because Mrs. Gurney seemed to suggest he ought to be more than he was. She had never done so beforehand; at a loss to deal with a dangerous new trend, Mr. Gurney behaved badly. He said, "You are talking through your hat, Mabel."

That finished it. Mrs. Gurney said no more until breakfast and very little in succeeding weeks. She observed the formalities, but killed conversation with barbed insinuations about women whose promise was wasted by feckless husbands. More than once Mr. Gurney was on the point of reminding her about her brother who threw up a job as a solicitor's clerk to sell second-hand cars.

Mr. Higgs' triumphant progress no longer entertained them. They were wilfully blind to his photographs in the *Examiner*, and deaf to the cheery clatter that penetrated the wall when he was at home. Fortunately Mr. Higgs was too much occupied to notice the coolness of his neighbours.

Of course, the day came when the mayoral car rolled up the road for the last time and Mr. Gurney took a mean delight in the vision of Mr. Higgs at the end of a bus queue. The frockcoat went with the other trappings and in his wellworn serge the fellow looked just like any other man.

Even with this consolation Mr. Gurney could not forgive Mr. Higgs. As a councillor he was still very much an Authorized Person, and at the next election Mr. Gurney did a most unworthy thing. He voted for Mr. Higgs' opponent whose politics he hated. By a tragic coincidence a number of other people voted for Mr. Higgs' opponent and, like Lucifer, Mr. Higgs fell. The Gurneys felt as if a stubborn blockade had been lifted, but the subject was too sore to permit comment. Mr. Gurney had the burden of his share in Mr. Higgs' ruin, and as soon as it was decent he risked saying to Mrs. Gurney, "I think I will pop round and give Higgs a hand with his garden."

"Do, dear," Mrs. Gurney replied placidly. "When it comes to gardening the poor little fellow seems to have no idea." [STOP TIMING]

Put your reading time here........................

1. Mr. Gurney was—
   (a) An outstanding man.
   (b) An ordinary man who had flashes of brilliance.
   (c) An important person.
   (d) A very ordinary person.
   (e) Exceptional in some ways.
2. One day his neighbour became.........................
3. Mr. Gurney's dislike of Mr. Higgs was caused by—
   (a) His jealousy of Mr. Higgs success.
   (b) Mrs. Gurney's jealousy.
   (c) The foolish figure which Mr. Higgs made.
   (d) Mr. Higgs' proud rejection of his neighbours.
   (e) Mr. Higgs' behaviour at the reception.
4. The breach with Higgs was healed—
   (a) When he became an Important Person.
   (b) When Gurney became an Important Person.
   (c) When Higgs became a councillor.
   (d) When Gurney became a councillor.
   (e) When Higgs stopped being a councillor.
5. This is a story of—
   (a) The petty jealousies of suburban life.
   (b) Small town politics.
   (c) Keeping up with the Jones's.
   (d) Two mediocrities.
   (e) The trials of married life.

The correct answers are at the bottom of page 72.

This passage has 920 words and you can find your speed from the following table.

Time	Speed	Time	Speed
1.20	690	2.40	345
1.30	612	2.50	325
1.40	551	3.00	306
1.50	503	3.10	290
2.00	460	3.20	276
2.10	424	3.30	263
2.20	395	3.40	251
2.30	368	3.50	240
2.40	345	4.00	230

Speed........................   Comprehension........................

Now carry on to the next exercise.

EXERCISE 14

The Waterman by George Bellairs

[START TIMING] There is an impression on this side of the Channel that the French are not very fond of water. The contents of their carafes are yellow and tainted looking; there is almost a total absence of baths if you get off the beaten track, and the plumbing is, to our eyes, fantastic. But a Frenchman might say that he has good wine to sell and is careful and thrifty where the fixed capital of his hotel is concerned. Why bother much about water? But that by the way, I am trying to tell the tale of the waterman of St. Divy. He lived in a kind of tenement in the tower of the over-large church. He was ecclesiastical firewatcher, bellringer, and factotum, and he carried on the trade of shoe-making in his spare time. He and Father Bellay, the priest, went fishing every Saturday, wet or fine, and it was a pity if you wanted to get married or buried on that day. You had to have the civil wedding ceremony performed at the mairie and wait for the rest until another time. Even then you were in difficulties, for the mayor was also the stationmaster, and you had to consult a time-table before fixing the fatal hour.

They say that if you don't wash your face for ten days in Brittany you can see the wind. There must have been a lot of wind-spotters in Divy. They just didn't bother. There were only three baths in the old town, too: one, which was always locked up, in the hotel; another at the chateau, and in which the count, said to be mad, immersed himself several times a day; and a third at the mayor's house, where they showed it to you as a part of an afternoon's pleasure, just as, over here, you might show a party your back garden or the family album. It was, therefore, surprising that they should make such a fuss about having water laid on at all. Its main use, as far as I could gather, was for swilling the streets, washing up, and boiling the local lobsters. Nobody drank it; it was said to be hard, so you washed in that caught in water butts, and the women did their laundry at the well their mothers had used before them. The town was proud of its water, for all that. They swore, in spite of their own contempt for it, that it was the finest in France.

Answers to Exercise 13—1 (*d*), 2 Mayor, 3 (*b*), 4 (*e*), 5 (*e*).

The funny part of it all was that the last place to have piped water was the fashionable villa suburb on the hill outside the old town. There they had baths and did the laundry indoors, but drew supplies by siphons from the stream. After a threatened revolution and political upheaval which almost overthrew the precariously balanced National Government the suburbans got their pipes but not their water. There they were, all their taps bright and their tiles polished ready for their baths, and nothing in the pipes because somebody had forgotten the law of gravity and pressures and levels and the main supply from the lower town hadn't the energy to reach the hilltop. Then they erected a water-tower and bought a small petrol engine to boost the water up to it. They appointed Grumello, the ecclesiastical odd-job man, as water bailiff. For a week or two the select residents of the upper town bathed and washed to their hearts' content. It was even said that in their initial enthusiasm they drank the water too.

Then a new shoe shop opened amid chromium and concrete in the lower town and began to sell the latest models from Paris and, what is more, mend them. Almost simultaneously all the taps ran dry and a drought set in on the hill. Grumello, in his eyrie among the jackdaws wasn't on the telephone, so the suburbans could not ring him up. Instead they had to make a pilgrimage to church, climb among the rafters, and ask Grumello what was going on. He said he was too busy. Never in his life had he been so pulled out with repairs. To emphasize this, he pointed to a pile of battered footwear which must receive his ministrations before he could even think about water. They were for his regular customers, and he couldn't let them down; now could he? Water was his spare-time job. On the other hand, if the people on the hill had been regular customers, too, in the way of soling and heeling, he'd have to look after them. As it was . . . he threw another handful of shoe-nails into his mouth to indicate that the interview was at an end.

There was a public meeting on the hill that night. Grumello wasn't going to blackmail them. They went to see the mayor in between trains. He shrugged his shoulders. Baths? He didn't see what they were bothering about. He'd been brought up in the hard school, he said, and told them of the days when he'd sluiced himself under the pump at four o'clock on a frosty morning on his father's farm. They left him still enjoying his icy ablutions in retrospect and went to see Father Bellay. The priest showed them his own spartan washing apparatus—a tin bowl with a hole in the bottom, and a plug, and a jug which he filled at the baptismal tap in the vestry. He also propounded a pet theory that total immersion in water removed valuable insulating and protective oils from the body and permitted the escape of vital energy. Meanwhile Grumello could be heard hammering nails overhead somewhere, to remind them the offer still stood.

The next day the priest, the mayor, and Grumello, returning from a record fishing, found a queue of customers, some of them with shoes which looked too good to repair, waiting on the stairs of the church tower. They had been there a long time, they said, but they were very pleasant about it. Towards evening there were explosive noises in the concrete pillbox which housed the petrol-engine and pump. " The water! The water! " shouted the hill-dwellers one to another as it gurgled in the tanks, and the night rang with songs in the baths and the joyful hiccuping and belching of emptying waste-pipes. [STOP TIMING]

Put your reading time here........................

1. This story is about—
    (a) A town in France with no regular water supply.
    (b) A town in Brittany where water is taken by cart.
    (c) A town in France which gets its water from Paris.
    (d) A town in Brittany which has piped water.
    (e) A town in Brittany where nobody washes.
2. Grumello refused to supply the villas with water because—
    (a) He didn't like the people who lived there.
    (b) He wanted to have a day fishing.
    (c) They did not pay him enough for the water.
    (d) He was too lazy to start the engine.
    (e) They did not give him their shoes to repair.
3. The people of the old town used the water for—
    (a) Drinking.
    (b) Swilling the streets and washing up.
    (c) Making tea and cocoa.
    (d) In the dyeworks.
    (e) For washing and bathing themselves.
4. Grumello had several other jobs one of which was
    ....

5. The only people who had baths lived in............................
The correct answers are at the bottom of page 76.

This passage has 1,060 words, and you can find your speed from the following table.

Time	Speed	Time	Speed
1.30	707	2.50	375
1.40	635	3.00	353
1.50	579	3.10	335
2.00	530	3.20	318
2.10	489	3.30	303
2.20	455	3.40	290
2.30	424	3.50	277
2.40	397	4.00	265
2.50	375		

Speed........................   Comprehension........................

You have reduced vocalization a great deal now, but you must always be on your guard against it, especially when you are reading something which contains dialogue, for there is always a temptation to take the parts and act the scene.

YOU AND YOUR EYES

WE have been mainly concerned, up to now, with the breaking down of the bad reading habits of the past, and they are well on the way to being banished, but you must continue the fight against them.

Now we come to the stage of introducing a new and positive reading habit. In section two the reading process was explained, how the eye sees and the movements it makes. The eye does not move steadily along a line of print, but moves in jerks, stopping from time to time. *It is only when the eye is stopped* that you are able to read, and a diagram of your eye movements at present would be something like this—

s————————s————————s————————s————————s

Everyone, with practice, can read better and faster.

—with your eyes stopping at each point where I have put s. You can see somebody else's eye movements if you stand behind them whilst they are reading and hold a hand mirror so that you can see one of their eyes but are not interfering with their reading. At first you will only be able to see the big sweep back to the beginning of the next line, but after a time you will be able to count the number of times that they stop. Get somebody to do the same for you and you will be able to work out how many words you are able to take in at a glance. This is called your eye span. Find out what your eye span is as you read the next exercise.

EXERCISE 15

Equal Clock Watching by Ian Crichton

[START TIMING] She used to work at the desk next to mine in

Answers to Exercise 14—1 (*d*), 2 (*e*), 3 (*b*), 4 Bellringer, Fire-watcher, Shoemaker, 5 The Suburb.

the Civil Service several years ago, and she is certain to be still there, in the same old brown suit and fur-lined boots. She was as kind as she was efficient, but it must have been exasperating that a male sitting beside her was doing the same work as she was and being paid more. Now she and all her friends have won their long campaign for the justice of " equal pay " to be recognized, and I am glad. The one who deserves sympathy now is my successor, who will have to listen to her triumphant crowing.

My employment was not " terminated," nor was I dismissed as " redundant ": I resigned. It was one of the best things that I have ever done, but most of the credit must go to her.

One long afternoon a few months after I joined the service we were clock-watching together. When she was bored she applied her efficiency to the problem of how to sneak glances at her watch without appearing to be anxious to go home. With her greater experience she was much better at this than I am. She employed a variety of ruses, and gave the impression that she was either winding a watch that had stopped or was worrying conscientiously about all the work she might not have time to finish, or—sitting so that the clock on the wall was behind her—was innocently powdering her nose.

Her skill impressed me, but I felt sure that this sort of thing was necessary only to us lowlier civil servants, and that the work became more interesting as we grew more senior. I thought enviously of our boss administering Great Britain as though proud to be a member of the finest Civil Service in the world. Then I happened to glance at him. All envy vanished and pity took its place. He had taken off his spectacles and was frowningly examining the glass—using the clock on the wall as a background.

So he was at it too. Then he went out of the room and I told my friend what had happened. I suggested that when one started pitying one's boss it was time to resign. She looked at me as she had done on my very first morning, when I had announced my firm but polite dislike of tea. On both occasions her expression varied between awe and a refusal to believe that anyone could be so odd.

In a hushed voice she asked me when I was going and what job I had got " outside." To all her queries I could only smile foolishly and shake my head. I just did not know what I would do, and began to wonder if I was making a big mistake. It would

F

be so easy just to sit tight and not say a word. I asked her if she thought it would be very foolish of me to leave.

Automatically she got up to make some tea. She always disdained trolleys of canteen tea, and sat huddled round her private spirit lamp, engrossed in her ritual. Her usual practice was then to go into the corridor and queue for canteen cakes, because if she was not queueing she would have to go on with her work, and that was to be avoided at all costs. If she timed it well she could join the queue when it was at its longest, and thus kill at least five minutes quite legitimately. Then she would return to her desk and kill another five in drinking and eating. I was slow to learn, but in a few weeks I had developed a passion for tea and cakes that vied with hers.

Now she paid me the compliment of foregoing her cakes, and as she sipped she answered my question. She told me how safe and secure the job was. She had calculated exactly how much her own pension would be and in what year she would be eligible for it. She knew she would be earning x in 1960, y in 1970, and so on. She also knew even more exactly that if she failed to move up the necessary grades her earnings would reach a certain height and stay there.

Then she put down her cup, and what she said astonished me. She admitted that she had been wanting to resign for years but felt that she was stuck fast in some nightmare mixture of office glue and red-tape. She urged me to give the boss my notice straight away, whether I had another job or not. She knew, and was kind enough to tell me, that it became progressively harder to break free and that I must go before it was too late.

"You're still unmarried," she said, "so you don't have to worry yet about a pension. Get a job where you won't have any idea what your income will be in 1960. You'll be a square peg in a square hole, and the sky will be your limit."

She smiled sadly, looking down at her fur-lined boots. " I make no apologies for those clichés," she said, " because you must remember that I am, after all, a civil servant." [STOP TIMING]

Put your reading time here............................

1. They spent one long afternoon doing nothing but...............
2. She liked to have her tea break—
    (a) As short as possible.

(b) When it best fitted in with her work.

(c) As long as possible.

(d) In the canteen.

(e) In a café nearby.

3. When the author told her he was leaving she—

(a) Encouraged him to go.

(b) Warned him he would lose his pension rights.

(c) Told him of the opportunities for promotion in the service.

(d) Disagreed with him about the Civil Service.

(e) Told him he would be a round peg in a square hole.

4. The female civil servant—

(a) Found her work interesting and absorbing.

(b) Found her work interesting at times.

(c) Found her work dull and monotonous.

(d) Found her work too difficult.

(e) Enjoyed the work because it was so easy.

5. The main impression of this passage is that—

(a) Civil servants are bored and disinterested.

(b) Lower grade civil servants are bored.

(c) The Civil Service is a pleasant and interesting job.

(d) The higher civil servants are keenly interested.

(e) The author enjoyed being a civil servant.

The correct answers are at the foot of page 80.

This passage has 870 words and you can work out your speed from the following table.

Time	Speed	Time	Speed
1.30	586	2.30	354
1.40	522	2.40	326
1.50	474	2.50	307
2.00	435	3.00	290
2.10	401	3.10	273
2.20	372	3.20	261
2.30	354	3.30	249

Speed...................... Comprehension......................

Did you work out your eye span, and find out how much you take in at a glance? Most people take in two or three words at once, but it is obvious that if they could take in more they would increase their speed of reading. For although eye movements are very quick, they take time, and there are so many of them to each page that any reduction will increase speed. Such a reduction can only come by increasing the eye span.

Answers to Exercise 15—1 Clock watching, 2 (*c*), 3 (*a*), 4 (*c*), 5 (*a*).

A HELPING HAND

INCREASING the eye span is not an easy process, and the next exercise has been printed in short lines to help you to do this. There is no point in timing this exercise for the form is not familiar, and you will not be able to read these short lines very quickly until you are used to them. It is purely a matter of trying to take in all the words in these short lines at a glance.

The eye is selective and you can widen your vision or narrow it when you wish. If you are looking at a line of five people, you can concentrate on one, or you can look at them all at the same time. This is what you must do with the next exercise, widen your vision and take in these three word lines without any eye movement. The arrangement of the material will help you to do this.

Get somebody to check if you are moving your eyes.

EXERCISE 16

Green Jerseys by M. E. Lowe

[DO NOT TIME THIS EXERCISE]
         It seems
     a long time now since
     as one of the first
     recruits
     of the Women's Land Army,
     I spent
     a strange day
     standing in queues
     at the Agricultural College
     in Leicestershire.
     There was the queue
     for gum-boots
     and the queue

for shirts, dungarees,
and green jerseys—
exciting new uniforms
which already seemed
to have the smell
of the earth about them.
For the next few years
it was to be
our comfortable habitual wear.

The most important queue
was the one
outside the Principal's office
where we
discussed our future
with a quiet,
sun-tanned man
who did us the honour
of taking us more seriously
as land workers
than we were yet able
to take ourselves.

Should we " do " live stock,
or general arable work,
dairying, horticulture,
or poultry?
We knew little
about any of them.
The modern school of thought
favoured arable work
because of the chance
to ride about on a tractor.
The longer-sighted
who were attracted
by the idea
of a career on the land
chose the more womanly jobs
like poultry, gardening,
and dairy work,

which they would
probably be allowed to do
when the war was over.
Dairying was the least popular,
though,
because almost everyone
was determined to get
into the open air
and stay there.
I started
with live stock
and went over to gardening.
Morning milking
brought me a friend
and an unforgettable experience.
They sent us out in pairs
to practice
at the farms round about.
I had been up early
but never before
the first bird
made its first cheep,
at pre-dawn.
Shattered
by the alarm clock
in what seemed deep night,
I found myself walking,
still half asleep,
in strange clothes,
through fields
of unbelievable silence.
Moonlight
drained the colour
from trees and grass,
from everything
except the purple,
opaque shadows
of the stacks.
As the frosted October air
passed our cheeks

and filled our lungs
we began
to feel wide awake,
but in an unfamiliar world
where night
would never end.
We stepped softly
on the crisped grasses
and spoke in whispers.
Jessica
was a commercial artist,
myself a journalist.
We neither of us
knew much about
work on the land,
but both remembered
" grandfather's farm,"
hers in Worcestershire
and famous for perry,
mine in Shropshire
where they bred
the Kerry ewes.
So our friendship
began this morning,
walking through the empty,
moon-coloured fields.

By contrast
the shippon
was filled with warm life
and rich smells.
After a few fears
and failures
and frustrations
we discovered
that there is
no pleasanter occupation
than hand milking,
with its soporific rhythms,
head against

the comforting side
of a solid cow.

Outside again
we found
a startling change.
Reality had come
with a sunrise
which turned
the frosted grasses
to a sentimental pink.
The sky
was unpaintably magnificent
over the flat fields—
the sort of sky
my old nannie
used to describe as
" just like
a Christmas card "—
her highest
words of praise.
And so to breakfast.
Those were
the early days
before rationing,
and I have
seldom tasted
bacon and eggs
so good.

The next weeks
were given
to the mastery
of new skills,
and new pains.
Every job
brought a pain
in a different place,
increasing until
it was about to be
unbearable,

then, as the muscles
adjusted themselves,
giving place
to a delicious sense
of ease and power.
About that time
a new job
was introduced,
and the process
began again.
Milking attacked
the inner forearm;
hedging between
the shoulder blades;
cutting mangolds,
the small of the back;
hoeing, a little higher up;
and carting dung,
the shoulders.
We learnt
a new respect
for the labourer
whose job
often looks slow and easy
when he is
really performing
miracles of rhythmic skill
and endurance.

There was
a very good cross-section
at the college
of all the sorts
who go to make the world—
and they were
rather good sorts in all.
Some girls were there
because they had been
to the hop fields
year by year

with London East End families,
and so felt
drawn to agriculture.
Others came
because they hunted
and were handy
with a horse—
so why not
with sheep and cows?
A girl from Ireland
rode like a centaur,
but found it difficult
to write or spell.
She often asked
odd questions
during lectures.
We had been told
to fertilize
glasshouse tomatoes
with a rabbit's tail.
" And would not
any other tail
have done? "
asked the clear, Irish voice
from the back of the room.

The bogy
of the bull
was soon dispersed
when we met him
face to face.
He was a little,
black Aberdeen Angus,
reassuringly hornless
and very tame—
a Ferdinand of a bull.
We soon learned
to smack him
on the back
with contemptuous familiarity.

We had
much more respect
for a batch
of bad-tempered
Irish heifers
which arrived
about that time
and gave us
our first experience
of maternity work.

The country round
was what Adrian Bell calls
" pudding country,"
just plain fields
and hedges and woods,
and then more woods
and hedges and fields,
but we loved it,
those of us
who had been starved
of open country
for some time.
Sherwood Forest
was a disillusionment;
it was too small
to hold our vision
of secure, leafy depths
protecting men
in Lincoln green—
but Charnwood Forest
was vast enough
and full of October colour.

We left
just before Christmas,
one to be a shepherd
in Scotland,
another to look after turkeys
in Lincolnshire,

a third to help
with a dairy herd
in Devon.
I grew vegetables
for an evacuated publishing firm
in Buckinghamshire,
and Jessica grew tomatoes
and kept rabbits
in Surrey.
We dispersed,
after living
cheek by jowl
in that strange,
vivid interlude.
Just occasionally
I met someone
who was " there,"
and we ask for news
of so-and-so
and wonder
what someone else
is doing now.

On the day in November
when the
Women's Land Army
was finally disbanded,
we all thought
of one another
with warmth
born of a shared adventure
which
we shall always remember
as one of the most real
and valuable experiences
in our lives.

1. The author is reminded of her experiences because—
   (a) She has met some of her old friends.
   (b) She has gone to work on a farm again.
   (c) The Women's Land Army is being revived.

(*d*) The Women's Land Army is being disbanded.

(*e*) She has been a member of the Women's Land Army.

2. The course started with—

(*a*) A test in Arithmetic and English.

(*b*) An interview with the Principal.

(*c*) Lessons in milking.

(*d*) Instruction in gardening.

(*e*) A day on a farm.

3. The author found early rising—

(*a*) Slightly uncomfortable but vaguely exciting.

(*b*) Uncomfortable and unpleasant.

(*c*) No break with her normal routine.

(*d*) Dull and boring.

(*e*) Very comfortable and most exciting.

4. Every new job—

(*a*) Involved little physical strain.

(*b*) Caused aches and pains in different parts.

(*c*) Was easily learned.

(*d*) Was very difficult to learn.

(*e*) Caused great mental strain.

5. All the girls involved—

(*a*) Came from farming people.

(*b*) Were excellent horsewomen.

(*c*) Had previous experience with animals.

(*d*) Had been hop picking.

(*e*) Were of different backgrounds and attainments.

6. The author thought that—

(*a*) Her time in the W.L.A. had been wasted.

(*b*) Although she had helped with the war effort, she would not do the same thing again.

(*c*) She had had a great and valuable experience.

(*d*) Women were out of place on the land.

(*e*) She had had a rather unpleasant experience.

You will find the correct answers at the foot of page 92.

I hope that you were able to take in those short groups at a glance. It was probably difficult, but remember that it is only necessary to widen the eye span by a small amount to effect a considerable improvement. Now try the same technique with the next exercise, which is printed in the ordinary way.

EXERCISE 17

One of Australia's Great Passions by N. J. N. Dixon

[START TIMING] There are moments when you might conclude that to the average Australian the two most important things in life are beer and betting—and as in Victoria he cannot get any beer after 6 p.m. in public places (an injustice which is exercising the state profoundly), betting is perhaps the greater passion.

There are fantastic lotteries in which even an hotel (or £100,000 instead) may be the first prize; there are shop lotteries called " caskets," there are horses with jockeys on their backs and there are horses pulling the little gigs at the trotting tracks; inevitably there are the greyhounds—and no doubt a dozen other ways of courting that queer factor called Chance. But the horse is the thing. I would not say that Australians love horses by and large, but they have a profound and peculiar knowledge of the behaviour of horses.

To-day I have been to my first Australian race meeting, at Melbourne's famous course at Flemington. It was the second most " important " meeting of the season. The really big affair comes in November with the Melbourne Cup day, which, to quote my informed guide, " stops the traffic in Australia." Factories, offices, even buses and trams, go out of action while this race is broadcast. Even children take portable radios to school.

It was quickly obvious early this morning that it was a race day in Melbourne. Newspaper boys were selling official race cards as readily as the newspapers containing the tips; there was a fine show of binoculars in the crowds streaming off the trains at Spencer Street Station—and (though this is purely deduction) the bank cashier who cashed my traveller's cheque gave me ten shillings too much. He did tell me that if I had not given it back the search for it probably would have ruined any chance he himself had of getting out to Flemington to-day!

And Flemington rewards a visit—especially on such a day as this has been, with the sun shining from a cloudless blue sky and a nice breeze tempering the heat to a barely acclimatized visitor from England. Of our English courses, only Goodwood perhaps can beat it for its setting and only the Royal Ascot meeting for its lawns and flowers. But Flemington's flowers are a gardener's pride and joy—beds of flowers set in the lawns (almost young parks) between the stands and the running track; flowers in rich colour and profusion around the enclosure in which the jockeys mount their horses; a flower-lined avenue along which the horses, already saddled, are led to the mounting-ring; banks of flowers rising all along the outer rails for as much of the six furlongs straight as forms a vantage point for the racegoers—which is almost half a mile of it.

The members' stand is a vast double-decker, with luncheon-room, the higher-price Tote offices, and other administrative offices beneath it. One half is women only, the other men only, and when filled (as it was) while a race is being run it presented an odd sight—one half almost as gay as the flowerbeds themselves, the other a study in black and white and looking rather like some-thing between a shareholders' meeting and a Rotarian convention.

At the back of this stand is a large paddock in which the bookmakers stand—the equivalent, probably, of our Tattersall's ring. The paraphernalia of " the old firm " seems to be the same the whole world over, the satchel, the blackboard—and the voice. But all the bookmakers were standing in almost regimentally straight lines under blue umbrellas with fringes, so that from a short distance it looked a bit like a tea-garden. Beyond the bookmakers are the Tote stalls for the more modest investors: the minimum stake is five shillings and your ticket is printed for you on a machine rather like those things one used to see on railway stations that stamped out your name and address on metal strips.

Above the stalls were great indicator boards with orange-coloured ribbons running up like mercury in a thermometer showing the money that was being invested on each animal both for a win and for a " place." If this was not enough for a gamble, you could go to another stall and couple the numbers of horses you thought might win two successive races. And finally, when the eighth race came along, and if you had any money left, you could go for the " Quinella," in which you select two horses and hope they finish first and second. This was, of course, none other than our now familiar forecast pool.

Meanwhile, back on the course, loudspeakers are keeping the crowd informed of all essential preliminaries—the saddling, the

---

Answers to Exercise 16—1 (*d*), 2 (*b*), 3 (*a*), 4 (*b*), 5 (*e*), 6 (*c*).

parade, the departure to the starting-point. In attendance on the horses all this time are two riders in red hunting coats and huntsmen's caps—the clerk of the course and his assistant whose functions thus differ vastly from the British clerk. The Australian clerks shepherd the troop to the start, rounding up the fractious and wayward, and at the starting-gate itself they take a big part in getting the horses quietly lined up for the " off."

The " off " itself comes dramatically, with the clang of a gong. There is no preliminary proclamation, as in England, " They're under starter's orders." The commentator has kept one informed of every detail of the lining-up process, and it was notable, even though some of the fields were about twenty strong, that in only one event was there a delay beyond the set time for starting the race. From the " off " the commentary was a sixty-mile-an-hour torrent of words; it was impossible to believe that the race-reader even paused to take a breath.

The commentary was taken right to the finish. There was no waiting for the judge's announcement. Only in the close finishes that had to be determined by photograph were the crowds held in suspense and the speed with which a photo-finish was determined was remarkable. So, too, with the weighing-in of the jockey and his accoutrements. Australian racing is highly streamlined: nowhere else is a man and his winnings separated for so short a time. After all, there is always the next race coming along —and the bars close at 6 p.m.

It was the favourites' day at Flemington and if I did not make a fortune, the Tote at least stood me a good lunch in the cafeteria, where the biscuits and cheese are " thrown in." A man at the entrance gate carried courtesy to a stranger to such lengths as to name eight horses he thought might win the eight races. When, incredibly, the first three of them did win, it seemed time to have some regard for the law of averages. The fourth won the St. Leger while we were tackling the lamb and mint sauce. As it seemed that the age of miracles had dawned, we very cannily took a " place " ticket on Lucky Stride in the Newmarket Handicap (notice how enduring are the ties with the Old Country), but the ticket for Lucky Stride remains a souvenir of Flemington.

We left the course as the jockeys were mounting for the sixth race: the time was 3.30 and it was already over three hours since Comic Lad had set the ball rolling. An elderly gateman directed

G

us to the taxi-park. He had left Liverpool forty-two years ago and was so moved at finding two Lancastrians in our little party that he shook hands twice all round and said we must not miss Cambridge in the 3.40. Cambridge, we recalled, was also one of the eight original prophecies, but we resisted another Tote barracks and found our car for Melbourne. Cambridge, we saw later in the evening papers, won the 3.40 in a photo-finish. We saw, too, that Somerset Fair had fulfilled our adviser's expectations in the seventh race. As I said, the Australian has a profound and peculiar knowledge of the behaviour of horses. [STOP TIMING]

Put your reading time here........................

1. The great passion which the author is discussing is
....

2. The most important race in Australia is the............................

3. The most impressive thing about the track was—
   (a) The wonderful weather.
   (b) The six furlong straight.
   (c) The accommodation for spectators.
   (d) The flowers.
   (e) Its popularity.

4. The greatest difference from an English racecourse was—
   (a) The speed of the whole performance.
   (b) The beauty of the course.
   (c) The running commentary.
   (d) The size of the field.
   (e) The rows of bookmakers.

5. The author got tips from—
   (a) A newspaper boy.
   (b) A bank clerk.
   (c) A jockey.
   (d) A man at the entrance gate.
   (e) The man in the cafeteria.

6. What was the name of the racecourse?............................

You will find the correct answers at the foot of page 96.

This passage has 1,350 words and you can work out your speed from the following table.

Time	Speed	Time	Speed
2.00	675	3.20	405
2.10	621	3.30	385
2.20	578	3.40	367
2.30	540	3.50	352
2.40	506	4.00	337
2.50	476	4.10	324
3.00	450	4.20	311
3.10	425	4.30	300

Speed.................... Comprehension........................

The next passage has slightly longer lines than Exercise 16 and you should try to take them in at one glance. Don't time this but get someone to check whether you are taking them in at one glance or whether you are making slight eye movements. Both of these are satisfactory, but it is wrong if you are making any big eye movements.

EXERCISE 18

The New Suit by George Bellairs

[DO NOT TIME THIS EXERCISE]

A man I know, in a burst
of arty-crafty enthusiasm,
started to make home-spuns.
They were very nice, too,
mottled brown warp and weft
with lovely
red, yellow and green flecks
scattered in the weave
like bright little burrs.
He taught himself
this ancient art,
and when he had
churned out enough material
he sold me a suit length.
At the first fitting
I handled the cloth
with delight.
It was soft and warm and woolly

and looked far finer
made up than
any of the masterpieces
of sartorial art
worn by the young gods
in the magazines
in the tailors' shops.
My tailor, however,
mysteriously shook his head,
and, with an old razor blade,
viciously ripped the coat
down the back,
wrenched a sleeve roughly
from its temporary moorings,
and divided the vest in two.
I thought the gesture
arose from the fact
that by supplying
my own superior material
I was saving one pound
two and sixpence.

Joseph in his famous coat
must have experienced
the same exhilaration as I did
when, clad in my new suit
with its burrs gently glowing
like flowers in bloom,
I started off for my holidays.
The politeness of station staffs
and dining car conductors
made me realize
what a superior figure
I must be cutting.
One of them even asked me
if I would like
a second helping of sweet. . . .

Answers to Exercise 17—1 Betting, 2 Melbourne Cup, 3 (*d*), 4 (*a*),
5 (*d*), 6 Flemington.

Crossing on the plane, too,
I felt dressed
in keeping with the luxury
and, shall we say,
nattiness of the travel.
It was good to be alive . . .
" What's the matter with your suit? "
said my host
when he met me at the airport.
I'd expected a comment
on the cloth, I admit,
and maybe a request
for the name of my tailor,
but this . . .
It wasn't good enough.
Peevishly, I told him so.
He led me without more ado
to a secluded spot
and there I removed my jacket.
It looked as if my tailor
had been at it again
with his safety razor!
The back seam had given
from top to bottom.
The cloth itself had pulled apart.
Hastily, I began
to go over my anatomy,
like a doctor probing
for a spreading disease.
In every part subject to pressure
the suit was giving way.
Shoulders, arms, trousers' seat,
knees were all fraying open,
just as though some sorcerer
had touched and smitten them
with a fearful plague.
" There's not enough
twist in the yarn,"
said my friend,
with a technical flourish,

but I was too busy to bother.
I was anxiously
holding myself together
in fear of total nakedness any time
and, in this twisted posture,
I clambered in the waiting car.

Strange to say,
there was a tailor
in my friend's remote village.
He worked on the roads as well,
and dug graves in his spare time.
He gave us a cordial welcome
when we sought him out.
" There's not enough
twist in the yarn," he said,
greatly to my annoyance
and my host's obvious delight.
Then he took my lovely jacket,
made an incision in the lining,
inserted his hand,
and turned the whole thing
inside out.
He bade me confirm his diagnosis
by an interior view,
like a surgeon
laying open a patient
to convince a sceptical physician.
He offered his services
whilst we waited,
although he could promise nothing
but a patchwork job
for the time being.
This would be a minor operation.
A major performance
would entail reinforcing
from within every inch
of cloth liable to tension.
I said it would be awkward
parading in underclothes

whilst Booiley
(this is phonetic:
I never knew how he spelled it)
did the job.
" I'll lend you a suit," said Booiley.
" One of my own I've just made."
I ought to tell you
that the tailor was almost a dwarf,
very thick set,
with short and powerful arms and legs;
in fact nearly as broad as long.
The suit went on easily to begin with,
but my arms and legs
kept on going after the sleeves
and trousers had finished.

Booiley leapt on the table,
sat cross-legged,
put on a thimble without a top,
and began to wax his thread.
" This came from the wreck
of the Lottie," he said,
indicating the beeswax.
" So did that . . . and those. . . ."
He pointed to a sewing machine
and a heap of needles and thread.
" She was wrecked
on the coast here;
bound from Bristol to India, they said.
It looked like a mothers' meeting
after a riot . . .
sewing machines and stuff
all over the beach."
His fingers flew to and fro.
I paraded about
in my borrowed plumes,
my elbows showing,
my suspenders indecently exposed.
My friend kept
flinging taunts about,

so I took a turn
in the little, quiet garden
of the cottage.
" There's all the time
in the world here, why worry? "
said the gnome as a parting shot.

I seemed more incongruous
in the garden than indoors.
Looking myself up and down,
I had the feeling
that it was a dream of the kind
where you find yourself
walking in pyjamas
down a busy thoroughfare.
A passing tramp
eyed me fraternally
and jays attacking a row of peas
fled with wild cries.
" Get a move on,"
I said churlishly
as I returned indoors.
" All the time in the world,"
replied Booiley patiently.
I came apart again during
a garden party.
Someone asked me
if it was the latest fashion
to have patent cloth in suits,
and my immediate reaction
was to shrink visibly
in the unholy garment
in an effort
to persuade the seams to behave.
For the rest of the holiday
I was seen about
in a suit of sober blue.
I felt very much out of place
among all the gay attire
of the local plage,

but it was more reassuring
than raiment which at any time
threatened to become,
like the Emperor's New Clothes,
nothing at all.
It was annoying,
because those red,
green and yellow burrs
would have put all else to shame.
Booiley took the suit
as I finished my holiday
and, from what I can gather,
has spent the winter with it.
I hear he is creating
a massive lining of heavy tape,
a sort of inner reinforcement
like a shadow-suit
of crossword squares,
and to this he plans to attach
the original with
its many embellishments.
My home-spun friend
has refunded my money.

1. The author begins by thinking that—
   (a) Home-spun cloth is better than other cloth.
   (b) Home-made suits are better than mass-produced suits.
   (c) Home-made cloth is not as good as other cloth.
   (d) Mass-produced suits are better than home-made suits.
   (e) There is no difference between home-made and mass-produced suits.

2. Station staffs and dining car attendants were polite and kind because—
   (a) They thought the author was very well dressed.
   (b) They thought he would tip them well.
   (c) His suit was of such superior cloth.
   (d) Home-spun cloth is worn by wealthy people.
   (e) His suit was splitting at the seams.

3. The trouble with the cloth was that............................

4. The tailor was—
   (*a*) A tall thin man.
   (*b*) Very small and thick set.
   (*c*) About the same size as the author.
   (*d*) Tall and very broad.
   (*e*) Very small and very thin.
5. The tailor was—
   (*a*) Able to remake the suit in a short time.
   (*b*) Too inefficient to do the job properly.
   (*c*) Able to remake the suit eventually.
   (*d*) Unable to remake the suit.
   (*e*) Too busy to remake the suit.
The correct answers are at the foot of page 104.

You should have increased your eye span a little on this passage, and that should lead to an increase of speed on the next exercise which is printed in the usual long lines.

EXERCISE 19

Danger by J. A. Cuddon

[START TIMING] Gin-coloured, thick and heavy—nitroglycerine might be mistaken for many things. Gunpowder, in a jam-jar on a kitchen shelf, could be for washing or baking. Guncotton—innocuous name!—like brittle, slender twigs, might pass for a pale macaroni. But a mine, washed up on a beach, lying comfortably, squat and obese in the sand, commands respect as well as curiosity. Its snail-horn warheads look tender and frail; and there is always a chance that some cunning and invisible process within it is preparing for destruction.

It is peculiar to be close to something which, with an uncertain temperament, may pass within a fraction of a split second from acquiescence to ruining, blasting anger. To be in a room full of bombs is almost as exciting as standing in a cage full of well-fed and apparently somnolent tigers. Both are hypersensitive creations. The advantage of tigers is that you can see and hear what they are doing, while bombs are immobile and silent. The disadvantage of both of them is that a single error may make them change their minds; and then it is usually too late to do anything about it.

I was made fully aware of such possibilities quite recently. It was in an area strangely desolate and closely guarded. A tract sprawling over many untenanted acres and harbouring one of the biggest ammunition manufacture and supply depots in the land.

To get there we took one of those shabby, middle-aged trains which, occasionally, are still to be seen shuffling along branch lines in remote places: trains long since relegated to a rustic and pensionable obscurity. After a short journey one of these coughed us out at an almost anonymous station—no more than a few planks and an office spawned in antiquity among weeds and grass —where one man appeared to combine all duties, assisted by a youth still ambitious for an old blue waistcoat and a porter's hat.

It was only a mile or so from there to the ammunition preserve but, as soon as we arrived, we were aware of a subtle difference in the atmosphere. The big gates, the barbed wire, the high railings, the armed guards, notices prohibiting smoking and lights —all had the effect of making us a little cautious and sensitive. But it was not these obvious signs which induced a feeling of inquisitive apprehension. It was quiet there; very quiet. There were not many people about and those that there were were silent and preoccupied, going about their business with an air of detached efficiency. A loud word or laugh surprised.

After a few introductory remarks on the pattern of the place we were conducted to what must be one of the oldest trains in existence. It consisted of two short wooden carriages—the paint-work blistered and flaked by years of exposure and neglect— which contained low, hard seats running from end to end, the contraption being drawn by a patriarch among engines. Rusty and asthmatic, it scuffled along on grinding wheels into an area of woods straggling among hairy, unkempt fields: fields of every withered colour—brown, mustard, dun, ochreous, parched and dyed by the constant August sun. Ultimately, rasping with the exertion, the train dropped us at the first depot—a huge, barn-like structure with a covered loading ramp alongside the rails.

The engine lapsed into a coma and again the silence of a destitute country surrounded us. But a silence informed by the whir and hum and buzz of innumerable insects; an undercurrent of life not immediately noticeable; a low-pitched accompaniment fabricated by the machinery of millions of wings, torn only infrequently by the cry of a jay and the long cackle of a magpie.

Over all, the light and the heat spread itself steadily, almost ponderously; the weight of it cutting shadows in slabs, in slim dagger-points and broad blades. The light carving weapons against itself and the heat pressing down on all the wounds.

Alert and absorbed we entered the building. A notice said " DANGER," and prohibitions were redoubled. We exchanged a few jocularities in an undertone but the laughter was a polite affair. Bombs are unpredictable things. Like tigers they are easily startled by sudden noises. In a lobby we were issued with rubber boots and buff-coloured coats and then led into the explosives-room.

It was rather like going into a big church to assist at a solemn ceremony; or into an operating theatre to watch a critical demonstration. The high, vaulted barn—well-lighted, proofed against the searching heaviness of the heat laid upon it, and smelling slightly of chemicals—revealed about a dozen men, clad like ourselves but wearing in addition masks, rubber gloves, and close-fitting white hats rather like large skull-caps. They were all small men with gnome-like faces and delicate, wrinkled skin, a little pale. When they moved they padded silently and precisely, the inattention of their eyes showing how they concentrated almost exclusively upon their work. Each knew exactly what he was doing and exactly how to do it. Speech seemed superfluous to them. The atmosphere was stretched tight, like the thinnest membrane.

Cautiously we moved among the work-benches while our guide —in a low voice—explained what was being done. Occasionally one of us managed to whisper a question; but it was difficult to concentrate—so mysterious were the rites and the air they engendered. One got the feeling that one was being watched; that a force inhabited there; lay waiting for a mistake. I glanced over my shoulder: one of the little men was looking at me with pallid, expressionless eyes. He did not seem to notice and bent again at his work.

Coming out it was a relief to feel the moist hand of the heat again; the flash of light in the eyes; to hear the stutter of a distant pheasant; to smell the scorched grass; to feel one's foot strike the ground with a reassuring crunch. In there it had been like

---

Answers to Exercise 18—1 (*a*), 2 (*e*), 3 Not enough twist in the yarn, 4 (*b*), 5 (*c*).

walking on glass, breathing fragile air, touching the most flimsy filaments of an inexplicable power: where every smothered cough was like a detonation; where a box, moved, caught the ear; where a bomb—snug in its straw—gripped the eye and made one wonder whether or not it was just going to do something. For half an hour I had felt as if I were looking down the blank stare of the barrel of a revolver, wondering if I should see what came out when it did come out.

On the way to the next depot I asked our guide how long the men worked at the explosives and he told me that some of the men had been there nearly twenty years. I think I should have blown myself up within a week. [STOP TIMING]

Put your reading time here.........................

1. Explosives are—
   (a) Terrifying in appearance.
   (b) Quite ordinary to look at.
   (c) Rather odd in appearance.
   (d) Somewhat frightening when seen.
   (e) Not pleasant to see.
2. The author compares bombs to a ferocious animal. What animal is it?............................
3. He went there by—
   (a) Motor bus.
   (b) Motor car.
   (c) Plane.
   (d) Train.
   (e) Motor cycle.
4. On arrival the author was impressed by—
   (a) The quietness.
   (b) The noise.
   (c) The peaceful atmosphere.
   (d) The happiness of the workers.
   (e) The sadness of the workers.
5. The protective clothing issued was—
   (a) Felt slippers and rubber aprons.
   (b) Rubber boots and raincoats.
   (c) Boiler suits and helmets.
   (d) Felt slippers and brown coats.
   (e) Rubber boots and brown coats.

The correct answers are at the bottom of page 108.

This passage has 1,140 words. You can work out your speed from the following table.

Time	Speed	Time	Speed
1.30	760	2.40	427
1.40	685	2.50	402
1.50	620	3.00	380
2.00	570	3.10	360
2.10	526	3.20	342
2.20	488	3.30	320
2.30	456	3.40	308
2.40	427		

Speed........................   Comprehension........................

THE HALF WAY TEST

You are now half way through the course and it is time for a test to compare your speed with your initial speed on Test 2, and to make sure that your comprehension has not fallen. For it is your speed that you are trying to improve whilst keeping comprehension at a satisfactory sixty to seventy per cent level.

This test is an extract from the same volume of short stories as Test 2, and is, therefore, of equivalent difficulty, so your score will be strictly comparable. It is 1,800 words and you should set yourself a target time for reading it which should not be more than five minutes. Do not vocalize the dialogue.

EXERCISE 20

Extract from *The Adventure of the Lion's Mane*
by Sir Arthur Conan Doyle

[START TIMING] It is a most singular thing that a problem which was certainly as abstruse and unusual as any which I have faced in my long professional career should have come to me after my retirement; and be brought, as it were, to my very door. It occurred after my withdrawal to my little Sussex home, when I had given myself up entirely to that soothing life of Nature for which I had so often yearned during the long years spent amid the gloom of London. At this period of my life the good Watson had passed almost beyond my ken. An occasional week-end visit was the most that I ever saw of him. Thus I must act as my own chronicler. Ah! had he but been with me, how much he might have made of so wonderful a happening and of my eventual triumph against every difficulty! As it is, however, I must needs tell my tale in my own plain way, showing by my words each step upon the difficult road which lay before me as I searched for the mystery of the Lion's Mane.

My villa is situated upon the southern slope of the Downs, commanding a great view of the Channel. At this point the coast-line is entirely of chalk cliffs, which can only be descended by a single, long, tortuous path, which is steep and slippery.

At the bottom of the path lie a hundred yards of pebbles and shingle, even when the tide is at full. Here and there, however, there are curves and hollows which make splendid swimming-pools filled afresh with each flow. This admirable beach extends for some miles in each direction, save only at one point where the little cove and village of Fulworth breaks the line.

My house is lonely. I, my old housekeeper, and my bees have the estate all to ourselves. Half a mile off, however, is Harold Stackhurst's well-known coaching establishment, the Gables, quite a large place, which contains some score of young fellows preparing for various professions, with a staff of several masters. Stackhurst himself was a well-known rowing Blue in his day, and an excellent all-round scholar. He and I were always friendly from the day I came to the coast, and he was the one man who was on such terms with me that we could drop in on each other in the evenings without an invitation.

Towards the end of July, 1907, there was a severe gale, the wind blowing up-Channel, heaping the seas to the base of the cliffs, and leaving a lagoon at the turn of the tide. On the morning of which I speak the wind had abated, and all Nature was newly washed and fresh. It was impossible to work upon so delightful a day, and I strolled out before breakfast to enjoy the exquisite air. I walked along the cliff path which led to the steep descent to the beach. As I walked I heard a shout behind me, and there was Harold Stackhurst waving his hand in cheery greeting.

" What a morning, Mr. Holmes! I thought I should see you out."

" Going for a swim, I see."

" At your old tricks again," he laughed, patting his bulging pocket. " Yes. McPherson started early, and I expect I may find him there."

Fitzroy McPherson was the science master, a fine upstanding young fellow whose life had been crippled by heart trouble following rheumatic fever. He was a natural athlete, however, and excelled in every game which did not throw too great a strain upon him. Summer and winter he went for his swim, and, as I am a swimmer myself, I have often joined him.

At this moment we saw the man himself. His head showed

above the edge of the cliff where the path ends. Then his whole
figure appeared at the top, staggering like a drunken man. The
next instant he threw up his hands, and, with a terrible cry, fell
upon his face. Stackhurst and I rushed forward—it may have
been fifty yards—and turned him on his back. He was obviously
dying. Those glazed sunken eyes and dreadful livid cheeks could
mean nothing else. One glimmer of life came into his face
for an instant, and he uttered two or three words with an eager
air of warning. They were slurred and indistinct, but to my ear
the last of them, which burst in a shriek from his lips, were
" the lion's mane." It was utterly irrelevant and unintelligible,
and yet I could twist the sound into no other sense. Then he
half raised himself from the ground, threw his arms into the air
and fell forward on his side. He was dead.

My companion was paralysed by the sudden horror of it, but
I, as may well be imagined, had every sense on the alert. And I
had need, for it was speedily evident that we were in the presence
of an extraordinary case. The man was dressed only in his
Burberry overcoat, his trousers, and an unlaced pair of canvas
shoes. As he fell over, his Burberry, which had been simply
thrown round his shoulders, slipped off, exposing his trunk. We
stared at it in amazement. His back was covered with dark red
lines, as though he had been terribly flogged by a thin wire
scourge. The instrument with which this punishment had been
inflicted was clearly flexible, for the long, angry weals curved
round his shoulders and ribs. There was blood dripping down
his chin, for he had bitten through his lower lip in the paroxysm
of his agony. His drawn and distorted face told how terrible that
agony had been.

I was kneeling and Stackhurst standing by the body when a
shadow fell across us, and we found that Ian Murdoch was by
our side. Murdoch was the mathematical coach at the establishment, a tall, dark, thin man, so taciturn and aloof that none can
be said to have been his friend. He seemed to live in some high,
abstract region of surds and conic sections with little to connect
him with ordinary life. He was looked upon as an oddity by the
students, and would have been their butt, but there was some
strange outlandish blood in the man, which showed itself not
only in his coal-black eyes and swarthy face, but also in occasional
outbreaks of temper, which could only be described as ferocious.

H

On one occasion, being plagued by a little dog belonging to McPherson, he had caught the creature up and hurled it through the plate-glass window, an action for which Stackhurst would certainly have given him his dismissal had he not been a very valuable teacher. Such was the strange, complex man who now appeared beside us. He seemed to be honestly shocked at the sight before him, though the incident of the dog may show that there was no great sympathy between the dead man and himself.

" Poor fellow! Poor fellow! What can I do? How can I help? "

" Were you with him? Can you tell us what has happened? "

" No, no, I was late this morning. I was not on the beach at all. I have come straight from the Gables. What can I do? "

" You can hurry to the police-station at Fulworth. Report the matter at once."

Without a word he made off at top speed, and I proceeded to take the matter in hand, while Stackhurst, dazed at this tragedy, remained by the body. My first task naturally was to note who was on the beach. From the top of the path I could see the whole sweep of it, and it was absolutely deserted save that two or three dark figures could be seen far away moving towards the village of Fulworth. Having satisfied myself upon this point, I walked slowly down the path. There was clay or soft marl mixed with the chalk, and every here and there I saw the same footsteps, both ascending and descending. No one else had gone down to the beach by this track that morning. At one place I observed the print of an open hand with the fingers towards the incline. This could only mean that poor McPherson had fallen as he ascended. There were rounded depressions, too, which suggested that he had come down upon his knees more than once. At the bottom of the path was the considerable lagoon left by the retreating tide. At the side of it McPherson had undressed, for there lay his towel on a rock. It was folded and dry, so that it would seem that after all he had never entered the water. Once or twice as I hunted round amid the hard shingle I came on little patches of sand where the print of his canvas shoe, and also of his naked foot, could be seen. The latter fact proved that he had made all ready to bathe, though the towel indicated that he had not actually done so.

And here was the problem clearly defined—as strange a one

as ever confronted me. The man had not been on the beach more than a quarter of an hour at the most. Stackhurst had followed him from the Gables, so there could be no doubt about that. He had gone to bathe and had stripped, as the naked footsteps showed. Then he had suddenly huddled on his clothes again— they were all dishevelled and unfastened—and he had returned without bathing, or at any rate without drying himself. And the reason for his change of purpose had been that he had been scourged in some savage, inhuman fashion, tortured until he bit his lips through in his agony, and was left with only strength enough to crawl away and to die. Who had done this barbarous deed? There were, it is true, small grottos and caves in the base of the cliffs, but the low sun shone directly into them, and there was no place for concealment. Then, again, there were those distant figures on the beach. They seemed too far away to have been connected with the crime, and the broad lagoon in which McPherson had intended to bathe lay between him and them, lapping up to the rocks. On the sea two or three fishing-boats were at no great distance. Their occupants might be examined at our leisure. There were several roads for inquiry, but none which led to any very obvious goal.

When I at last returned to the body I found that a little group of wandering folk had gathered round it. Stackhurst was, of course, still there, and Ian Murdoch had just arrived with Anderson, the village constable, a big, ginger-moustached man of the slow, solid Sussex breed—a breed which covers much good sense under a heavy, silent exterior. He listened to everything, took note of all we said, and finally drew me aside.

" I'd be glad of your advice, Mr. Holmes. This is a big thing for me to handle, and I'll hear of it from Lewes if I go wrong."

I advised him to send for his immediate superior, and for a doctor; also to allow nothing to be moved, and as few fresh footmarks as possible to be made, until they came. In the meantime I searched the dead man's pockets. There were his handkerchief, a large knife, and a small folding card-case. From this projected a slip of paper, which I unfolded and handed to the constable. There was written on it in a scrawling hand: " I will be there, you may be sure. Maudie." It read like a love affair, an assignation, though when and where were a blank. The constable replaced it in the card-case and returned it with the other things to the pocket of the Burberry. Then, as nothing more suggested itself, I walked back to my house for breakfast, having first arranged that the base of the cliffs should be thoroughly searched. [Stop Timing]

Put your reading time here.........................

1. At this time Sherlock Holmes was living in—
   (a) His flat in Baker Street.
   (b) A cottage on the Welsh Coast.
   (c) A large house on the Downs.
   (d) At a small school.
   (e) A small house on the Sussex Downs.
2. Doctor Watson was—
   (a) Living in the same house.
   (b) A rare and infrequent visitor.
   (c) Living in a house nearby.
   (d) Out of the Country.
   (e) No longer a friend of Holmes.
3. The beach consists of—
   (a) A long and unbroken stretch of sand.
   (b) Rocks and rock pools.
   (c) Sand and shingle interspersed.
   (d) Steep cliffs backed by sand dunes.
   (e) Steep cliffs falling into the sea.
4. The coaching establishment consisted of—
   (a) About ten boys and two masters.
   (b) About fifteen boys and three masters.
   (c) About twenty boys and several masters.
   (d) About twenty-five boys and several masters.
   (e) About thirty boys and several masters.
5. Stackhurst and Holmes were—
   (a) Acquaintances.
   (b) Fairly friendly.
   (c) Not particularly friendly.
   (d) Great friends.
   (e) Neighbours but not very friendly.
6. On this day the beach was very attractive because—
   (a) The wind was blowing hard.
   (b) It was calm again after a gale.
   (c) A gale was blowing up.

   (*d*) Holmes had been overworking.

   (*e*) It was very hot and sultry.

7. During the morning Holmes met—
   (*a*) Stackhurst and two other men.
   (*b*) Stackhurst, Watson and McPherson.
   (*c*) McPherson, Watson and Murdoch.
   (*d*) His old housekeeper and Stackhurst.
   (*e*) His old housekeeper and two men.

8. McPherson was especially fond of swimming because—
   (*a*) He excelled at it.
   (*b*) He could not take part in more strenuous sport.
   (*c*) He did not like any other sport.
   (*d*) The weather was so hot.
   (*e*) He was fond of sun bathing.

9. Write down the words which McPherson said when he was dying................................

10. McPherson was—
   (*a*) Completely dressed.
   (*b*) Wearing swimming trunks and a Burberry.
   (*c*) Wearing trousers, a Burberry and a hat.
   (*d*) Wearing a Burberry and a pair of canvas shoes.
   (*e*) Wearing a Burberry, trousers and a pair of canvas shoes

11. His back was—
   (*a*) Covered with bruises.
   (*b*) Covered with dark red lines.
   (*c*) A mass of old scars.
   (*d*) Crushed and shattered.
   (*e*) Not particularly damaged.

12. Murdoch was—
   (*a*) A hasty tempered mathematician.
   (*b*) A mild mannered classicist.
   (*c*) A hasty tempered classicist.
   (*d*) A mild mannered mathematician.
   (*e*) An ordinary teacher of no outstanding qualities.

13. On one occasion—
   (*a*) Murdoch pushed McPherson through a plate-glass window.
   (*b*) McPherson pushed Murdoch through a plate-glass window.

(c) Murdoch threw McPherson's dog through a plate-glass window.

(d) McPherson threw Murdoch's dog through a plate-glass window.

(e) McPherson and Murdoch had a stand up fight.

14. Holmes sent Murdoch—
   (a) Back to school.
   (b) To the village for a doctor.
   (c) To bring Doctor Watson.
   (d) To the village for the police.
   (e) To see if anyone was on the cliff top.

15. When Holmes looked round—
   (a) There were several people on the beach nearby.
   (b) There was nobody else on the beach.
   (c) There was only Stackhurst and himself on the beach.
   (d) There was only the body and himself on the beach.
   (e) The only others on the beach were a long way off.

16. When Holmes examined the path, he found—
   (a) A confusing mixture of footprints.
   (b) Only McPherson's and Murdoch's footprints.
   (c) Only his own and Stackhurst's footprints.
   (d) Only two sets of McPherson's footprints.
   (e) Only one set of McPherson's footprints.

17. It was clear that—
   (a) McPherson had not gone in the water.
   (b) McPherson had gone in the water.
   (c) McPherson had not dried himself.
   (d) McPherson had dried himself.
   (e) McPherson had forgotten his towel.

18. The body was found—
   (a) On the beach by the lagoon.
   (b) Half in and half out of the water.
   (c) Half way up the cliff path.
   (d) At the top of the cliff.
   (e) Huddled in a small cave.

19. The constable was—
   (a) An excitable Welshman.
   (b) A ponderous Sussex man.
   (c) Dark and slightly built.

(d) Fair and very fat.

(e) Rather rude to Holmes.

20. When he had finished Holmes—

(a) Went home to ring Watson.

(b) Got in touch with Scotland Yard.

(c) Went to the school with Stackhurst.

(d) Assisted in the removal of the body.

(e) Went home for breakfast.

The correct answers are at the foot of page 116.

This passage has 1,800 words, and I hope you did it in less than five minutes. Work out your speed from the table.

Time	Speed	Time	Speed
2.30	720	4.00	450
2.40	675	4.10	436
2.50	635	4.20	415
3.00	600	4.30	400
3.10	568	4.40	385
3.20	540	4.50	372
3.30	514	5.00	360
3.40	491	5.10	348
3.50	469	5.20	337
4.00	450	5.30	327

Speed........................   Comprehension........................

Compare your results with those you had for Passage 2, and you will see how you have improved.

READING THE NEWSPAPER

You have read an exercise printed in three word groups and one printed in four word groups. Now we are going to try a slightly longer line of five or six words, which is the standard line of a newspaper. The following extracts are printed as nearly as possible as they appeared in the paper, and here is a short one to start with. If you have a wide eye span, you should be able to take in a line at a glance, that is, to fix your eyes on the middle of the line and see the whole line. Don't leave any part unread; you must see and read every word.

EXERCISE 21

" *Prêt-à-Porter* "
From Phyllis Heathcote

PARIS
[START TIMING] Development of the
ready-to-wear business is an outstanding
characteristic of the dressmaking industry
in France since the war. In the old days
it was difficult to find a wearable " prêt-
à-porter "—certainly not one with a label
inside the collar. There were, of course,
dress, coat, and suit departments in the
great stores, but no woman with any
pretensions to style or good taste would
have thought of dressing that way.
Nearly everybody had her " petite
couturière " (or her " tailleur "), who
made for her according to her own ideas
and with her own materials. These little
dressmakers were good—most of them
set up in business after years of first-class
training and experience in one of the big
houses—and their prices were very

Answers to Exercise 20—1 (*e*), 2 (*b*), 3 (*c*), 4 (*c*), 5 (*b*), 6 (*b*), 7 (*a*),
8 (*b*), 9 The Lion's Mane, 10 (*e*), 11 (*b*), 12 (*a*), 13 (*c*), 14 (*d*),
15 (*e*), 16 (*d*), 17 (*a*), 18 (*d*), 19 (*b*), 20 (*e*).

reasonable. The only drawback as far as
I could see was that they invariably lived
on a fifth floor, with no lift. . . .

They still exist, of course, but there are
already fewer of them, and if the production of good ready-made clothes con-
tinues to develop at the present rate and
if the dressmakers continue to run up
their prices, then it seems to me that they
are doomed in the end to disappear—
except, perhaps, in the provinces. And
that would be a thousand pities. For
these are real craftswomen and represent
a lively, personal, unstandardized, and
creative element in fashion—and conversation—in France.

But to come back to the ready-mades.
From being an anonymous, unpretentious
industry its higher reaches are now beginning to command attention and a sort of
grudging respect. A new set of names we
never heard of a few years ago is creep-
ing into the currency. And like their
big brothers of the Haute Couture, the
"prêt-à-porter" manufacturers now send
out expensive-looking invitation cards
requesting us to view their collections and
drink their champagne. . . . Among the
names in this new category are Gattengo,
Basta, Waser, Pierre Billet, and, for
" jeunes filles," Lempereur. The latest
arrival is Jacques Fath-Université, a
collection specially designed for junior
clients.

Although inspired by the great fashion
houses and by what has already been
shown, these displays of ready-made
clothes tell us how the ordinary
woman is likely to interpret current
styles. For instance, the straight, long,
slim, spindling button-through coat, often
in corduroy, though launched tentatively
by the Haute Couture a season or so
back, has come into its own in the
" prêt-à-porters ": so that to-day every
other woman you meet in Paris is dressed
in some version of this garment. Indeed,
particularly among younger women, it is
beginning to amount to a uniform. (It
seems to me that this practical style is the
perfect answer to the problem peculiar to
the British weather of discovering a comfortable, warm, waterproof garment that

keeps tidy and attractive-looking in both wind and rain.)

These, briefly, are some of the main points of the prêt-à-porter collections: Coats inspired from the straight overcoat or slim redingotes. Narrow, sloping shoulders on coats and suits, small arm-holes, short basques to suit jackets. Pleated skirts—a few shaped ones flaring out under the jacket basque. Waists softly marked without any sign of taping. In the dresses the sweater line predomi-nates. Fabrics in favour are wool and silk mixtures, alpaca weaves, shantung weaves, tweed, fancy flannels, cashmere, Shetland weaves, a great many cottons of all kinds, and corduroys. Colours: beige running through all the shades to brown, lighter greys than last year, yellows, a new steel blue. [STOP TIMING]

Put your reading time here...................

1. Prêt-à-porter means—
   (a) The name of a firm of clothiers.
   (b) Ready for anything.
   (c) Waterproof.
   (d) Ready-made.
   (e) Second-hand.

2. In the old days, most women—
   (a) Made their own clothes at home.
   (b) Bought ready-made clothes in shops.
   (c) Had their clothes made by a small dressmaker.
   (d) Never had any new clothes.
   (e) Wore second-hand clothes.

3. Dressmakers are tending to disappear because—
   (a) The clothes they make are not good enough.
   (b) They are pricing themselves out of the market.
   (c) They do not charge enough.
   (d) Women prefer to make their own clothes.
   (e) They find the job dull and monotonous.

4. The manufacturers of prêt-à-porter are—
   (a) Anonymous tailors working in back street premises.
   (b) Now well-known firms who label their garments.
   (c) Small dressmakers working in garrets.

(*d*) Linked with the big department stores.

(*e*) Not particularly successful at the moment.

5. The prêt-à-porter business has—

(*a*) Had little effect on the clothes of the Paris women.

(*b*) Had only a slight effect on the clothes of the Parisiennes.

(*c*) Caused uniformity in coats worn in Paris.

(*d*) Caused Parisiennes to wear startling colours.

(*e*) Emphasized the difference between the poor and the rich.

You will find the correct answers at the foot of page 120.

This passage has 590 words and you can work out your speed from the table below.

Time	Speed
1.10	505
1.20	442
1.30	395
1.40	354
1.50	321
2.00	295
2.10	272
2.20	252
2.30	236

Speed....................... Comprehension.......................

I expect you suffered a drop in speed on this exercise. It was caused by the change from the usual type and lay-out. These shorter lines make for quicker and easier reading, so once you are used to them you should make further increases in speed.

EXERCISE 22

From Alistair Cooke
NEW YORK, JANUARY 13

[START TIMING] Costa Rica and Nicaragua do not like each other very much at the moment. But beyond that it would be rash to say who is fighting who, where the " troops " are recruited from, whose equipment they are using, and whether an exchange of insults between the two heads of State, and a splatter of bullet marks on some buildings in San José, the capital of Costa Rica, constitute a war by any modern or even medieval definition.

The "New York Times," with its usual professionalism, has three war correspondents diligently seeking out the details of the fighting, but so far even the grand strategy evades them. Yesterday, for instance, Colonel Francisco Orlich, who is described as the commander of the Costa Rica "Government Forces in the Field," went on a "tour of interrogation" of rebel prisoners. There were eight of them, dressed in no other uniform than dungarees. They would not identify themselves and a Costa Rican officer was not even sure that they were any sort of Costa Rican, rebel or loyalist. "They don't seem," he said, "like our people." However, one was recognized as a Costa Rican and they were all promptly sent off to the penitentiary.

Challenge to a Duel

What is sure is that aircraft variously identified as "rebels" or fugitives from the Venezuelan Air Force, have been strafing five or six Costa Rican towns. The actions of ground troops are accurately described as "confused." A force of "air-borne rebels" claimed to have taken Villa Quesada on Tuesday and yesterday Costa Rican troops announced that they had recaptured it. It is a remote village at the end of a mountain road and, from this morning's dispatch filed from there by the "New York Times" man, it would seem that Colonel Francisco Orlich is in command of the situation. If so, the "air-borne rebels" of the agency dispatches would be those same eight men in dungarees.

The Costa Rican Government has suspended civil liberties without saying which ones; and it is assumed that the country is on a war footing if only the battle grounds can be identified and used.

The only straightforward quarrel is that between President Figueres of Costa Rica and President Somoza of Nicaragua. Yesterday President

---

Answers to Exercise 21—1 (*d*), 2 (*c*), 3 (*b*), 4 (*b*), 5 (*c*).

Figueres accused Venezuela of sending its planes in to help the rebels. Venezuela retorted that the charge was "ridiculous." The President of Nicaragua replied to Mr. Figueres even more explicitly. "Damn liar," he said. He thereupon challenged President Figueres to meet him at the border "with revolvers."

Symptons of Instability

Although this latest Latin-American collision sounds at this distance even more Ruritanian than the eruption in Guatemala last summer, the United States is concerned about it as one of many symptoms of instability in the Latin-American republics. The Council of American States voted yesterday in Washington to ask any American States "that are in a position tc do so " to send aircraft into Costa Rica on observation missions. To-day, American planes attached to the Caribbean Air Command will leave their bases in Panama. The Council also asked all the Governments to "deny their territory to any military action against the Government of any other country."

The State Department is looking anxiously on the present disturbance as yet another of the sporadic upheavals that have embittered Latin-American relations in the past two years: the attempt in April, 1953, on the life of Peron; the Communist plot in British Guiana the following October; the threat to the life of President Somoza for which Nicaragua blamed Costa Rica last April; the military junta in Paraguay last May; the brush between the Army and uprising of students in Colombia in June; the Gautemalan affair in July; the suicide of Vargas, the deposed President of Brazil; and the assassination of President Remon of Panama this month.

Causes of Unrest

The United States is not much afraid of any organized coup from that "hostile outsider" whose identity needs no gloss. It suspects rather that all these eruptions spring from widespread economic and social unrest, especially in those countries whose peoples are thoroughly aware for the first time that they live under nearly-feudal regimes. Dr Milton Eisenhower, the President's brother, delivered a long and disturbing report to the President in November, 1953, after a so-called fact-finding tour of South America. Last January came the report of the Randall Commission stressing the essential need of the Latin-American republics for freer trade and for the more imaginative use of the resources of private enterprise.

President Eisenhower is reliably said to feel that the recommendations of the Randall Commission apply far more urgently to Latin America than to Europe; and that is why he will fight to extend the reciprocal trade treaties for three years, to lower tariffs across the Rio Grande, and to simplify Customs procedures which at present suffocate in a bog of incompetence and red tape orderly trade between the United States and the Central-American republics in particular.

That is why, too, he is sending Vice-President Richard Nixon on a goodwill tour of South America. It may explain why, in the face of damning evidence accumulated by the Democratic National Committee, he yet felt himself obliged to praise the Vice-President so fulsomely at his press conference yesterday. [STOP TIMING]

Put your reading time here.......................

1. Costa Rica and Nicaragua are—
   (a) Fighting desperately with each other.
   (b) Threatening to attack each other very shortly.
   (c) Not really fighting each other.
   (d) Fighting together against Mexico.
   (e) Quite friendly with each other.
2. One side claim to have captured—
   (a) Eighty uniformed men.
   (b) Eight men in overalls.
   (c) Eight hundred paratroopers.
   (d) Eight captains of artillery.
   (e) Eighty foreign nationals.

3. Planes have bombed—
   (a) Five or six Costa Rican towns.
   (b) Several Venezuelan towns.
   (c) The capital of Costa Rica.
   (d) Rebel ground forces.
   (e) Supply dumps and marshalling yards.
4. The two Presidents have been—
   (a) Shooting at each other with revolvers.
   (b) Calling each other names.
   (c) Appealing to UNO.
   (d) Threatening to start an Atom War.
   (e) Trying to reach a peaceful settlement.
5. The United States is concerned because—
   (a) They have many holdings in Costa Rica.
   (b) They think that the fighting might spread to themselves.
   (c) They are a peace-loving nation.
   (d) There are many Americans in the two countries.
   (e) They think it indicates general instability in Central America.
6. President Eisenhower has decided—
   (a) To enforce peace by using American forces.
   (b) To stop all trade with the two countries.
   (c) To increase trade with the two countries.
   (d) To call a Pan-American conference.
   (e) To take no action.

The correct answers are at the foot of page 124.

This passage has 870 words and you can find your speed from the table below.

Time	Speed
1.30	580
1.40	522
1.50	474
2.00	435
2.10	401
2.20	372
2.30	350
2.40	326
2.50	307
3.00	290

Speed...................... Comprehension......................

You should have recovered your speed on that one and be able to improve it on the next exercise.

EXERCISE 23

[START TIMING] Snow fell heavily across the south part of England and Wales yesterday, reaching a depth in some places of six inches in a few hours, stranding traffic in many areas and stopping bus services at towns as far apart as Maidstone and Swansea. The snow was still falling from the Kent coast to Bristol at 11.30 p.m., but in Devon and Cornwall, where earlier the deepest of the drifts had formed, it turned to rain in the evening. At midnight the first reports of serious flooding came in.

At Truro, in Cornwall, the flooding was the most serious for 60 years. The main road through the city was impassable, with water rising halfway up shop windows. Many people were driven upstairs; others in the streets could not reach their homes. Motorists abandoned cars with the water up to the petrol filler caps. Civil Defence rescue squads, Red Cross, and the W.V.S. were called out, and a rest centre was opened in a Methodist schoolroom.

At Bude, where traffic in the outlying districts had been brought to a standstill by deep snow drifts, several roads were flooded last night to a depth of several feet.

In Kent the snow, which was being driven by a wind off the sea, was described as one of the worst blizzards for years. On the main coast road between Folkestone and Dover traffic was brought practically to a standstill, and Dover Hill, on the main road just outside Folkestone, was closed to buses and cars. For nearly two hours there was an electricity failure in parts of Romney Marsh.

Five-Mile Traffic Jam

Only a part of Northern England and North Wales escaped the day's storm,

Answers to Exercise 22—1 (*c*), 2 (*b*), 3 (*a*), 4 (*b*), 5 (*e*), 6 (*c*).

and with 81 counties in Britain under
snow last evening the R.A.C. was moved
to describe traffic conditions in one
word: " Chaotic." Ice on the hills and
minor collisions stopped long lines of
vehicles in many places. Some drivers
gave up because the snow was falling
so thickly that they could not see. The
longest traffic jam reported was at High
Wycombe, Bucks, where a series of
collisions held up a line of vehicles for
five miles.

All London's main roads remained
open to traffic but shortly before midnight motorists were advised to drive
with great caution, and not to journey
to the West Country or Wales until conditions improved. Trains from South
Wales were arriving an hour late.

All air services had to be guided into
London Airport last night by radar,
and for four hours visibility on the run-
ways was cut to six hundred yards.
Several services were held up or can-
celled. At Wandsworth Stadium greyhounds ran up to their knees in snow.

Lancashire's " Blanket "

Early this morning Lancashire and
North Wales were benefiting from a
blanket of cloud which prevented the
temperature from dropping as rapidly
as had been expected. At midnight the
temperature was 29 deg. and an hour
later had only dropped another ·56 of a
degree at Manchester Airport. The
" blanket " first began to break up over
Blackpool and North Wales, where the
temperature immediately dropped quite
noticeably, and the same was expected
to happen over Manchester later.

Scotland had another day of snow, but
the 68 railway passengers and crews
who had spent Wednesday night in the
three trains cut off by snowdrifts in
Caithness were rescued. Some had been
in the trains—stranded at Altnabreac,
Georgemas Junction, and Bower—for 36
hours when rescue teams, clearing drifts
up to ten feet deep, reached them.
Several had found shelter in cottages or
in station buildings; others who stayed
in the trains kept up their spirits by

I

singing hymns. The travellers at Altnabreac had been without food for 24 hours
when the relief train reached them at
7 a.m.

South-bound passengers who had the
heart for a further journey through the
snow were travelling to Inverness last
night. The ten who wished to go north
to Thurso were still waiting for the line
to be cleared.

The nineteen passengers of a B.E.A.
plane from Orkney to Aberdeen, which
became snowbound on Wick airport on
Wednesday afternoon, were still
stranded in Wick last night. One of
them, an Orkney boy of ten who
was going to Aberdeen for hospital
treatment, was taken to hospital in
Wick. Two B.E.A. engineers who left
Renfrew yesterday to free the snowed-
up plane were able to get only as far
as Inverness.

Drifts of up to seven feet completely
blocked all main roads in the Orkney
Islands. Bus passengers, caught by the
blizzard on Wednesday afternoon, were
still sheltering in farms, and hotels were
packed with stranded travellers.

The snow prevented a wedding from
taking place at Wick and a wedding and
a funeral in the Hebrides. The Hebrides
wedding was to have been solemnized
at Barvas, Lewis, and men were
still working late last night to clear the
road to the bride's home six miles
away. They were encouraged by an
open invitation extended to all diggers.

Sea Smashes Wall

In Northern England a high sea hit
the east coast. Some streets at Clee-
thorpes were flooded for over an hour
when waves 15 ft. high swept over the
coastal railway embankment and under-
mined a part of it. British Railways
are to start work on Monday on a new
defence wall which will cost £8,000. At
Scarborough about 120 tons of concrete
from a bathing-pool crashed outwards
as the sea flooded the pool and smashed
down 60 feet of a surrounding wall.

The ice caused an unusual accident at
Audlem, Cheshire. Friction generated
by the spinning wheels of a lorry set fire

to the tyres. The lorry was severely damaged, but its load of grain was saved.

A burst in a trunk water main near Peel Bridge deprived 7,000 homes in Ramsbottom, Holcombe Brook, Tottington, Walshaw, and parts of Bury of their supply for 12 hours yesterday. Water carts served some of them, and the supply was restored in time for supper by engineers of the Irwell Valley Water Board, who worked by floodlight.

At sea, Dutch rescue services had a busy day helping ships in distress. A helicopter rescued fifteen of the crew of the Norwegian ship Gatt (1,700 tons) which ran aground on Wednesday night off a pier at the Hook of Holland. She sprang a leak that overwhelmed the pumps and quenched the boiler fires. Tugs and lifeboats could not reach her through high seas, but seven of the crew of 22 got ashore by means of a rope stretched between the ship and the pier.

Last night a Dutch seagoing tug took in tow the Swedish ship Bohus (2,083 tons) which had reported herself " cracked aft midships " off the Dogger Bank, and another Dutch tug went out to the Swedish motor-ship Boreland (2,646 tons) which had engine trouble 40 miles west of Texel Island.

Several ships and a Dutch aircraft failed to find any survivors from an upturned vessel, possibly a fishing-boat, seen from the British ship Ludhan Queen about sixty miles east of Denmark yesterday morning.

Three other ships were known to be in trouble last night: the Italian Onorato (5,781 tons) drifting with her steering gear out of action, the Norwegian ship Vard (1,918 tons), and a Norwegian steamer Kya which was aground on the south coast of Sweden. [STOP TIMING]

Put your reading time here.........................

1. Yesterday it snowed—
    (*a*) In northern Scotland and the Orkneys.
    (*b*) In southern Scotland and the Pennines.
    (*c*) In Lancashire, Yorkshire and North Wales.

    (*d*) In the south part of England and Wales.

    (*e*) In Jersey and the Channel Isles.

2. In Cornwall—

    (*a*) The frozen snow made roads impassable.

    (*b*) Traffic was able to proceed normally.

    (*c*) Floods made roads impassable.

    (*d*) There was little snow.

    (*e*) The snow turned to rain early in the morning.

3. As a result of the storm, almost all over the country—

    (*a*) Roads were soon cleared by snowploughs.

    (*b*) Roads were impassable and traffic was at a standstill.

    (*c*) Roads were flooded.

    (*d*) All air services were cancelled.

    (*e*) Travelling was difficult but rarely impossible.

4. Early this morning—

    (*a*) Temperatures in Lancashire were the lowest in the country.

    (*b*) There was a heavy fall of snow in Lancashire.

    (*c*) Rain began to fall in the north of England.

    (*d*) Snow and sleet reduced visibility in North Wales.

    (*e*) Lancashire was kept warm by a blanket of clouds.

5. In Scotland and the Orkneys—

    (*a*) Most of the marooned people did not get clear yesterday.

    (*b*) All the people held up were able to resume their journey.

    (*c*) A Pan-American plane was held up at Renfrew.

    (*d*) The snow melted quickly causing floods.

    (*e*) Nobody was seriously inconvenienced.

6. At sea—

    (*a*) Conditions were normal for the time of the year.

    (*b*) There were many ships in distress owing to the high seas.

    (*c*) A ship ran aground on the Goodwin Sands.

    (*d*) Dense fog caused collisions in the Mersey and Thames.

    (*e*) A B.E.A. plane crashed into the North Sea.

You will find the correct answers at the foot of page 130.

This passage has 1,200 words and you can find your speed from the table below.

Time	Speed	Time	Speed
1.50	655	2.00	600
2.00	600	2.10	553

Time	Speed	Time	Speed
2.20	514	3.10	378
2.30	480	3.20	360
2.40	450	3.30	340
2.50	423	3.40	327
3.00	400	3.50	313
3.10	378	4.00	300

Speed........................ Comprehension........................

You have become accustomed to this form of presentation now, and I want you to find out your eye span on the next exercise and see if you are taking in these short lines at a glance. So get out your mirror again and ask somebody to count your stops for a few lines.

EXERCISE 24

Better Craftsmen, but Slower

[START TIMING] In the building industry, a man starts to be a craftsman when he is forty, reaches a high standard at fifty, and then retains his skill but loses his speed, according to one of the employers quoted in the Nuffield Foundation's third report on the later life in the building industry: *Ageing Men in the Labour Force*, published yesterday.

The report, prepared by Mr F. Le Gros Clark and based on the collective experience of 78 building firms and general foremen, finds " some evidence " that at least 60 per cent of building craftsmen remained "thoroughly active and efficient " into their mid-sixties. It finds also fairly common agreement that elderly operative builders would be wise to leave constructional work for " the more restrained tempo " of maintenance and repairs.

Not many foremen favoured gangs made up wholly of older and slower men, believing that their tempo would be that of the oldest and slowest. One said that old men together were " quarrelsome and contentious ": if they were to be isolated there was a preference for having them working individually, or, at most, with one or two selected younger men who could both benefit from their experience and help them out. Group bonus schemes caused difficulties when older men worked in the same gang as younger, but, given compatibility of temperament, they would mix, and, according to one foreman, " the younger men usually do their best to make things easy for the old."

Craftsmanship

Many foremen liked to have grades of experience and skill mixed in a gang, even where greater experience went with a slower pace. The younger men could learn " the knacks and refinements of their work " from the older. Only they knew " how to steer round difficulties "; the younger craftsmen had had " too little experience of high class work " and the presence of their seniors seemed to give stability and a steady rhythm of work.

Of these " slighting references " to young craftsmen the report says that, while they may reflect no more than the mood of each passing generation of craftsmen, they may contain " a modicum of truth." It goes on:

" There has been a break in the transmission of skill and experience, and the post-war generation is in process of acclimatizing itself to new methods of construction. It has not yet completely done so, and in some instances the training the young men received may not have produced good all-round craftsmen. Undoubtedly the training schemes will improve; in the meantime, it is questionable whether many of the young bricklayers or carpenters of to-day are as well equipped for skilled finishing and alteration work as were their fathers at the same age, though the training of plumbers and plasterers is probably more traditional.

" The fact that on group bonus contracts some men in their sixties, and even in their late fifties, fail to maintain the pace (or have a rooted dislike for this mode of production) creates a problem

---

Answers to Exercise 23—1 (*d*), 2 (*c*), 3 (*e*), 4 (*e*), 5 (*a*), 6 (*b*).

of a special kind. It disturbs what has always seemed to be the natural relations between the old and young.

"There are many knacks and shifts that cannot be taught in a training course, or, if taught, will not be fully assimilated until they are met in practice. . . . So far as the mere pace of production discriminates against the older man, there is risk that the full transmission of skill will suffer, that there has to be more 'making good' on a site than should have been necessary, and that the task of supervising the younger men is made more difficult."

One remedy which the report suggests is that the tempo of work on a contract might be gradually increased, so that, by the time construction is under way, the older operatives might be drafted out of the gangs on to the finishing and interior processes. Meanwhile they would have done much in the early weeks both to train the younger men and to set a smooth rhythm of excavation and construction.

No Wasted Energy

The worth of such men is well described by an employer who writes—

"Many men above the normal retiring age have proved valuable servants. They were conscientious, knowing from experience the best way to approach a job, adopting good, economical methods of doing work, having clever manipulation of their tools, using their energy wisely, and taking advantage of every opportunity for improvisation. While their movements in walking and climbing are slower, that is often offset by their plodding ways; and every movement of a tool in their hands is achieving its purpose."

The report believes that the building industry could possibly employ 10-15 per cent or more of elderly men provided their numbers were carefully distributed. Ten per cent of "manifestly elderly men" was about the upper limit a foreman could comfortably handle on a large building site, but on maintenance, or where the quality of the work was the main consideration, the proportion could rise much higher. Maintenance could, "without damaging costs," employ 15 per cent or more of elderly men, though it must be said " emphatically " that to overweight the maintenance side of the industry with the " over sixties " would be bad economics.

Ageing craftsmen should not be " automatically drafted " to maintenance, but the transition should be easy if they wished to make it, which might mean reconsidering some current superannuation schemes. There was already a tendency among older men to gravitate to this side of the work; it was advisable for them to make the transition in their fifties, while they were still vigorous and able to adapt themselves to work of a type for which the new methods of construction to which they had grown accustomed might have given them little guidance. [STOP TIMING]

Put your reading time here........................

1. In the building industry the best workers are—
    (a) Between twenty and thirty.
    (b) Between thirty and forty.
    (c) Between forty and fifty.
    (d) Between fifty and sixty.
    (e) In no particular age group.
2. Older men in the building industry are best suited for—
    (a) Retirement.
    (b) Maintenance work.
    (c) Working in gangs with younger men.
    (d) Working in gangs of older men.
    (e) Instructing apprentices.
3. The older men have—
    (a) Less skill than the younger men.
    (b) Equal skill with the younger men.
    (c) A restricted outlook on the trade.
    (d) Nothing to teach the younger men.
    (e) Greater skill than the younger men.
4. Older workers should be transferred to maintenance—
    (a) In their early fifties.

(*b*) In their late sixties.

(*c*) Completely.

(*d*) Only as a last resort.

(*e*) When they are unfit for anything else.

5. The main theme of this article is that—

(*a*) There is no place for the older worker in building.

(*b*) Older workers are better for all classes of work.

(*c*) There is a place for older workers in building.

(*d*) Building needs more old men.

(*e*) In building the accent is on youth.

You will find the correct answers at the foot of page 134.

This passage has 900 words and you can find your speed from the table below.

Time	Speed
1.20	675
1.30	600
1.40	540
1.50	490
2.00	450
2.10	415
2.20	385
2.30	360
2.40	337
2.50	318
3.00	300

Speed......................   Comprehension......................

I expect that you were able to take in those lines in either one or two glances. Two will do quite well, for it would not be true to say that unless you can take in such a line at a glance you will never be a really quick reader. You have often seen runners taking short strides beating those who take long strides. The length of your eye span, like the length of your stride must vary with individuals, but all inefficient readers can increase their eye span to some extent.

WHERE TO START

WHATEVER the length of your eye span, your starting point is very important. This is a line from exercise 23.

driven by a wind off the sea, was

If you have a four word span, your eye movements were

s   s   s

driven by a wind off the sea, was

and if you had a slightly shorter span then your eye movements were

s   s   s

driven by a wind off the sea, was

In both cases, part of your first eye span included the margin where there are no words at all, and in the first case the last eye span also included part of the margin.

There will be a marked reduction of effort and consequent increase in efficiency if you fix your eyes at first on the second or even third word of the line, then your eye movements would be

s   s

driven by a wind off the sea, was

and you would only make two stops or fixations because you are not wasting any of your peripheral vision as it is called. In addition you would very much reduce that large sweep back which is so obvious when you are watching people's eye movements through a mirror.

Try to start at the second or third word of each line of the next exercise (which you should not time) and get somebody to see if you are reducing eye movements.

Answers to Exercise 24—1 (*c*), 2 (*b*), 3 (*e*), 4 (*a*), 5 (*c*).

EXERCISE 25

[DO NOT TIME THIS EXERCISE]

Machinery for the Mills

Firms engaged in the production and processing of textiles are still, in the main, in a much stronger financial position than they were before the war. They are better supplied with resources for undertaking capital expenditure, both for obtaining better results from their original classes of trade and for developing new classes. In most sections the numbers of firms have decreased, but the numbers which are able and willing to buy new machinery remain larger.

In Lancashire, although the re-equipment subsidy scheme is no longer available the spinning section of the cotton industry is still undertaking much re-equipment, and the weaving section provides a considerable demand for looms, both automatic and non-automatic, and for winding and other machinery. Uptwisters for yarns spun from man-made fibres have attracted increasing attention in the last few years, while looms specially designed for weaving the new yarns are another fairly recent development. Most of the producers of synthetic yarns and staples, moreover, are renewing or extending their plants on a large scale.

On the export side the full returns for 1954 when they are published during the next ten days or so, will probably show that the year's total shipments were slightly smaller, both in value and in quantity, than those of 1953, and much smaller than those of 1952, for which totals of 2,253,723 cwt and £50,441,914 were recorded. For the eleven months ended November exports were 1,430,742 cwt, valued at £35,361,562 in 1954, against 1,543,534 cwt, valued at £37,376,883 in 1953. There was a large increase last year in shipments to Pakistan, with smaller ones in those to Australia, Poland, Turkey, Greece, Egypt, Peru, Uruguay, and Argentina. Exports to Italy, France, Belgium,

Brazil and the United States, however, decreased rather sharply and brought the total figures down. The year's trade nevertheless appears to have been reasonably satisfactory in view of the foreign competition, the import restrictions, and the credit difficulties which were encountered.

Research and Production

The size and range of the demand for textile machinery are large and it is not surprising to find that both in research and in production expansion is being undertaken. Textile Machinery Makers Ltd. announces that it intends to extend its research facilities by the provision of new buildings and equipment at its research centre, T.M.M. (Research) Ltd., Helmshore. The T.M.M. research centre has been in operation for eight years and is now regarded as the foremost organization engaged in research and development in spinning machinery. Important contributions to technological progress have already been made as the result of work done at Helmshore and demands on the services of the research centre have increased to the point where additional space and facilities will be required in the near future. The new buildings will provide an increase in the existing floor-space of 60,000 square feet by 60 per cent and permit extension in all sections, including those concerned with machinery or spinning cotton, cotton waste, wool, and man-made fibres. It is expected that the building extensions will be completed before the end of this year.

Earlier in the week it was disclosed that Platt Brothers, Ltd., had decided to reconstruct its Hartford works at Oldham at a cost of some £750,000. The company's East works, also at Oldham, was closed two years ago, but it appears that, for some years at any rate, production will not all be transferred to the new works at Barton.

1. Firms producing textiles are—

   (a) Not as well placed as they were before the war.

   (b) Very much in the same position as in 1939.

(*c*) Better placed than their American competitors.

(*d*) In a better position than the machinery makers.

(*e*) In a stronger position than before the war.

2. Most new machinery—

(*a*) Is paid for by the re-equipment subsidy.

(*b*) Is for the processing of synthetic yarns.

(*c*) Is for the spinning of cotton.

(*d*) Is spread over all branches of the textile industry.

(*e*) Is for the spinning and weaving of cotton.

3. The exports for last year were—

(*a*) Smaller than 1952 but bigger than 1953.

(*b*) Bigger than 1952 but smaller than 1953.

(*c*) Bigger than 1952 and bigger than 1953.

(*d*) Smaller than 1952 and smaller than 1953.

(*e*) About the same as 1952 and 1953.

4. The research centre is concerned with—

(*a*) Research into machinery for wool as well as cotton and rayon.

(*b*) Research into machinery for cotton only.

(*c*) Research into machinery for any fibre.

(*d*) Research into methods of cultivating cotton.

(*e*) Research into improvement of the staple cotton.

You will find the correct answers at the foot of page 138.

Put your comprehension score here.......................

You should have reduced your eye movements quite a lot by starting part of the way along the line. See if you can keep up this improvement on the next slightly longer passage.

EXERCISE 26

From our own Correspondent

PARIS, JANUARY 13

[START TIMING] The Council of Ministers of the O.E.E.C. opened its two-day meeting here under the chairmanship of Mr R. A. Butler, in order to take further steps towards the liberalization of trade and credit in Europe and to prepare for convertibility at a later stage. The atmosphere was markedly more confident than that which prevailed not so very long ago.

For one of the member States this

cheerfulness must have been almost thwarting. For while the other members were discussing an increase in the liberalized sector of trade from 75 to 90 per cent France was promising to reach 75 per cent by April, and that with the help of compensation taxes which though reduced have not yet been abolished. Thus, though France was able to boast of improved productivity and better balanced trade, the general standard was already being raised by the achievement of others.

The statement made by M. Faure was a mixture of reported progress and explanation why it could not be even better. Expansion, he said, had been successfully achieved without inflation, but only very patient methods could reduce the disparity between French and other prices. Mechanization for the reconversion of antiquated undertakings was permitting a noticeable reduction, however. A committee of experts was to report within the next two months on causes delaying liberalization.

The French Programme

France's balance of payments had improved steadily. She would cease to ask for the benefit of Article 3c of the liberalization code as soon as she was able to notify that liberalization had in fact reached 75 per cent and would thus recover within the O.E.E.C. the prerogatives as well as the responsibilities of full membership. The liberalization of a further 23 per cent, however, involved certain adjustments, which made the delay of two months necessary.

As to the level of compensation taxes, those of 15 per cent had been reduced to 11 and those of 10 per cent to 7, while more than half of the categories of goods recently liberalized were paying less than 11 per cent. This process would continue.

Since April, M. Faure continued, imports of the liberalized categories had increased by 40 per cent. France accepted for herself in principle the goal of 90 per cent liberalization with the suppression of 10 per cent of the quota still maintained, but meanwhile he was bound to make these three points:

1. It was impossible to foresee the consequences of the O.E.E.C. proposals on the French balance of payments. France after renouncing the use of Article 3c must re-examine her attitude before putting the new programme into force.

2. The application of 75 per cent liberalization within each category of goods would create serious difficulties for French agriculture.

3. The present O.E.E.C. discussions must be reconsidered in the light of the conclusions reached at the next meeting of the G.A.T.T., with its much larger membership.

British Stability

Addressing the British representatives in an interval during his arduous labours as chairman, Mr Butler said:

" The fact that the United Kingdom is in great heart and enjoys economic stability has obviously contributed greatly to our influence in the affairs of Europe and increased our general respect. The position at home of employment, consumption, and production, all at their peak, is in itself very satisfactory. High production means that we are increasing imports, since the factories require more raw materials, which is a reason for watching our exports very carefully. Recent export figures themselves show that we have kept them well in mind. There are already some indications of a possible shortage of manpower.

" To have achieved full employment, high production, and high consumption without inflation is something of an achievement which can only be maintained thanks to the care of modern economic science. If this can be main tained we will have achieved something very worthwhile. There is at present no ground for self-satisfaction; we must maintain our efforts and watch against inflation, since this would immediately involve an increase of costs and make more difficult our competition with such other exporters as Japan, Germany, and the United States.''

Mr Butler welcomed President Eisenhower's statement to Congress indicating that priority would be given in his legislative programme to measures for widening trade. He went on to recall that when the present Government came into office severe measures had been necessary and some savage cuts had had to be made in imports. These had been very well received by other Powers. There had never been any retaliation, and it was now up to Britain to give a lead for further liberalization. There was every hope that further liberalization would be agreed on, and in this connexion the French initiative announced by M. Faure was a welcome one. [STOP TIMING]

Put your reading time here.........................

1. The atmosphere was—
   (*a*) Rather pessimistic compared with last year.
   (*b*) Rather more confident than last year.
   (*c*) About the same as last year.
   (*d*) Much less hopeful than last year.
   (*e*) Very hopeful compared with last year.

2. Which country has not made much progress?
   ....

3. M. Faure said that—
   (*a*) France would never reach 90 per cent liberalization.
   (*b*) Other countries were impeding French efforts.
   (*c*) There were special difficulties for the French.
   (*d*) France was opposed to liberalization.

4. Mr. Butler said that Britain's influence was due to—
   (*a*) American support.
   (*b*) The long history of British Free Trade.
   (*c*) The part we played in the war.
   (*d*) The diplomatic efforts of Mr. Eden.
   (*e*) Our strong economic position.

5. Britain must guard against—
   (*a*) Inflation.
   (*b*) Deflation.
   (*c*) Rising labour costs.

(*d*) Increased taxation.

(*e*) Poor salesmanship.

The correct answers are at the foot of page 142.

This passage has 780 words and you can find your speed from this table.

Time	*Speed*
1.30	520
1.40	468
1.50	425
2.00	390
2.10	360
2.20	333
2.30	312
2.40	292

Speed...................... Comprehension......................

Reduced eye movement means increased speed.

K

LONG LINES AGAIN

Now let us consider the eye movements for a line of normal length if there is an eye-span of three normal words. This is the second line of Exercise 1, with each stop shown by—

s⎯⎯⎯⎯⎯⎯s⎯⎯⎯⎯⎯⎯s⎯⎯⎯⎯⎯s⎯⎯⎯⎯⎯s
the Arctic circle is familiar to thousands of visitors from lower

If you fix your eye on the second word to start with you will eliminate one movement like this—

s⎯⎯⎯⎯⎯s⎯⎯⎯⎯⎯s⎯⎯⎯⎯⎯s
the Arctic circle is familiar to thousands of visitors from lower

If you have a slightly wider eye-span your eye movements starting at the first word would be—

s⎯⎯⎯⎯⎯⎯s⎯⎯⎯⎯⎯s⎯⎯⎯⎯⎯s
the Arctic circle is familiar to thousands of visitors from lower

So that if your eye started at the third word you would reduce your movements by one like this—

s⎯⎯⎯⎯⎯s⎯⎯⎯⎯⎯s
the Arctic circle is familiar to thousands of visitors from lower

In both cases the biggest eye movement of all, from the end of one line to the beginning of the next, is also greatly reduced.

Try fixing on the second or third word in the next exercise which has the normal length of line.

Answers to Exercise 26—1 (*b*), 2 France, 3 (*c*), 4 (*e*), 5 (*a*).

EXERCISE 27

North of the Limpopo by Patrick Monkhouse

[START TIMING]   A previous article described the attempt now being made in Southern Rhodesia to improve African farming by making land ownership individual instead of communal. Suppose that comes off in itself—as the indications are that it will—what are the secondary consequences likely to be? If peasants grow and sell more they will buy more, too. There should be a substantially greater demand for consumer goods, a stimulus to industries supplying them, and an increased demand for industrial labour. There should also become available an increased supply of industrial labour. Can supply and demand be brought to meet? This operation is a vital, and not a simple one.

There are believed to be about 315,000 Africans farming in the reserves and about 270,000 working for wages (in the towns or on European farms). The groups overlap, for many have a foot on both sides of the line and work in a town while retaining land in a reserve. This is healthy for neither farming nor industry; it makes for a shifting and unstable labour force in industry and for half-hearted work on the land. It is expected that as holdings in the reserves gradually become individually owned a good number of the smaller and uneconomic holdings will be sold, as the sellers know they can buy land again when they want it; and families will move more or less permanently into the towns. A continuing increase in population will in any case have a similar effect.

The Minister for Native Affairs, Mr. Fletcher, has indeed expressed the opinion that Africans will tend to leave the towns, because prospects on the land will be better. It is hard to see this happening, at any rate for some time to come. The general expectation is that as the many small and uneconomic holdings become saleable they will be sold for cash to a neighbouring farmer—thus building up holdings of economic size—and the seller will seek full-time work in a town. The reverse process might occur if there was a rapid increase in the number of "native purchase" farms.

The prospects of permanent African employment in industry depend on four things. There must be industrial jobs going. The workers must have, or be able to get, skill enough to do them.

They must not be kept out by artificial obstacles from work which they can do. And they must be able to get tolerable accommodation for their families as well as for themselves. There are question marks to all these conditions now.

To take the last first, family accommodation is still far too limited. Municipal authorities have long built barracks for single men and so perpetuated the " one foot in the reserve " policy. This is changing. Salisbury has built at Highfield a council-house estate of 1,000 cottages to let; these are readily taken up by married men. A more important experiment is just beginning; Salisbury and Bulawayo are each building 3,000 houses for sale. A 99-year lease can be bought by instalments and sold if the occupier leaves. In addition, big employers commonly build married quarters for their staffs. But the growth of secondary industries which is likely in the next few years, and which is needed if the attempted disentangling of rural and urban work is to succeed, will call for a good deal more than is now in sight.

There has in fact been a very rapid growth in industry since the war. The rise has flattened out in the last two years. But soon the Kariba hydro-electric scheme will give a fresh stimulus to development; and the new Federal tariff will also have a protective effect on some industries, particularly textiles and hollow ware. The field for employment will continue to expand.

In most industries, however, African participation has been limited to unskilled or very slightly skilled work. This is not because Africans are inherently bad workers. The unstable background common hitherto has led to much shifting of jobs and therefore to small opportunity of acquiring skill. For instance, 60 per cent of the Rhodesian railways' African staff have less than four years' service. Serious technical training is negligible. There is nothing comparable to the Royal Technical College at Nairobi or even to the twenty trade schools capped by the Hodgson training centre in Northern Rhodesia. Some mission schools give a basic training in a few trades. Otherwise employers must arrange training for their own recruits.

Some do so, with good results. I visited a weekly newspaper office, staffed entirely by African linotype operators and printers (as well as journalists); a doubling and weaving mill with a score of Lancashire overlookers and 250 African operatives, among them a few women, a significant development; a factory for making farm carts, dumping wagons and the like, where Africans had taken over all the production work on the floor, including welding and the operation of a turret lathe. There was here a European supervisor with an African deputy for each section of a dozen men or so; this year a supervisor was away for three months and the deputy carried on quite effectively. A recent conference on grades of labour in engineering found a certain amount of racial overlap about the middle of the list and a solitary African working alongside Europeans in grade one.

It is said that a distinguished American visitor was lately discussing with a Government official in Salisbury the prospects of more African development in industry. The official said that there had been some success in simple repetitive work. " Yes," said the American, " simple repetitive work like we do at Detroit."

In some of the older-established trades like building, the European unions present a solid barrier which Africans cannot pass. In major building contracts Africans play only a humble part. But even in building, African craftsmen are working for small African contractors as well as for the Government's Native Engineering Department. Sometimes social convention plays a similar part. A garage-owner told me that he had an African panel-beater who was as good as any of his European staff who accepted the man as a fellow-craftsman. But it was hard to make full use of him because so many customers specified that their work must be done by a European.

African clerks and storemen are getting an inconspicuous footing. A business man said, " Of half a dozen applications I had lately to fill a clerical vacancy, an African's was the best. I would like to have taken him—but not just yet. I'd rather someone else broke the ice." This attitude is probably common; many people are inclined to be liberal, but wait for someone else to give a lead. Others think that too bold a lead would provoke a reaction, and prefer to let the slow thaw do its work.

One can feel a certain impatience at the well-to-do European's timidity in social practice, and yet sympathise with the European artisan's jealousy of African advancement. His wages are relatively high (and add to the high cost of everything) but so are his expenses. His dwelling is modest; not for him the gracious living of Salisbury's smart suburbs, where a house may cost £50 a month to rent, and £7,500 to buy. His wife has

African help in the house, but she may have to go out to work herself to pay for it; and the growing number of wives employed in clerical jobs adds to those who have something to lose from African advancement in that field.

Yet in the long run, and not so very long, there is no security to be had in the defence of a sectional interest. Their best hope, too, lies in the steady expansion of the national economy, and there will be no steady expansion without African advancement in industry, accepted, encouraged, and prepared for by a more resolute programme of technical training than has yet been attempted. Without more African employment in industry, the land use policy will not work; and if the land use policy fails, Southern Rhodesia will drift into dangerous waters. [STOP TIMING]

Put your reading time here.......................

1. The main point of this article is—
    (a) The future of the African.
    (b) The farming future of the African.
    (c) The drift into the towns.
    (d) The industrial future of the Africans.
    (e) The colour bar.

2. Of the African population—
    (a) About twenty per cent live in the reserves.
    (b) About a quarter work in the towns.
    (c) About a third live in the reserves.
    (d) More than half work for wages.
    (e) More than half work in the reserves.

3. It is generally expected that—
    (a) There will be a drift to the towns.
    (b) There will be a drift to the country.
    (c) There will be little movement of population.
    (d) There will be an increasing number of small farms.
    (e) The small farmer will disappear.

4. One way to increase African employment in industry is—
    (a) To build more barracks for single men.
    (b) To find work for married women.
    (c) To work a three shift system.
    (d) To build more married quarters.
    (e) To build more roads.

5. Write down an important influence on future industrial development. ....

6. Africans are usually only semi-skilled because—
   (a) They have not the necessary intelligence.
   (b) They have no industrial background.
   (c) They do not stay at the job long enough.
   (d) They do not work hard enough.
   (e) They will not work long hours.

7. Give one example of skilled work which is being done by Africans...

8. Name one trade where European trade unionists are operating a colour bar...

9. The European artisan—
   (a) Welcomes African participation in industry.
   (b) Fears that the African will drive him out.
   (c) Is not afraid of the African worker.
   (d) Sees his standard of living threatened.
   (e) Operates a rigid colour bar everywhere.

10. The author considers African advancement in industry essential because—
    (a) It is a matter of elementary justice.
    (b) Industry cannot develop otherwise.
    (c) The land use policy will fail without it.
    (d) The only alternative is farming.
    (e) Africans are employed in similar jobs elsewhere.

You will find the correct answers at the foot of page 148.

This exercise has 1,350 words and you can find your speed from the following table.

Time	Speed	Time	Speed
2.00	675	2.50	476
2.10	622	3.00	450
2.20	578	3.10	425
2.30	540	3.20	405
2.40	506	3.30	385
2.50	476	3.40	366

Speed...................... Comprehension......................

Now do the next exercise and have somebody check your eye span to see if you have reduced eye movements by starting in a different place.

EXERCISE 28

Cotton and Purchase Tax

[START TIMING] The House of Commons discusses to-day the state of the cotton trade and the fears in Lancashire that it is heading for a slump. There are various causes. Possibly imports of foreign cotton cloth and yarn are not the most important. But of one serious handicap there is no doubt—the effect of purchase tax on the quality of Lancashire's trade and therefore on its volume.

The Chancellor of the Exchequer and the Minister of State at the Board of Trade have both been in Manchester lately to explain the difficulties of the Government in checking Indian imports. Both had suggestions to make to the industry about ways in which it might help itself. " We must make full use of our technical expertise and our ability to compete in specialized and high-class work," said Mr. Butler; Lancashire's main difficulty was shortage of export orders rather than imports of foreign cloth, said Mr. Low. Lancashire's case for the abolition of purchase tax accepts both the importance of specialization in higher grade work and the need for more export orders as articles of faith and claims that the tax is the greatest impediment to the realization of these aims.

The " D " scheme under which the tax is levied fixes an arbitrary price level—or " D " level—for different textile fabrics and stipulates that those cloths whose price is above that level should bear tax, while those priced below it escape. The public reaction to this, the industry claims, has been a steadily hardening refusal to buy any textiles which bear tax. Public resistance is further stiffened by the attitude of retailers for whom goods above the " D " level constitute a business risk as well as a poor selling line. For them a fall in raw material prices is exaggerated by the tax decline that accompanies it. For example, if a cloth falls in price by about 12 per cent to the " D " level it sheds $6\frac{1}{2}$ per cent tax at the same time so that the retailer is faced by a possible mark-down of 18 per cent. The public and the retail trade having set their faces against taxed textiles, the trade has no alternative

---

Answers to Exercise 27—1 (*d*), 2 (*e*), 3 (*e*), 4 (*d*), 5 Kariba hydro-electric scheme, Federal tariff, 6 (*b*), 7 Turret lathe operator, Linotype operator, cotton operative, welder, 8 Building, 9 (*d*), 10 (*b*).

but to produce the cheaper lines which escape it, while the more expensive " quality " lines, which Mr. Butler commended to the industry's efforts, decline.

It is not difficult to find corroborative evidence. Firms in the doubling section report that, since doubled yarn in such things as fine poplin shirtings almost inevitably puts the price above the " D " level, the demand for their product is falling very markedly. One firm making these shirtings says that its production has fallen by a half in the past four years, another that it is only making a third of what it made in 1951. Furnishing fabrics are another section of the industry in which Lancashire has long been noted for fine qualities, and here too the standard of the bulk of manufacturers' production is being forced down below the " D " level by the tax on everything above it.

One of the most famous firms in this field reports that in one class of goods only 0·8 per cent of its production is now in the tax-bearing price range. Before the present restrictions 18 per cent was in this price range. Further evidence can be found in the figures for purchase tax receipts from the various classes of textiles. The " D " scheme was introduced at the beginning of the financial year 1952. The yield of the tax in 1952—3 for the groups covering textiles was £43·7 millions: by 1953—4 it had declined to £38·8 millions. The figure for 1954—5 is expected to show a considerable further decline.

Another side to the picture is the decline in the number of craftsmen in the industry who are capable of producing the high-quality work. Many firms have a large proportion of their jacquard and box looms standing idle. The operatives who worked them have left the industry as the demand for their services disappeared, and no new ones have been trained to replace them. The same is true of machines for the finer types of finishing and their operatives.

In export markets Lancashire is often competing in countries which have textile industries of their own capable of producing the lower and medium ranges perfectly well. Thus it is in the better qualities that Lancashire stands its best chance. Now it is rarely economic to produce lines for an export market alone. What is needed to bring down costs and put a cutting edge on our competitive effort is long runs in particular lines. But if the home market will not take part of the production because tax makes it too expensive then only short runs are possible. Again, if something should go wrong with an export order and the customer does not take it after it has been made, it stands little chance of finding an alternative sale at home because its high quality makes it liable to a high rate of tax. Thus purchase tax increases risk for the potential exporter as well as dulling his competitive edge.

Examples of troubles in the export markets are as easy to find as examples of difficulties at home. A manufacturer of high-quality bed-spreads finding no sale for them at home has had to drop them from his range completely, even though there was a keen export demand. A firm making screen-printed poplins has had to reduce its range drastically. At a show in America it was criticized by buyers because it offered only a dozen designs. A maker-up of cotton frocks had to restrict his designs to bring them below the " D " line, and as a consequence their export possibilities were greatly reduced. Comparisons with the conditions under which competitors in other countries work further irritates the British exporter. West Germany, France and Italy suffer no such difficulties, and in many cases their Governments offer State help to exporters of such high-quality lines as velvets and fine poplins.

A further burdensome aspect of the tax affects both Lancashire's efficiency at home and its attempts to compete abroad. This is the cost of collection. Inevitably in an industry which still produces an immense variety of products the administration of purchase tax is far more complex than in one given to standardization, such as the motor-car industry. The chairman of a large textile concern has recently said that making out an invoice with the necessary purchase tax calculations produces " a Chinese puzzle that no one outside the trade can understand." A large wholesale firm estimates that the calculation and addition of the tax involves 20 per cent more clerical labour, while a firm selling dress fabrics reckons that its additional clerical costs due to the tax work out at about 7d. per invoice. Another firm worked out its annual extra cost at £6,000. These extra costs inevitably find their way into the price.

The Chancellor will no doubt argue that to make a special case of textiles would be to invite petitions for similar treatment from other industries. The answer is that none of them has problems so heavy and pressing as cotton. Or he may say that to release textiles from the tax would create an inflationary tendency—the very thing he warned the country against last month. The answer to this is a denial that the abolition of purchase tax would make the public buy more textiles, as the abolition of purchase tax from cars would inevitably send sales of cars mounting. The man in the street is not doing without a shirt because of the tax, and his wife is not doing without curtains or a frock. They are simply not buying shirts and frocks that bear tax. If the tax were lifted they would buy the same number of goods but of somewhat better quality. This would cost the country no more in imports nor would it be seriously inflationary internally, but it would right the distorted pattern that the purchase tax has imposed on the industry, and it would enable it to go forward with more confidence and competitiveness in world markets. [Stop Timing]

Put your reading time here......................

1. Purchase tax is—
   (a) Having no effect on the cotton trade.
   (b) Causing people to buy less cotton.
   (c) Causing people to buy synthetic cloth.
   (d) Causing people to buy cheaper cloth.
   (e) Not important enough to need action.

2. The " D " scheme—
   (a) Varies the tax due according to the cost of the cloth.
   (b) Has had little effect on demand.
   (c) Imposes the same tax on all cloth.
   (d) Has reduced demand for all cloth.
   (e) Imposes tax only on the most expensive cloth.

3. As a result of the " D " scheme, manufacturers—
   (a) Have been forced out of business.
   (b) Have increased their turnover.
   (c) Have carried on much as usual.
   (d) Have concentrated on producing cheap cloth.
   (e) Have concentrated on producing dear cloth.

4. Lancashire's exports should be—
   (a) Goods of all qualities.
   (b) Mainly high-quality goods.
   (c) Mainly low-quality goods.
   (d) Protected by Empire Preference.

(*e*) Goods of medium quality.

5. Cloth cannot be made for export alone because—
  (*a*) The cost of transport is too great.
  (*b*) The market is too small.
  (*c*) The home demand is too great.
  (*d*) There are not enough skilled workers in Lancashire.
  (*e*) Purchase tax has to be paid.

6. Another disadvantage of purchase tax is—
  (*a*) The time wasted in assessing it.
  (*b*) The cost of collection.
  (*c*) Its effect on demand for all goods.
  (*d*) The odd prices at which goods have to be sold.
  (*e*) The difficulty of working out the right amount.

The correct answers are at the foot of page 154.

This passage has 1,350 words and you can find your speed from the following table.

Time	Speed	Time	Speed
1.50	736	3.00	450
2.00	675	3.10	426
2.10	623	3.20	405
2.20	578	3.30	385
2.30	540	3.40	365
2.40	506	3.50	352
2.50	476	4.00	337
3.00	450		

Speed........................   Comprehension........................

SECTION FIFTEEN

RHYTHM

You have now stopped head movements, reduced vocalization, and increased your eye span, and the result is that you are reading much faster and have an entirely different rhythm to your reading. There is no looking back and you should read each exercise at the same speed throughout, not starting slowly and finishing fast but at the same pace throughout. Adopt a pace which is fast but economical of movement and of effort, and which will therefore be less tiring.

Get somebody to time you over two of the pages of the next exercise, they will see by your eye movements when you start on the next page, and find out if you are maintaining the same pace throughout.

EXERCISE 29

Iraq's Northern Defences by M. Phillips Price, M.P.

[START TIMING] The treaty between Turkey and Iraq and the accession of the United Kingdom to it opens a new chapter in the history of the Middle East. For the first time since the Arab League's foundations a State has broken away from it and its Egyptian leadership and has taken an independent line. Not only has Iraq lined up with Turkey, hitherto always a little suspect to Arabs as the residuary legatee of the old Ottoman Empire, but it has also shown that it regards the quarrel with Israel as not the only basis of Arab foreign policy. Being nearer to the danger in the north the Iraqis are not impressed with the neutralism of Mr. Nehru and Colonel Nasser and incline more to the attitude of Pakistan.

The recent debate in the House of Commons on the pact and our accession to it hardly did justice to this aspect of the Middle East situation. The fears of Israel, which figure so much in the speeches of the Opposition, are of course understandable; but

153

so are the fears of the Iraqis, which has caused them to take this step. If circumstances endanger her security, she ought not to forget her guarantees under the tripartite treaty. If that does not satisfy her its provisions can be strengthened.

On the other hand, nothing will create more resentment in the Arab world and delay in Arab-Israel settlement than a feeling that Israel is obstructing a defence system of the Middle East against aggression from the north. Turkey, Iraq, and, in a sense too, Pakistan are the extreme right wing of the N.A.T.O. defence lines. Hence the importance of this treaty.

Under the pact it will be possible to organize the defence of this right wing. But how do we envisage an aggression from the north? One must, of course, lay plans against the possibility of a Russian attack, with conventional weapons supported by tanks and even with atomic bombs, through Persia. In this case a chain of air bases from Eastern Turkey along the headwaters of the Tigris and the Great Zab would be necessary. Along with this would come radar stations, scattered supply depots from south-east Turkey to Upper Iraq, and bases for the ground forces of Turkey and Iraq to be reinforced by troops of Britain or other N.A.T.O. countries flown out there in an emergency. All this has now become possible under the pact and was not so before. It is the only way strength can be given to Iraq so as to give her a chance to hold the line till assistance comes to her. Some Opposition speeches last week sneered at Iraq's will to defend herself and pointed to Israel as the only country with an army of any importance. This treaty makes it possible for at least one Arab country to defend herself from the north and create conditions under which it could feel that the effort was worth making. Given an attack with modern weapons this is the kind of defence with dispersed bases and chains of airfields that would be needed and would link up with similar schemes of defence in Suez, Cyprus, and Iskanderun.

But it is very much more likely that a Russian offensive in this part of the Middle East would take an altogether different form. It is the kind of offensive which has only been tried by Russia in Korea, and even then only under cover of the North Korean army. For it is part of the philosophy of Russian communism to rely for the spread of its ideas and its political system by exploiting social weakness and national separatist movements. Civil war and internal disturbances thus created could be used as an excuse for intervention, as it frequently was in Chinese Turkestan (Sinkiang) in the days before the Chinese Communist Revolution.

There is plenty of material for this kind of offensive all along the Iraq-Persian frontier and particularly in north-west Persia itself. Here are national minorities; Russian communism ever since the famous Baku conference of the Comintern in September, 1920, has laid itself out to use nationalist movements along the Russian borders as a means to extend Russian power, as the Tsarist regimes once did, and in these days to spread the Communist political system throughout the East. In Turkey, of course, this cannot happen. The republic is too strong, too united, and too firmly anti-Russian. There was a weakness once in Eastern Anatolia, where in the Hakkiari highlands and in the country round Lake Yan the Khurdish tribes were a dissident element in the early days of the republic. But the Ankara Government has adopted a wise policy towards these Khurds and the grant of equal citizenship to Turks and Khurd alike has resulted in a pacification of this hitherto turbulent area. This part of Turkey, according to all reports, has now been assimilated to the democratic republic.

A similar problem presents itself to Iraq where a large Khurdish population is found along the Persian frontier from Sulelmaniye to the headwaters of the Great Zab. Iraq is adopting a different method to the Turks and by recognizing the Khurdish language is slowly gaining their confidence and hopes ultimately to assimilate them politically. They hope to do the same with the Assyrians.

The main danger lies in Persia, where the disaster of the Musaddiq era has weakened the central government. Thus the assassination of some important person might let loose disorder which the Russians could exploit by infiltration from the Caucasus. There are still disruptive elements among the Khurds, Lurs and Kashgais. Much depends on the succcess of the Shah in getting his agrarian reform programme adopted by the big landowners. This progressive and popular young monarch knows that the best defence of his country is a contented peasantry and loyal tribesmen.

If Persia is the weakest spot in this defence and Turkey the strongest, Iraq lies somewhere between the two. But Iraq has its agrarian problem. The big oil revenues which the Government has at its disposal for irrigation and flood control of the Tigris and Euphrates could be largely dissipated by the land-owning interests, which could drain off into their own pockets the increased wealth that should go to the Arab peasant and the Khurdish tribesmen. It is true the Iraq Government has large areas of " Mir," or state land, which can be improved and distributed but other large areas belong to the sheiks and even larger areas have never been properly surveyed or apportioned as regards ownership. The Bagdad bazaar has rowdy elements which Communists and fellow-travellers can exploit, as they did successfully when they wrecked Sali Jabr's Portsmouth Treaty in 1947. Since then there has been a government of progressive young Arabs and Khurds under the Premiership of Jamali, who during 1953 tried to deal with some of Iraq's most urgent social problems. They have been obstructed and have resigned. The present Prime Minister, Nuri Said, is the ablest and most experienced of all Arab statesmen, but it is yet to be seen if he thinks social reform sufficiently important to need much attention.

Thus the defence of this part of the Middle East has to be based on plans which the new pact makes possible. They must provide, first, against the event of conventional weapons being used and, secondly, as is more likely, against Communist infiltration and guerilla warfare. In the latter event airfields with Iraqi airmen, trained by the British, could support ground forces in the rough country on the Persian border against insurgents led by local Communists trained in the Caucasus. One well-known character, the Mullah Mustafa, from Northern Iraq, has been in Baku for years and, it is believed, is being kept ready to come forth if conditions should be favourable.

It is against this kind of offensive that military defence has to be organized. The other form of defence is social reform in Persia and Iraq, and this means, in fact, ensuring that the improvements financed by oil revenues go to provide better living conditions for peasants and tribesmen. The defence pact and our accession to it can do a lot, but social welfare in these countries is an equally important bulwark against the most likely form of Russian aggression. [Stop Timing]

Put your reading time here........................

1. Iraq has—
   (a) Remained within the Arab League.
   (b) Maintained its treaty obligations with Egypt.
   (c) Made a treaty with Israel.
   (d) Made a treaty with Turkey and Britain.
   (e) Made a treaty with Pakistan and India.

2. Opposition in this country was caused by—
   (a) Fears for the survival of the Arab League.
   (b) Fears for the survival of Israel.
   (c) Fears that the treaty would be ineffective.
   (d) A desire to placate Egypt.
   (e) A desire to placate Pandit Nehru.

3. The military threat to Iraq is—
   (a) From the East by Russia.
   (b) From the West by Israel.
   (c) Through Turkey by the Western Powers.
   (d) Through the Persian Gulf by India.
   (e) Through Persia by Russia.

4. Iraq is also threatened by—
   (a) The possible stirring up of civil war.
   (b) Aggression from Turkey.
   (c) A strong anti-British Opposition.
   (d) A strong Iraq Communist party.
   (e) A Fascist Army group.

5. The main danger lies in Persia because—
   (a) It has not a strong government.
   (b) The Shah is reactionary and unprogressive.
   (c) The central government has been weakened.
   (d) There is a larger anti-British group.
   (e) There is a strong Communist party.

6. The internal dangers in Iraq are two of—
   (a) Inflation and re-armament.
   (b) Nationalization of the oilfields.
   (c) The power of the rich landowners.
   (d) The big oil revenues.
   (e) The progressive Arabs and Khurds.
   (f) The rowdy elements in the bazaar.

The correct answers are on page 160.

This passage has 1,400 words and you can find your speed from the following table.

L

Time	Speed	Time	Speed
2.00	700	3.20	420
2.10	646	3.30	400
2.20	600	3.40	381
2.30	560	3.50	365
2.40	525	4.00	350
2.50	494	4.10	336
3.00	466	4.20	323
3.10	442	4.30	311
3.20	420		

Speed........................   Comprehension........................

Were you maintaining that easy rhythmic style of reading which saves time and effort? I am sure that you are well on the way to that. Read the next passage all at the same pace and see if you can raise your speed slightly on this type of exercise.

EXERCISE 30

A College in Bengal by Michael Lane

[START TIMING] Monsoon days are warm and sticky in Bengal. The rooms of our college hostels have their doors and shutters ajar—there are no windows—and a subdued murmur as of intoned prayer rises into the oppressive evening air. The period of compulsory study has begun. Hostel wardens, going their rounds, observe their students closely: for them to have their noses in a book is not sufficient—it must be an approved textbook.

There is no good translation of the verb " to study " in colloquial Bengali. Instead we use the verb " to read," and this is precisely what the students do. Their elders who guide them on the arduous road from matriculation to graduation in the University of Calcutta and who all bear the title of " professor "—though chairs are few and benches hard!—are described as " causing to read " in their several subjects the pupils in their charge. This is the usual translation of the English verb " to teach." Again this is accurate: for how many can understand sufficient English to take notes at a lecture? So few have the ability to read more than one English book in each subject that what they do read takes on the character of inviolable revelation, to be expounded in the lecture room and committed to memory

by devotional chanting morning and evening at the exhortation
of the professors.

Since the studium generale of twelfth-century Europe the
wheel has come full circle; again the learned tongue is not that
of the common people: again the authority of the writer is not
to be questioned, but believed, and again scholars may be very
young or very poor, and require a strict watch to be maintained
by warden or tutor. Only the spirit is different: for here the
spirit of true learning is long fled.

As the standard of the students' English falls year by year in
India, the task of " reading " becomes more difficult. In his
second year, the average student may be unable to understand
his written examination questions, and even in his fourth and
final year he will be happier if you explain things to him in
Bengali rather than in English. Although English is the medium
of instruction, the use of Bengali is on the increase in lecture-
room and laboratory. In the latter it is of necessity interlarded
with a high proportion of English technical words—an ugly
misalliance of Bengali verbs and pronouns with " burette " or
" voltage " or " filtrate " inflected with Bengali case-endings.
Meanwhile a section of the public loudly demands a lower
examination pass mark in English. Yet the majority of textbooks
are in English, and are likely to be so for many years.

It took me some time to adjust myself to examination standards
where the pass mark is 36 per cent and the first division begins
at 50 per cent, and where the suggestive words " candidates should
use their own words as far as possible," appear at the head of the
question paper. This devaluation is a result of the frantic desire
of parents that their children should have a college education at
whatever sacrifice of academic standards. Those who have passed
matriculation in the third division besiege the college annually
clamouring for admission to the intermediate courses. There is
constant pressure on colleges to increase their number—the class-
rooms overflow, people elbow one another in corridors and
laboratories, and library and common-rooms facilities are
negligible.

The more reputable institutions—Government and missionary-
founded colleges—resist the pressure in the face of constant
criticism though they are nevertheless full to capacity. The less
reputable run three shifts a day—morning, afternoon and evening

—and number their students in thousands. Some are as large as English universities. From all the colleges the pursuit of truth and learning could hardly be more remote, especially as the exclusively research and postgraduate " University " of Calcutta is completely cut off from the dependent but exclusively under-graduate " affiliated colleges," whose teachers have little leisure or aptitude for study and research.

Other characteristic figures in our colleges are the " casual students." This most appropriate name designates those who have failed once (or twice, or more) and are returning to do battle again. I have not yet seen anyone write " failed B.A. " after his name, but I have heard in many cases " I failed by only ten marks in my practical examination," or " I failed an honours degree by only four marks." Infallible examiners, who can assess a script with such minute accuracy! Perhaps this is the product of the rigid syllabus and the single prescribed textbook—no differences of opinion are needed, and an answer can be assessed to a single mark. These casual students are loosely attached to the college, attend some lectures and practical classes in the laboratory. They provide, of course, a useful addition to the college income and are ready to pay fees for private tuition by the professors in their spare time.

There is general recognition that for all students the teaching diet of the college is best supplemented by this private tuition. It is a kind of scholastic black market. At college you receive the bare rations of teaching at a controlled price. But if you have the money and the necessity you can take your fill elsewhere at much higher prices.

Nobody would attempt to persuade our students that they were aiming at anything except passing their examinations, and those who have any interest in a subject for its own sake are the merest handful. After all, the majority are there because their parents sent then, and they have a large number of subjects to study. Most of them are unfitted for listening to lectures, for seeking their own information, for judging critically and for the abstract generalization. Among science students the standard of mathe-matics is appallingly low—I know twenty-one year old degree students who cannot divide a number by four except by long

Answers to Exercise 29—1 (*d*), 2 (*b*), 3 (*e*), 4 (*a*), 5 (*c*), 6 (*c*), (*f*).

division. The joys of a liberal school education have not been theirs yet: from primary school days they have been taught only routine subjects in a routine way, and have studied for long hours, reciting their books in a traditional monotone. Application to the discipline of academic study at college level is spurring a jaded horse.

In our college we also have women students—they are perhaps 10 per cent of the number. But this cannot be called co-education: it is scarcely co-existence. Women students have no opportunity of mixing freely with the men: this is considered dangerous by local opinion. The women students are shepherded from one lecture to another by the professor, or they huddle in a small partitioned area of the entrance hall. They sit carefully apart on one side of the classroom, usually where they are unable to see the blackboard. Until recently they did at least join with the rest of the college in concerts of songs and music that are so much loved in India. Now the University, remote but all-powerful, has decreed that no woman student shall take part in any public performance of any kind on college premises. Even conservative local opinion is shocked. This determination to maintain an apartheid of the sexes would be incredible anywhere else in the world. However most of the colleges have no voice whatever in the affairs of the University. A college principal in Calcutta said to me, " I have no dealings at all with the Vice-Chancellor." After all, what is one college with a thousand students among the scores of thousands of students who are caused to read for a Calcutta degree.

The critics here have their own special remedies: most expect the Government to spend more money. But he would be a bold man who attempted the task of reforming either public opinion or the college educational system, so tangled in the problems of poverty and over-population. [Stop Timing]

Put your reading time here........................

1. During the compulsory study periods—
   (a) Students can read what they like.
   (b) Absolute silence is the rule.
   (c) Books in the vernacular are read.
   (d) An approved textbook must be read.
   (e) There is little supervision.

2. The student's ability to read English is—
   (*a*) A great help to them in their studies.
   (*b*) At quite low level.
   (*c*) At a high level.
   (*d*) Unimportant in their studies.
   (*e*) Useful but not essential to their studies.

3. In the author's opinion the students are—
   (*a*) Carrying on the tradition of the best English universities.
   (*b*) Learning in the American style.
   (*c*) Quite unsuited to university education.
   (*d*) Of low average intelligence.
   (*e*) Working as students did in the Middle Ages.

4. The Indian examination standards are—
   (*a*) Very low.
   (*b*) A little lower than in this country.
   (*c*) About the same as those in England.
   (*d*) A little higher than in England.
   (*e*) Very high.

5. Indian colleges are crowded because—
   (*a*) India needs more graduates.
   (*b*) Parents want their children to have a college education.
   (*c*) Standards of entry are low.
   (*d*) There are not enough colleges.
   (*e*) Education is fairly cheap in India.

6. What is a casual student?...............................

7. The aim of university education in India is—
   (*a*) To produce men of wide vision and attainment.
   (*b*) To give a wide background of culture.
   (*c*) To turn out as many scientists as possible.
   (*d*) To get the students through the examinations.
   (*e*) To provide an adequate supply of civil servants.

8. Amongst science students the standard of...............................
is very low.

9. Women students are—
   (*a*) Kept apart from the men.
   (*b*) Allowed to mix to some extent.
   (*c*) Allowed to mix with the men during lectures.
   (*d*) Allowed to take part in concerts.
   (*e*) Not allowed in the university at all.

The correct answers are at the foot of page 164.

This passage has 1,300 words and you can find your speed from the table below.

Time	Speed	Time	Speed
2.00	650	3.10	410
2.10	600	3.20	390
2.20	557	3.30	371
2.30	520	3.40	354
2.40	487	3.50	343
2.50	459	4.00	325
3.00	433	4.10	312
3.10	410	4.20	300

Speed........................ Comprehension........................

READING WHITE PAPERS

You have built up your speed on material of moderate difficulty which has become somewhat more difficult as you have gone through the book. Now you must learn to read the most difficult material with which the executive regularly comes into contact, namely Government White Papers, and most of the following exercises will be based on extracts from them.

There is no need to become apprehensive at the thought of reading them quickly, although you will find that you cannot read them at the same speed as you read the last test. Let us try some and see how you get on with them. The next three exercises are extracts from a Government publication about Selenium, a rather rare chemical.

EXERCISE 31

Selenium, Occurrence

[START TIMING]   Selenium (Atomic No. 34, Atomic Wt. 78·96) is a semi-metal. It exhibits a number of electro-positive characteristics and exists in a number of allotropic forms. It melts at 220·2°C and boils at 684·8°C. When any variety of selenium is maintained at 200–220°C for some time it is converted into metallic selenium. This, because of its electrical properties, is at the present time the most important form of selenium.

Selenium is widely distributed in the earth's crust (for figures of distribution and concentration see[1] but nowhere does it occur in other than very small amounts. It occurs in its most concentrated form in sulphide ore bodies. There is no known deposit which is worth working for the selenium content alone and it seems likely that selenium will remain a by-product of various metallurgical processes.

Answers to Exercise 30—1 (*d*), 2 (*b*), 3 (*e*), 4 (*a*), 5 (*b*), 6 One who has failed previously, 7 (*d*), 8 Mathematics, 9 (*a*).

(i) *Copper*

Selenium occurs in some, but not all, sulphide ores of copper, though figures for the selenium contents of various copper ores do not appear to be published. The content varies depending on the mine of origin, and probably does not remain constant even for a single mine. The bulk of the world's production of selenium arises from anode muds accumulated in the electrolytic refining of blister copper. In the present state of shortage, additional sources must be sought, and some possibilities are listed below; none of these sources is likely to provide major additions to the supply.

(ii) *Pyrites*

Pyrites may contain small and varying amounts of selenium. For example, Spanish pyrites contain only 0·002 per cent to 0·003 per cent but Cyprus pyrites contain 0·015 per cent. In general, cupriferous pyrites contain more selenium than others.

The selenium would not, of course, be extracted from the pyrites directly. The best hope is that it might become concentrated in some part of the plant in which the pyrites are processed. Thus, in the manufacture of sulphuric acid by roasting pyrites, the selenium may become concentrated in the gas cleaning section of the plant. Again, it may prove possible to recover selenium from sulphur prepared from pyrites. Thus, " The Noranda Mines, Ltd." is at present operating a pilot plant for the roasting of pyrites in preparation for building a commercial plant to roast about 350 tons of pyrites daily. This plant will produce 60 tons of sulphur daily containing about 0·10 per cent of selenium and 0·06 per cent of tellurium. Recovery of the selenium and tellurium from this material would result in the production of about 40,000 lb of selenium per year and perhaps 25,000 lb of tellurium. If a method could be found for recovering the selenium from the sulphur thus produced, a considerable increase in the production capacity of selenium would be realized. However, at this time there is no known means to remove the selenium from the sulphur economically[2].

(iii) *Sulphur*

Natural sulphurs may contain traces of selenium and there is a reference in the literature[1] to a native sulphur of volcanic origin which contained 5·18 per cent. This sort of concentration is thought to apply only to incrustations in the immediate vicinity of volcanoes. We are not aware of any evidence of selenium occurring in sulphurs imported into the U.K. (other than those prepared from pyrites).

(iv) *Uranium*

Selenium is associated with uranium-vanadium ores found in the Colorado Plateau region of the U.S.A.

(v) *Soils*

Certain soils have been found to contain selenium which becomes concentrated in the vegetation; the plants then become toxic to animals. The cultivation of crops to remove the selenium has been suggested, and plants have been found which concentrate the selenium to 10,000 parts per million (p.p.m.) or above; an average of 800 p.p.m. has been quoted[2]. It is just conceivable that a special crop of this nature might be ashed for selenium recovery. Such soils have been reported to occur in Ireland.

(vi) *Other Sources*

Small quantities of selenium may possibly occur where sulphide ores are smelted and in various metallurgical refining processes. Possible examples of this kind include the smelting and refining of zinc, lead, and precious metals. The difficulty here is that, to the producers of the major metal, selenium is an undesirable by-product for which demand, until recent years, has been small. It has been rare for a complete analysis of the raw material to exist. [STOP TIMING]

Put your reading time here......................

1. Metallic selenium is important because—
    (*a*) It is a valuable metal.
    (*b*) Of its magnetic properties.
    (*c*) Of its electrical properties.
    (*d*) Of its use in nickel plating.
2. Selenium is generally found—
    (*a*) In its pure state.
    (*b*) Mixed with gold and silver ores.
    (*c*) Mixed with iron ore.
    (*d*) Mixed with copper ore.
    (*e*) Mixed with soil.
3. Two other sources of selenium are—
    (*a*) Sulphuric acid.
    (*b*) Hydrochloric acid.

(c) Calcium carbonate.
(d) Pyrites.
(e) Sulphur.
(f) Chromium.

The correct answers are at the foot of page 168.

This exercise has 720 words and you can find your speed from the following table.

Time	Speed	Time	Speed
1.30	480	2.20	309
1.40	432	2.30	288
1.50	392	2.40	270
2.00	360	2.50	252
2.10	333	3.00	240
2.20	309		

Speed........................   Comprehension........................

You may have read that rather slowly because you thought that it was going to be much more difficult than it really was. Now that you know what the standard is, you can relax a little and read the next extract.

EXERCISE 32

Selenium in Coloured Glass

[START TIMING] The table given at the beginning of this section indicates that about three-quarters of the selenium used in the manufacture of coloured glass goes into selenium rubies which are used in motor car rear lights, aircraft wing tip lamps, ships' lanterns, railway signal lenses and signalling lamps of various kinds; only about one quarter goes to purely decorative ware. The manufacture of selenium rubies is confined mainly to three firms; the following brief description applies in detail only to one of the three firms but the broad principles are of general application.

(i) *Plant and Process*

In contrast to the manufacture of glass containers, selenium ruby glasses are made in individual covered pots and the process involves a relatively high proportion of manual handling.

The proportion of selenium in the mix is very much higher than in the case of mixes for decolourized glass; a batch of total weight 1,400 to 1,500 lb may contain from 1 to 10 lb of selenium, depending on the type of glass required. The preparation of the batch mix is carried out by hand, the mixing being done with shovels on the floor of the mixing shop.

The ceramic pot in which melting is carried out is made by the firm itself and is some 4 ft high, being totally enclosed except for a vertical opening some 11 in. × 9 in. at the top of the front of the pot. Twelve of these pots are arranged round the periphery of a circular furnace, so that the mouth of each pot registers with a corresponding hole in the outside furnace wall. The furnace may be coal or gas fired and the flames pass down flues situated at the base of each side of each pot. The melt is, therefore, not exposed directly to the flame as it is in the case of the continuously operating furnace used for the manufacture of decolourized glass. The temperature in the furnace itself is steady at about 1,400°C. Each time the pot is charged with the glass mix the mouth of the pot it stoppered while " founding " takes place; at the conclusion of founding the temperature of the glass inside the pot reaches about 1,300°C. The stopper is then removed so that the glass may cool to working temperature which is about 1,100°C or less. The mix is then " gathered " in appropriate amounts by hand, using a long steel rod with a ceramic tip. The " gather " is made from within a ring of ceramic material which floats free on the surface of the molten glass with much of its body below surface level; this serves to keep the surface within the ring free from scum. The pot is usually filled and worked three or four times per week.

Each " gather " of glass on the rod is dropped by the operative into a warm or hot mould and immediately pressed in a single hand-operation by the moulding operative. Two or three articles at a time are taken on a carrier from the moulding operative to the automatic lehr where it is cooled to room temperature over a three-hour period.

It is understood that only about three firms can thus produce a selenium ruby in a single cold stamping operation; other firms employ a re-heating furnace to obtain the full development of the selenium colour, which " strikes " at a temperature a little above the annealing temperature.

Answers to Exercise 31—1 (*c*), 2 (*d*), 3 (*d*), (*e*).

The development of batch compositions and operating conditions designed to produce a particular selenium ruby is largely a matter of experiment based on long experience. There is a constant danger of minor variations causing deterioration of quality in the finished product and it may be a matter of considerable difficulty to re-establish satisfactory conditions. For these reasons manufacturers are understandably reluctant to indulge in any variation of their conditions for experimental or other purposes unless it is absolutely essential.

Glasses for signalling lamps must conform with rigid B.S. specifications, but it is understood that no specification is in force in this country which covers the colour and light transmission of selenium rubies for car rear lamps, which is one of the major uses. The Americans, however, appear to be very much more critical and, to avoid trouble with cars destined for export, British manufacturers require adherence to close limits or to the appropriate specification of the American Car Manufacturers' Association. The manufacturers of car accessories also lay down rigid dimensional tolerances for these lenses.

(ii) *Recovery of Selenium*

Such economies as may be effected in the normal running of this manufacturing process have probably been made already under the pressure of the rising price of selenium, though it is not certain how far such economies have been carried in view of the reluctance of manufacturers to vary their process. However, one point does not yet seem to have been explored. As with decolourizing, it seems obvious that a considerable loss of selenium probably occurs during the melting process. It is likely that such loss as there is would have occurred by the end of the founding period and this receives some support from the observation that there is no significant change in the selenium colour throughout the three or four days that the pot may be in operation. So far it has not proved possible to obtain comparable analysis of selenium in the finished glass resulting from such a mix. However, there are indications in the literature[8] that the loss may amount to as much as four-fifths of the selenium in the original mix. It seems probable that most of it escapes to the atmosphere during the founding period through the crude plug in the mouth of the pot, some as selenium vapour but a considerable proportion probably as selenium dioxide. One reported attempt at recovery did not meet with success.

(iii) *Alternatives to Selenium*

Before the advent of selenium, copper and gold rubies were made; their manufacture required the use of skilled hand labour and so far as is known none are made in the country at present. It is said to be unlikely that either could be made to yield a purity of colour and degree of light transmission which would make it suitable for the manufacture of the various types of lenses for which selenium rubies are used. This would not, of course, apply to purely decorative ware. Ruby glass can also be made with neodymium, but its price and scarcity prohibit its use.

An alternative to selenium rubies for the manufacture of signal lamps of various kinds is, however, appearing; this is plastic, dyed with organic dyestuffs. The largest manufacturer of motor car accessories is shortly producing a design of rear lamp which can be made either in selenium ruby glass or in dyed plastic and other similar designs will follow. Lenses for ships' lamps made in a similar material are at present undergoing long term trials suggested by the National Physical Laboratory. The colour and light transmission characteristics of the plastic appear to be quite satisfactory, though in the case of car rear lamps, for example, very small lenses cannot be used because the plastic is affected by the heat of the light bulbs. Where complex and sharply defined mouldings are required plastic may have the advantage. On the other hand it may perhaps scratch more easily in use.
[STOP TIMING]

Put your reading time here........................

1. Most of the selenium used in coloured glass is—
    (*a*) Made into red reflectors.
    (*b*) Made into glasses of different colours.
    (*c*) Made into ornamental glassware.
    (*d*) Made into red lamp glasses.
    (*e*) Made into leaded lights.
2. The manufacturing process of selenium glass is—
    (*a*) Very highly mechanized.
    (*b*) Partly mechanized.
    (*c*) Mainly hand work.
    (*d*) Entirely hand work.

3. In the manufacture of the glass—
    (a) The method is that used for ordinary glass.
    (b) The melt is exposed directly to the flame.
    (c) The melt is sometimes exposed to the flame.
    (d) The melt is not exposed directly to the flame.
4. The temperature of the furnace is—
    (a) 1,100 degrees C.
    (b) 1,300 degrees C.
    (c) 1,400 degrees C.
5. Selenium rubies can be produced—
    (a) By a simple mechanical device working automatically.
    (b) By a single cold stamping by hand.
    (c) By a rather complicated combined furnace and stamper.
6. The manufacture of selenium rubies is—
    (a) A simple and straightforward process.
    (b) A matter demanding little experience.
    (c) A complicated business about which little is really known.
    (d) A complicated business in which much experiment is carried out.
7. Selenium rubies for car rear lamps for America are—
    (a) To the same specification as those for this country.
    (b) Made to much closer limits than those for this country.
    (c) Made much bigger than those for this country.
    (d) Made much smaller than those for this country.
8. Name a possible alternative to selenium rubies......................

The correct answers are at the foot of page 174.

This passage has 1,200 words and you can find your speed from the following table.

Time	Speed	Time	Speed
2.00	600	3.00	400
2.10	555	3.10	378
2.20	514	3.20	360
2.30	480	3.30	342
2.40	450	3.40	327
2.50	423	3.50	313
3.00	400	4.00	300

Speed...................... Comprehension......................

Now that you have become somewhat accustomed to this style of writing, you should be able to read the next passage at quite a high speed. Don't be put off by the fact that it is rather longer than the others for your new reading technique is more economical of effort than your old one.

Exercise 33

Selenium in the Glass Industry

[Start Timing] general

Selenium finds two contrasting uses in the glass industry, the first and older use being the manufacture of coloured glasses, particularly ruby glasses, and the second being the decolourizing of ordinary white glass. Decolourizing in this context means a masking of the green colour due to the iron content of the raw materials from which the glass is made to give a clear, brilliant and colourless glass.

The glass industry can be divided into the following three main groups—

A. Glass containers

This is the largest manufacturing group judged by tonnage or value of output, and its products are for three main uses, namely—

1. Foods and Drinks (two-thirds of the total).
2. Medicines, Drugs, Chemicals (one quarter of the total).
3. Other Goods such as Paints, Varnishes, Toilet Preparations, Oils and Inks.

B. Sheet, plate and other constructional glass (including safety glass)

C. Other glassware

1. Domestic Glassware:
   (*a*) Mouth-Blown
   (*b*) Hand-Pressed
   (*c*) Automatic Machine-made
2. Illuminating Glassware
3. Laboratory, Medical and Scientific Glassware
4. Optical Glass
5. Glass Tubing and Rod
6. Machinery Glassware
7. Lampblown Glassware
8. Stained Glass
9. Buttons, Beads, Jewellery
10. Glass Fibre Products.

The second group (*B*) uses no selenium (except for " Special White " Plate and some " Cathedral Rolled " Plate, which are produced in very small amounts) since these glasses are so thin that decolourizing is unnecessary, and the third group also uses a negligible amount for decolourizing. Decolourizing is therefore confined almost exclusively to the glass container trade. Of the coloured glasses containing selenium, selenium rubies for lenses and reflectors are the most important.

The following table gives an indication of the distribution of selenium within the glass industry—

End Use	% Selenium Used
Globes and Shades	3·5
Lenses and Reflectors	13·4
Bulbs and Valves	1·25
Stained Glass	0·25
Containers and Domestic	80·1
Other uses	1·5

DECOLOURIZING

(i) *Glass manufacturing process*

In the production of glass on a large scale, such as for window glass, glass containers, etc., the melting is carried out in continuously operated " tanks " ranging in capacity from 50 tons or less to 1,200 tons, with outputs of 10 to 100 tons of glass per day. Where small outputs are required, however, glass is still made in pots and " day-tanks " in small unit batches.

The colour of the glass obtained depends on the types and amounts of any colouring agents in the raw materials, on the composition of the " base " glass, on the temperature of melting and on the conditions (oxidizing or reducing) in the melt. Certain colours are very sensitive to melting conditions, so that glasses made from identical batches may differ noticeably in colour even if made in furnaces which are substantially identical in design. The reasons for such differences are not easily determined; slight differences in the shape of the " ports," causing the flames to play across the glass at slightly different levels, may be sufficient to account for the differences in some cases. For these reasons it is not always possible to specify exactly the mixtures which will operate satisfactorily in all tanks, it being necessary, in some cases, to make final adjustments to suit each particular tank. This is

M

particularly true when making sensitive colours or when some very delicate balance is required, as in decolourizing, in order to obtain a substantially colourless glass. Not unnaturally, therefore, changes from an established procedure are avoided whenever possible.

(ii) *Decolourized glass containers*

The use of selenium for decolourizing glass seems to date from about the time of the first world war. Although large continuously operating furnaces or " tanks " were introduced in the glass industry about 50 years ago it appears that these furnaces could not have been used for the continuous manufacture of decolourized glass without selenium.

The output of the furnaces may vary from 10 tons to about 100 tons per day. In a large installation the raw materials for the glass mix are stored in large quantities in gravity feed storage hoppers from which they are fed directly to the weighing and mixing room. The mixed ingredients are fed into hoppers whence their delivery is mechanically controlled directly and continuously onto the surface of the molten glass in the furnace. The molten glass is likely to reach a depth of three to four feet in the furnace, with the flames playing directly on, or slightly above, the surface. The temperature at the entry end of the furnace will be in the neighbourhood of 1300°C–1400°C rising to about 1450°C–1550°C and cooling off again to about 1250°C towards the end of the furnace.

At the working-end of the furnace the molten glass may be fed in measured quantities either by gravity or by suction into a multiple head forming machine. This is usually a rotary machine containing two sets of moulds; a primary set brings the glass charges roughly to shape with the neck formed. These partly rigid blanks are then transferred automatically to the final moulds, where after one revolution of the machine they are blown out to their final shape. They are transferred, still red-hot, to the annealing furnace or lehr where they are cooled to approximately room temperature over a period varying with the dimensions of the container.

Answers to Exercise 32—1 (*d*), 2 (*b*), 3 (*d*), 4 (*b*), 5 (*b*), 6 (*c*), 7 (*b*), 8 Dyed plastic.

The manufacture of the moulds, with the exception of the original casting, is usually undertaken by the container manufacturers themselves and represents a very considerable capital investment in machines, machine tools and stocks of moulds. The design of the moulds may have a considerable influence on the details of the production process since the thickness of the glass container will, of course, affect its cooling rate. Within fairly wide limits the moulds can be transferred from one forming machine to another of the same type but the forming machines themselves can only be transferred from one tank furnace to another providing the method of feeding in the glass is the same. For general efficiency the furnace must be kept running at a rate of output not far short of its maximum and this requires careful production planning for a long way ahead. Obviously, if several orders for small containers instead of large ones have to be on the same furnace the output will drop, and it is often a matter of extreme difficulty to maintain a nice balance in the pull on any one furnace. The furnace itself will probably run for an average of $1\frac{1}{2}$ to 2 years at a stretch (producing quantities of glass of an order of one hundred tons per day all the time). This operating life is controlled by the life of the refractory lining of the furnace. A large factory may house six or more of these furnaces but the majority have fewer. It should be obvious from this description that a continuous furnace of this kind represents an enormous capital investment and is a singularly inflexible instrument of industrial production.

(iii) *Mechanism of decolourizing*

A representative batch composition (main ingredients only) for a glass mix might be as follows—

Sand	1,000 parts
Limestone	250 parts
Anhydrous sodium carbonate (soda ash) .	300 parts
Felspar	100 parts
Sodium sulphate	10 parts
Arsenic trioxide	0·5 parts

Many minor variations are possible; for example, sodium nitrate may be used in part replacement of the sodium carbonate; borax may be included; or the felspar may be replaced by alumina. A typical composition of the final glass arising might be as follows—

Silicon oxide . . . . . 73 to 74%
Aluminium oxide . . . . 0·5 to 2·0%
Calcium oxide . . . . . 9·5 to 10·5%
Sodium oxide . . . . . 15·0 to 16·0%
Sulphate . . . . . . 0·1 to 0·3%
Arsenic trioxide . . . . . 0·01 to 0·05%

Apart from these main ingredients, selenium may be used in quantities varying from $\frac{1}{4}$ oz to 1 or 2 oz per 2,000 lb of batch. A trace of cobalt oxide is also used in most cases often less than 1 g per 2,000 lb of batch. All the above quantities are subject to considerable variations from one manufacturer to another.

Basically, a glass mix of the above kind without selenium will give a glass of a green colour, the intensity of which will depend on the iron content and on the conditions of melting. The contribution of the sand to the iron content of the finished glass is of first importance in that it is the greatest single batch constituent. Certain sands, of which there is a very limited supply in the British Isles, have exceptionally low iron contents (0·010 to 0·015 per cent Fe_2O_3) and with other precautions permit the manufacture of a glass having a minimum of colour, without the use of selenium. Several continental countries have extensive deposits of sands of low iron content. To obtain a colourless glass some selenium is necessary whatever sand is used. In this country sand purification processes have been developed to allow certain British sands with a higher initial iron oxide content to be used in conjunction with selenium to make a decolourized glass. In the United Kingdom the very large quantity of sand used annually in the manufacture of containers comes partly from the British Isles and partly from the Continent. In general it is not possible to decolourize a glass containing more than 0·07 per cent Fe_2O_3 even by the use of selenium; this amount of iron in the finished glass corresponds roughly to 0·02 per cent to 0·04 per cent Fe_2O_3 in the sand.

It has been known for a long time that the green colour of the glass will be much reduced if it is made under oxidizing conditions, and this is the function of the arsenic (preferably with a little nitrate) in the batch mixture. Recent work by Professor Moore and his co-workers[5] shows that much of the resultant ferric iron can exist in the glass in a colourless form, probably four-coordinated with oxygen atoms forming corners of four silica tetrahedra. Supporting evidence for this suggestion has been obtained by a study of the magnetic susceptibility of various glasses, since iron in this form in glass has an abnormally low susceptibility; there is an analogy with ferric phosphate, in which the iron is four-coordinated, ferric phosphate being also colourless and having an abnormally low susceptibility. Whether this theory ultimately finds general acceptance or not it appears to offer a satisfactory explanation of the main facts, since the amount of iron left in the blue ferrous state will be only a fraction of the original iron present. With selenium present the ferrous iron appears to form some iron selenide, giving a pale brown or yellow colour to the glass, which, with any yellow colour due to any trace of ferric iron remaining in the un-coordinated form will be neutralized by the addition of the traces of cobalt already mentioned.

(iv) *Alternatives to selenium*

It is difficult on *a priori* grounds to suggest what materials might be tried as alternatives to selenium, though considerable efforts have been made at replacement.

(*a*) *Manganese dioxide*. Manganese dioxide is used to decolourize glass melted in individual covered pots, though the resultant glass may sometimes be without the full brilliance characteristic of a selenium decolourized glass. The main disadvantage of manganese dioxide is that it is very readily reduced to the colourless form and requires very much more careful control of oxidizing conditions than is normally possible in an open continuous furnace.

(*b*) *Tellurium*. Tellurium has also been suggested as a possible alternative to selenium on the grounds of its association with selenium in the periodic table and the similarity of some of its properties. Preliminary experiments carried out at the Department of Glass Technology at Sheffield University indicated that by itself tellurium gives no colour to ordinary glass, but in the presence of small amounts of iron it gives a strong green colour to the glass. Trials carried out by firms on the manufacturing scale show that it offers no promise as an alternative to selenium.

(*c*) *Cerium dioxide*. Cerium dioxide can be used for glass melted in pot furnaces and gives a good, clear, decolourized glass, particularly in combination with manganese dioxide.

Unfortunately the effect is considerably diminished above 1400°C (i.e. at the higher temperatures of the tank furnace) and so the material is of little or no practical use for large-scale modern manufacture of containers.

(*d*) *Neodymium oxide.* It has been claimed that this can be used as a decolourizing agent, preferably in combination with cerium dioxide, but its scarcity and cost prohibit its use.

(*e*) *Nickel oxide.* Nickel oxide can be used as a decolourizing agent in glasses in which the alkali is present as potash, but gives brownish colours in soda glass, such as is used for glass containers.

(*f*) *Lithium nitrate.* Lithium nitrate has been reported to have some decolourizing power but experimental trials failed to show any such effect.

It would appear therefore that no satisfactory alternative to Selenium is even in sight at present.

(v) *Economy of selenium*

Many conditions, e.g. size of furnace, composition of raw materials, etc., vary considerably from one firm to another. It is not possible therefore to recommend any maximum or minimum figure for the proportion of selenium in a given batch of glass. However, in the last two years the glass industry and the Department of Glass Technology at Sheffield have devoted much attention to the problem of economizing in selenium. Some factors that have emerged as being important in controlling the actual amount of selenium used are as follows—

(*a*) *Antimony oxide.* Antimony oxide was formerly used as well as arsenic in the batch mix but has been found to require a higher consumption of selenium. As a result, many manufacturers appear to have stopped using it.

(*b*) *Arsenic oxide.* It has been found desirable to restrict the use of arsenic oxide to the minimum possible in order to economize in selenium.

(*c*) *Sodium nitrate.* Small amounts are desirable but an excess will again increase consumption of selenium.

(*d*) *Sodium sulphate.* Sodium and other sulphates are used to aid the melting of the glass batch. They also suppress the pink selenium colour and their use must be cut down to an absolute minimum.

(*e*) *Working temperatures.* The pink colour of the selenium "strikes" at the annealing temperature and at a temperature immediately above it. Since thick-walled ware will remain in this temperature zone longer than thin-walled ware, two different results can be obtained from the same furnace at the same time. Conservation of the sensible heat in the glass containers between the forming machine and the hot chamber of the lehr is beneficial and may lead to an economy in selenium.

(*f*) *Foreign materials.* Traces of iron and chromium may be picked up by the various ingredients of the glass batch during storage and handling in the works. This can generally be avoided by improved tidiness and cleanliness.

The details of the action of these factors will not be described here, since they have been examined carefully by the glass industry and the Department of Glass Technology, and the results made available to the whole industry. However, it can readily be seen that it will require good and careful management to control all these factors and keep them all at a level which will ensure the lowest possible consumption of selenium. Moreover, the glass manufacturer has many other things to look after besides his consumption of selenium. No uniformity of practice from one factory to another can therefore be expected. Nonetheless, the glass industry has been active in obtaining quantitative results indicating the relative importance of these various factors and in transmitting these results to the industry. In this connexion, two important papers have been published which between them should give glass manufacturers all the information they need to cut selenium consumption down to the minimum practicable level[6, 7]. In these papers the following proportions are suggested as representing good modern practice—

Arsenic Oxide	. . .	1 lb per 2,000 lb batch
Sodium Nitrate	. . .	3 lb per 2,000 lb batch
Selenium	. . . .	$\frac{1}{2}$ oz per 2,000 lb batch

The articles also indicate that firms have succeeded in cutting down their consumption of selenium by amounts varying from 20 per cent to over 80 per cent during 1951-3. It now seems likely that the more efficient firms at least are operating with the smallest amount of selenium possible, at least without major modifications to plant and process. Some firms may yet be able to economize still further but it is likely that any further economies which can be effected in this way will be marginal only.

(vi) *Recovery of selenium*

It has so far proved impossible to obtain comparable figures on (*a*) percentage of selenium in a given batch mix and (*b*) the percentage of selenium in the finished glass resulting from this mix. However, selenium melts at 220·2°C and boils at 684·8°C, whereas the temperature in a tank furnace is about 1450°C, so that there would not seem to be much doubt that a proportion of the selenium is lost from the furnace during the melting process. The use of selenites has been suggested in order to reduce volatilization losses, but it is believed that in practice decolourizing could be carried out equally well by using an amount of selenium element equivalent to the selenium added as selenites.

Any selenium volatilized will presumably go up the chimney with the flue gases, though at the moment it is an open question how much of any escaping selenium goes free into the atmosphere, and how much might be found in the flue dusts. It appears that little attention has been given to this problem, and no figures have so far been obtained. Until such figures are obtained it is impossible to say whether selenium recovery, either from flue dusts—or from the escaping gases—would be worthwhile. [STOP TIMING]

Put your reading time here........................

1. The two most important uses of selenium are—
    (*a*) In the manufacture of laboratory glassware.
    (*b*) In the manufacture of glass containers.
    (*c*) In the manufacture of sheet glass.
    (*d*) In the manufacture of stained glass.
    (*e*) In the manufacture of domestic glass.
    (*f*) In the manufacture of lenses and reflectors.
2. The manufacture of glass is—
    (*a*) An easily controlled process.
    (*b*) A process in which experiment is easy and frequent.
    (*c*) A fairly difficult process.
    (*d*) A process which it is not easy to forecast.
    (*e*) An extremely difficult process where experiment is avoided.

3. The manufacture of glass containers is—
    (a) Still mainly a hand process.
    (b) Mainly a hand process but mechanization is coming in.
    (c) More mechanized than hand work.
    (d) Almost completely mechanized.
4. Glass containers are still—
    (a) Mainly blown by glass blowers.
    (b) A product of a mechanical moulding process.
    (c) Made from the finest glass.
    (d) Not made from decolourized glass.
5. A continuous furnace—
    (a) Is a recent innovation in the glass industry.
    (b) Lasts for less than a year.
    (c) Will produce a thousand tons of glass a day.
    (d) Operates at a temperature of 2,000 degrees C.
    (e) Is extremely expensive and inflexible.
6. The colour of the glass without selenium depends mainly on—
    (a) The temperature of the furnace.
    (b) The amount of iron in the sand and the conditions of melting.
    (c) The amount of copper in the sand and the conditions of melting.
    (d) The amount of limestone used.
    (e) The conditions of melting and the amount of felspar.
7. To obtain a colourless glass............................is essential.
8. As an alternative to selenium—
    (a) Tellurium has proved successful.
    (b) Nickel oxide is moderately successful.
    (c) Nothing has proved successful.
9. On economy in selenium—
    (a) Many unsuccessful experiments have been carried out.
    (b) Recovery of selenium from the waste gases is quite simple.
    (c) There are several ideas but they are difficult to put into practice.
    (d) Glass manufacturers are not interested.
    (e) The maximum amount is now recovered.
10. Write a brief answer to the following—
Is the consumption of selenium an important factor in the cost of glass containers?........................

You will find the answers to questions 1 to 9 at the foot of page 184. Look back in the passage to see if you have a sensible answer to question 10.

This passage has 3,000 words and you can work out your speed from the table below.

Time	Speed	Time	Speed
5.00	600	7.00	428
5.10	582	7.10	419
5.20	562	7.20	409
5.30	545	7.30	400
5.40	529	7.40	391
5.50	514	7.50	382
6.00	500	8.00	375
6.10	486	8.10	367
6.20	473	8.20	360
6.30	461	8.30	352
6.40	450	8.40	346
6.50	439	8.50	339
7.00	428	9.00	333

Speed........................   Comprehension........................

SECTION SEVENTEEN

THE LEVEL OF DIFFICULTY

You will readily accept the idea that the reading material which you have to deal with in the course of your daily life varies a great deal in difficulty. In this book the difficulty of the exercises has increased very much since the beginning.

It is a cardinal point of effective reading that you do not read everything at the same speed. That is one of the marks of inefficiency. You should read everything as fast as possible, but that will not be the same speed for everything.

Now that you have to some extent conquered the slowing effects on all your reading of vocalization and a narrow eye span, and you have proved to yourself that you can read twice as fast and remember just as much, your speed should be decided by the difficulty of the material to you. The last two words are important, for the level of difficulty is a personal matter, and it is a mistake to accept some wide and sweeping criterion such as that all Government White Papers are very difficult to read. It depends on what they are about. That is the key to assessing the difficulty of a passage; how difficult is the subject matter to you. It may be a very abstruse treatise on physics, but, if that is your line you will not find it difficult.

When you start to read you should be able to assess the difficulty of a passage and read it at the maximum speed consistent with reasonable comprehension. That does not mean that you should go back to all your old bad habits; it means that you must have a variable speed of reading. The next exercises are taken from Government White Papers and you must use your own judgment of their difficulty to decide the speed at which you are going to read. Do not stop dead at the tables of figures, but get a general idea of them.

The first one is quite short and will let you see what you have to deal with.

EXERCISE 34

The National Insurance (Industrial Injuries) Act, 1946. First Quinquennial Review

[START TIMING]

Pneumoconiosis

19. The after history of pensions awarded for pneumoconiosis is very different. At the initial examination the disease is usually in an early stage and the case is assessed at a correspondingly low disability level. Any degree of disability, however low, ranks for a pension; no gratuities are payable. The disease may remain stationary for long periods or may become worse; it is therefore rare for a life assessment to be given unless the disease has reached the 100 per cent level. It follows that virtually the only cessations are those due to the death of the pensioner, and that the great majority of cases in payment are on a provisional basis. The statistics can be summarized as follows—

Year	Total awards from July, 1948, to end of year (in thousands)	Pensions in payment at end of year (in thousands)			Ratio of (5) to (2)
		Provisional	Final	Total	
(1)	(2)	(3)	(4)	(5)	(6)
1949	7·6	7·3	0·2	7·5	0·99
1950	10·9	10·4	0·3	10·7	0·98
1951	14·5	13·4	0·5	13·9	0·96
1952	18·8	16·9	0·7	17·6	0·94
1953 (app.)	23·4	20·5	1·0	21·5	0·92

The last line of the table shows that of 23,400 pensions awarded up to the end of 1953, 92 per cent were still in payment at that date, less than five per cent of these being on a final basis. The remainder of the table shows the corresponding position at

Answers to Exercise 33—1 (*b*), (*f*), 2 (*e*), 3 (*d*), 4 (*b*), 5 (*e*), 6 (*b*), 7 Selenium, 8 (*c*), 9 (*c*).

earlier dates. It is clear that so far as pneumoconiosis cases are concerned an extended analysis of reassessment, on the lines of Table 2, is not needed. The estimation of the future cost of pneumoconiosis pensions is, however, attended by difficulty in other respects. These are dealt with in the paragraphs which follow.

20. It is extremely difficult to obtain any firm indication of a trend in the numbers of new cases coming forward each year. About eighty per cent of them arise in the coal-mining industry, and for these the Ministry of Fuel and Power has published statistics which cover the period from July, 1943, when the range of lung conditions caused by dust was widened to include all cases to which the term " pneumoconiosis " is now applied. Up to July, 1948, the figures show the number of coal-miners with pneumoconiosis who were certified each year under the Workmen's Compensation Acts; thereafter—apart from a diminishing residue of compensation cases—they indicate the numbers diagnosed under the Industrial Injuries Act. The progression of the figures from year to year during the period 1943-53 is, however, very erratic for a number of reasons. In the early years of the period they include a substantial backlog of cases which, prior to 1943, were not eligible for compensation. Mainly for this reason the numbers rose to a peak of nearly 6,000 cases in 1945. Thereafter there was a substantial decline but the numbers rose again to about 6,000 in 1949. This may well have been due to the fact that, unlike diagnosis under the Industrial Injuries Act, certification under the Workmen's Compensation Acts entailed suspension from work; numbers of men who would otherwise have presented themselves for examination before July, 1948, may have deferred doing so on this account. After 1949, the annual numbers fell steadily to about 3,400 in 1952, but since then they have again risen appreciably. How much of this rise is due to the intensification of measures for detecting the disease at an early stage it is impossible to say, but it would not be surprising if, for this reason, the numbers showed some further increase in the near future. Moreover, it can hardly be expected that the new cases coming forward would yet reflect such beneficial results as may have been achieved by devices for the suppression of dust in the mines. A secondary factor which may lead to some slight increase in the numbers is the recent extension of title to pension to cases with an initial disability rating of less than five per cent.

21. It will be clear from the preceding paragraph that estimates of the number of new pneumoconiosis cases arising in future years can only be conjectural. Although, for reasons already given, there may be no reduction in the annual numbers of awards in the immediate future, the circumstances do not seem to warrant an assumption that the long-term trend will be other than downward. I have therefore based my calculations on the arbitrary assumption that in twenty years' time the annual number of new cases will have fallen to one-half, and by the end of the century, to one-quarter, of the current level.

22. It is equally difficult to foresee what changes are likely to occur in future years in the average rate at which pensions are payable. With the passage of time, the disability rating of cases of long standing will tend to increase; on the other hand, for reasons indicated in paragraph 20, the total number of pensions in payment may in future years contain a higher proportion than in the past of early stage cases with very low assessments. The position is as yet too immature to enable any tendencies of this kind to be discernible in the statistics; the average rate of pension has, in fact, remained steady at about 30 per cent, and in all the circumstances I have based my estimates of cost on the assumption that it will continue at this level.

23. The material so far available for investigating the mortality of pneumoconiosis pensioners has, like the other statistics, been collected on a sampling basis and is meagre in the extreme; it has been quite impracticable to analyse the experience according to degree of disablement or duration of award as well as by age attained, although these are clearly relevant factors. On this account estimates of the rate at which the body of pensioners will increase year by year, and of the dimensions which it will ultimately attain, are necessarily highly speculative. [STOP TIMING]

Put your reading time here.........................

1. For this disease—
   (*a*) A gratuity is usually payable.
   (*b*) A pension for a short period usually meets the case.
   (*c*) A varying permanent pension is usually necessary.
   (*d*) The same rules apply as for injuries.
2. The estimation of future cost is difficult because—
   (*a*) The number of new cases is difficult to gauge.

(b) People recover so quickly.

(c) Preventive measures may cause the disease to die out.

(d) There is an alarming increase in the incidence of this disease.

3. The annual numbers—

(a) Have increased steadily over the last ten years.

(b) Have varied greatly but are now falling.

(c) Have varied greatly but are now steady.

(d) Were steady for a long time, but now are variable.

(e) Have varied greatly but are now rising.

4. Of the new cases of pneumoconiosis—

(a) Twenty per cent are coal miners.

(b) Forty per cent are quarry workers.

(c) Sixty per cent are coal miners.

(d) Eighty per cent are coal miners.

(e) Ninety per cent are coal miners.

5. The main trend of new cases has been assumed to be—

(a) Upwards.

(b) Stationary.

(c) Downwards.

(d) Impossible to foresee.

You will find the correct answers at the foot of page 188.

This exercise has 900 words and you can work out your speed from this table.

Time	Speed	Time	Speed
1.30	600	2.20	385
1.40	540	2.30	360
1.50	490	2.40	337
2.00	450	2.50	317
2.10	415	3.00	300
2.20	385		

Speed....................... Comprehension.......................

That was a fairly short exercise so that you would get accustomed to the difficulty of this type of material. You should be able to read it at a good speed with reasonable comprehension. Try and increase your speed on the next exercise which is also quite short.

EXERCISE 35

Cmd. 9372. Final Report of a Court of Inquiry into a Dispute between the British Transport Commission and the National Union of Railwaymen

[START TIMING]   *Background to the dispute*

5. The National Union of Railwaymen (N.U.R.) represents a wide range of railway employees, but the dispute before us was confined to those known as " conciliation staff "—that is, the non-salaried workers within the scope of the Machinery of Negotiation for Railway Staff described in paragraph seven below, including the locomotive and traffic staff, those engaged in signal and telecommunications work and those employed in the handling of baggage, goods and rolling stock. The precise number and details of both salaried and conciliation staff within the scope of this Machinery, for the week ending 27th March, 1954, are set out in Appendix 1. Of the conciliation staff, the locomotive grades are represented jointly by the Associated Society of Locomotive Engineers and Firemen (A.S.L.E.F.), which has the majority of members, and the N.U.R., and the other sections (Traffic Permanent Way, Goods and Cartage, etc.) by the N.U.R. alone. The total number of conciliation staff as stated to us by the British Transport Commission is about 350,000.

6. The Machinery also covers about 90,000 salaried staff whose representation is shared between the Transport Salaried Staffs' Association (T.S.S.A.) and the N.U.R., the former having the majority of members. We were informed that negotiations about the salaries of these grades were proceeding between the two Unions and the Commission, and they were therefore agreed to be outside the scope of our inquiry.

7. The present Machinery of Negotiation for Railway Staff was set up under an Agreement of 1935 between the Railway Companies on the one hand and, on the other, the N.U.R., the A.S.L.E.F. and the T.S.S.A. (then known as the Railway Clerks' Association) and is still in force as between these three Unions and the British Transport Commission. At the national level the Machinery consists of three stages—

Answers to Exercise 34—1 (c), 2 (a), 3 (e), 4 (d), 5 (c).

(*a*) Discussions between the Union or Unions concerned and the Railways Staff Conference. If there is failure to agree either side may refer to

(*b*) the Railway Staff National Council, which is a joint body consisting of representatives of the Commission and of all three Railway Unions. Failing settlement, a major matter may be referred on agreed terms of reference to

(*c*) the Railway Staff National Tribunal, which consists of an independent Chairman and two members not connected with the Railway industry. The Chairman is appointed by agreement or failing agreement, by the Ministry of Labour, and the other two members are nominated respectively by the Commission and the Union or Unions concerned. The awards of the Tribunal are not necessarily binding upon the parties.

8. Clause 18 of the 1935 Agreement provides as follows—

" In no circumstances shall there be any withdrawal of labour or any attempt on the part of the employees to hamper the proper working of the Railway until any matter under dispute has been submitted through the proper channels to the higher Management or, if such matter is within the scope of the Machinery of Negotiation, until the provisions thereof have been fully utilized." [STOP TIMING]

Put your reading time here.........................

1. The dispute concerned—
    (*a*) Salaried workers.
    (*b*) Only locomotive drivers and firemen.
    (*c*) Most non-salaried workers.
    (*d*) Mainly signalmen.
    (*e*) Porters and other station workers only.

2. The negotiating machinery consisted of—
    (*a*) Two stages and arbitration by the Minister of Transport.
    (*b*) Three stages of arbitration.
    (*c*) One meeting and one arbitration committee.
    (*d*) Discussions and then arbitration.
    (*e*) Discussions, then discussions by a joint body, then arbitration.

3. Under the 1935 agreement, the Unions agreed—
    (*a*) Never to go on strike again.

(b) Never to go on strike until all the machinery had been employed.

(c) Not to go on strike without first meeting the employers.

(d) Not to go on strike in time of Emergency.

(e) Not to go on strike over pay dispute.

The correct answers are at the foot of page 192.

This passage has 480 words and you can work out your speed from the following table.

Time	Speed
0.50	576
1.00	480
1.10	411
1.20	360
1.30	320
1.40	288
1.50	261
2.00	240

Speed......................   Comprehension......................

Now try the next exercise. Do not be put off because it is longer. With extracts of this type, the correct answers to the questions form a summary of the main points of the passage, and as you read you should be sifting the information and retaining that which is important.

EXERCISE 36

National Insurance (Industrial Injuries) Act, 1946

[START TIMING]

Scope of the Act

1. The system of industrial injury insurance introduced by the Act of 1946 came into operation on 5th July, 1948. Its purpose is to provide benefits for insured persons who incur injury caused by accidents arising out of and in the course of their employment. These benefits are also payable in respect of certain prescribed diseases. Broadly speaking, the Act applies to all civilians who are insured under the National Insurance Acts as employed persons. It does not extend to members of the Forces; on the other hand, its provisions cover certain small groups of persons

who are classed as "self-employed" for the purpose of the National Insurance Acts. Throughout the period covered by this review the number of persons insured under the Act has varied but little from a total of 20½ millions, of whom almost exactly one-third are women.

2. Unlike the main National Insurance Act, the Industrial Injuries Act has no counterpart in previous legislation. Its provisions differ radically from those which, under the Workmen's Compensation Acts applied to injuries sustained by employed persons before 5th July, 1948. Compensation under the old system was assessed by reference to loss of earning capacity; benefit under the new consists of a fixed weekly payment, for a limited period, in cases where the injury causes incapacity for work, followed by a pension or lump sum of an amount determined (on a scale analogous to that employed for war pensions) by reference to the extent of the impairment sustained. With one important exception the question of earning capacity does not enter into the computation of benefit payments under the Industrial Injuries Act. There is the further fundamental distinction that claims for workmen's compensation, if not settled by agreement between the claimant (or his representatives) and the employer (or his insurers) were the subject of legal adjudication in local courts. Under such a system the need for systematic central collation and analysis of statistics of the nature and incidence of industrial accidents and diseases was not apparent, and although periodical returns of the numbers and amounts of compensation payments were collected from employers and insurers in certain industries and published in summary form by the Home Office, they provided only a very general basis for estimates of the expenditure which the introduction of the Industrial Injuries Act would entail. Financially therefore—if not administratively—the Act was something of an adventure into the unknown; the assessment, in terms of weekly contributions payable by all insured persons and their employers, of the cost of the benefits which it provided could be no more than a tentative process subject to review in the light of actual experience of the working of the scheme.

Contributions

3. Although the risk of injury varies greatly between one

industry and another, the principle of the Act is to spread the cost of the benefits evenly over the whole body of insured persons by means of weekly contributions from them and from their employers. These contributions, which are not payable in respect of periods when the person is unemployed or incapable of work, are at present at the following rates. (The rates quoted have been increased by the National Insurance Act, 1954.)

	Insured Person	Employer	Total
Men	4d.	5d.	9d.
Women	3d.	3d.	6d.
Boys } (under age 18)	3d.	3d.	6d.
Girls }	2d.	2d.	4d.

There is an Exchequer supplement equal to one-fifth of the income from the contributions of insured persons and employers. The relative amounts of the weekly contributions for men, women, boys and girls are determined broadly by the consideration that although the basic rates of benefits are the same for both sexes the additions in respect of dependants are payable to men to a greater extent than to women; for juveniles the Act prescribes lower basic rates.

Benefits

4. There are three types of benefits—

(i) Injury benefit is payable (for a period not exceeding twenty-six weeks) during total incapacity for work following an industrial accident or the onset of an industrial disease. The weekly rate of benefit payable for persons aged 18, and over is 55s., with additional allowances for dependants at the same rates as those payable under the National Insurance Act. Juveniles under age 18 without dependants receive benefits at lower rates.

(ii) Disablement benefit is payable from the end of the injury benefit period, in respect of a loss of physical or mental faculty. Payment of this benefit is not dependent on incapacity for

Answers to Exercise 35—1 (*c*), 2 (*e*), 3 (*b*).

work. If the degree of disablement is assessed at less than 20 per cent, the benefit normally takes the form of a gratuity; in other cases a weekly pension is paid, the rate of pension being determined according to a scale based on the degree of disablement. The rate for 100 per cent disablement is 55s. per week, while for 20 per cent disablement it is 11s. per week. The maximum amount of the gratuity, i.e. for 19 per cent disablement for life, is £185. Additional benefits—special hardship allowance, unemployability supplement, constant attendance allowances, increase of benefit during approved hospital treatment and allowances for dependant—are also payable in certain circumstances. By far the most important of these is the special hardship allowance, which is described in detail in later paragraphs. Expenditure on the other types of supplement is inconsiderable.

(iii) Death benefit is payable on the death of an insured person as the result of an industrial accident or prescribed disease. The main benefit is a widow's pension (payable in the majority of cases at the rate of 37s. per week) with allowances for children, but there are also benefits for other dependants of the deceased. Both the nature and the amount of the benefit vary according to the relationship to the deceased and the extent of the dependence, and there are provisions limiting the benefit payable in respect of any one death.

Injury benefit is not payable to persons suffering from the lung diseases pneumoconiosis and byssinosis; they may qualify for disablement benefit from the onset of the disease. Disablement gratuities are not payable in respect of pneumoconiosis; for any degree of disablement of one per cent or more a pension is payable.

5. The extent of the benefit transactions under the Act can be indicated by a few round figures. About three-quarters of a million awards of injury benefit are made each year. The number of persons becoming entitled to disablement benefit has tended to increase year by year; the provisional number for 1953 is about 85,000, of whom 34,000 were awarded gratuities and 51,000 pensions. In many of these cases the disability is only temporary; some two-thirds of the pensions (or three-quarters if pneumoconiosis pensions are excluded) are terminated for this reason within a few years of award. The annual number of awards of death benefits slightly exceeds 2,000. These figures give a broad

measure of the extent of the industrial injury risks to which the insured population as a whole is subject although, for the reason indicated in paragraph 3, the rates derivable from them cannot be regarded as representative of any particular industry.

Supplementary Schemes

6. Section 83 of the 1946 Act enables the Minister to approve schemes, submitted by a body representing insured persons of any class and their employers, for supplementing the rights conferred by the Act. One such scheme has been approved, and is in operation, for colliery workers; it contains its own provisions for periodical actuarial reviews. The Act provides that no part of the funds required for a supplementary scheme shall be derived from money provided by Parliament. The transactions of the scheme do not therefore affect the Industrial Injuries Fund in any way and are outside the scope of this review.

Northern Ireland

7. Section 84 of the Act of 1946 enables arrangements to be made between the Governments of Great Britain and of Northern Ireland for co-ordinating the systems of industrial injuries insurance in the two countries so as to secure that they operate as far as possible as a single system. For this purpose a Joint Authority has been established, with power to make any necessary financial adjustments between the two Industrial Injuries Funds. The Authority has decided, however, that consideration of this matter should be deferred until the first quinquennial actuarial reviews of the schemes of both countries have been completed. The estimates given in this report of the future progress of the Great Britain Fund are therefore subject to such adjustments as may be found to be necessary when the results of the reviews for both countries have been considered. In view, however, of the relative dimensions of the two systems—the insured population of Northern Ireland is less than one-fortieth of that of Great Britain —it is unlikely that the inclusion of the adjustments would materially affect any of the conclusions reached in this report. [Stop Timing]

Put your reading time here........................

1. The Act applies—
   (a) To all residents of Great Britain.

(b) To all British people at home and abroad.

(c) To all employed under the National Insurance Act and to soldiers serving at home.

(d) To all employed persons under the National Insurance Act and to all members of the Forces.

(e) To all employed persons under the National Insurance Act.

2. The new Act—

(a) Is a development of the Workmen's Compensation Act.

(b) Has its benefits based on loss of earning capacity.

(c) Is quite different from any previous Act.

(d) Uses the local courts as appeals courts.

(e) Came into force on 2nd July, 1946.

3. The contributions—

(a) Are the same for the whole body of insured persons.

(b) Are the same for the insured person and the employer.

(c) Are in proportion to the benefits received.

(d) Are assisted by a contribution from the Exchequer.

(e) Are the sole sources of income.

4. Injury benefit is paid for—

(a) Two months.

(b) Four months.

(c) Between five and seven months.

(d) Between eight and nine months.

(e) Indefinitely.

5. Disablement benefit—

(a) Is always a weekly payment.

(b) Is a gratuity and a weekly payment.

(c) Lasts for 26 weeks.

(d) Is never more than £2 a week.

(e) Is a gratuity or a weekly payment.

6. Each year there are—

(a) About three quarters of a million awards for disablement.

(b) About three quarters of a million awards for deaths.

(c) About half a million awards for death.

(d) About half a million awards for disablement.

(e) About half a million gratuity awards.

7. The new Act—

(a) Does not apply to Northern Ireland.

(b) Does apply to Northern Ireland and their statistics are included.

(c) Does apply to Northern Ireland and their statistics are not included.

You will find the correct answers at the foot of page 198.

This exercise has 1,500 words and you can work out your speed from this table.

Time	Speed	Time	Speed
2.30	600	3.50	391
2.40	562	4.00	375
2.50	529	4.10	360
3.00	500	4.20	346
3.10	470	4.30	333
3.20	450	4.40	321
3.30	430	4.50	310
3.40	409	5.00	300
3.50	391		

Speed...................... Comprehension......................

You have now adjusted your speed to the difficulty of the material, and although you are not able to read these exercises at the same speed as you can read the simpler exercises, you should be able to read them a good deal faster than your original speed on comparatively easy material.

EXERCISE 37

National Insurance (Industrial Injuries) Act, 1946. *Quinquennial Review*

[START TIMING]

IV. THE MAIN FACTORS DETERMINING THE COST OF BENEFITS

Injury Benefits

14. It will be seen from Table 1 that, if allowance is made for the introduction of higher benefit rates in 1952, there has been little variation in the cost of injury benefit from year to year. This is due to the relative stability of the factors which determine the amount of the annual expenditure, viz., the number of awards and the average periods during which benefit is payable.

Statistics of rates of awards and average durations of benefit are given, by sex and age, in Table F of Appendix 3. It will be noted that the rates of awards for men are several times as great as those for women—a reflection of the fact that many more men than women are employed in industries where the accident risk is heavy. On the other hand, the average duration of benefit is greater for women than for men—at most ages very considerably greater. The age analysis shows that for both sexes the average duration increases steadily with age; this, however, is not a feature of the awards rates, at least so far as men are concerned. Doubtless one of the main explanations of the course of the men's award rates—a slight but steady downward trend as the age advances—is that in the heavier and more hazardous industrial processes there is a higher proportion of younger men than in those occupations which make smaller demands on vigour and physique. It is commonly accepted also that the accident risk is lessened with growing skill and experience and that the older and more experienced worker has a more cautious attitude towards occupational risks.

Disablement Benefit

15. The award of disablement benefit rests on a medical assessment of the degree of disability. In the great majority of cases the initial assessment, i.e. that made on the first examination of a claimant, is naturally tentative, and if the existence of disability is established a provisional award is made for a limited period. When, at the end of this period, a case in which a provisional pension has been awarded comes up for reassessment, the result may be either (i) the termination of the pension or (ii) its continuation on a provisional basis for a further period (with a second reassessment at the end of that period) or (iii) its confirmation for life. In cases (ii) and (iii) the degree of disability recorded on reassessment may, of course, differ from that recorded on first examination. The cases in the first of these three categories are of three types. If the disability has disappeared completely, the pension is terminated forthwith; if it has fallen below the 20 per cent level an appropriate gratuity is substituted for the pension (about three-quarters of the terminations are of this type); or if it can be foreseen that the disability will persist only for a short further period, the case is disposed of by limiting the currency

of the pension to that period, which is usually from three to six months. Cases in which a gratuity has been awarded on the first examination may likewise be subject to further assessments; in a small proportion of these cases the degree of disability recorded on reassessment is 20 per cent or more, so that a pension becomes payable.

16. The circumstances described above, considered in conjunction with the wide range of possible benefit rates and the variety of supplementary payments which a disablement benefit may attract, make it clear that any initial award may develop quite a complicated case-history. Disablement benefit is administered locally, and a simple system had to be devised whereby the local offices could transmit, for central collation and analysis, such particulars of a sample of these histories as would yield informative statistics for administrative and actuarial purposes. Some experience of the actual working of the assessment system was necessary before this could be done.

17. Reverting to the three categories of cases described in paragraph 15, it is evident that the reassessment process for a particular batch is not complete until every one of them has been transferred from category (ii) to either category (i) or category (iii). Until this stage has been reached no reliable estimate can be made of the dimensions of the long-term liability, as distinct from the short-term liabilities represented by payments of pension on a provisional basis and the gratuities (or temporary payments for a limited further period) awarded in terminating cases. The disposal of the early provisional assessments has extended over a longer period than might have been expected, and the statistics available for the purposes of this review are barely sufficient to display the complete working out of the reassessment process, even for the awards made in respect of accidents occurring (or diseases developing) in the first six months of the operation of the Act.

18. The following table covers all disablement pensions other than those awarded in respect of pneumoconiosis, to which special conditions apply (see paragraph 19). It relates to pensions awarded in respect of injuries sustained in each of the years 1948 to 1951, and shows for each of the four batches the

Answers to Exercise 36—1 (*e*), 2 (*c*), 3 (*c*), 4 (*c*), 5 (*e*), 6 (*a*), 7 (*c*).

proportion of cases in categories (i), (ii) and (iii) respectively at the end of one, two, . . . years after awards.

TABLE 2

Disablement pension awards (excluding pneumoconiosis cases)

	Period (yrs.) elapsed since award	Year of accident (or onset of disease)			
		1951	1950	1949	1948
Proportion of cases terminated	1	0·59	0·54		
	2	0·70	0·67	0·63	
	3		0·71	0·68	0·70
	4			0·71	0·72
	4½				0·73
Proportion of cases still in payment on a provisional basis	1	0·32	0·36		
	2	0·14	0·16	0·18	
	3		0·06	0·08	0·09
	4			0·03	0·04
	4½				0·03
Proportion of cases which had been confirmed for life	1	0·09	0·10		
	2	0·16	0·17	0·19	
	3		0·23	0·24	0·21
	4			0·26	0·24
	4½				0·24

It will be seen that, when analysed in this way, the assessment record displays a fairly definite pattern. On a broad view, the table indicates that during the first five years or so of the operation of the system rather more than half the pensions were terminated within a year of the initial award. At the end of a further year the proportion of cessations grew to about two-thirds; thereafter it increased much more slowly towards a limiting figure of apparently 75 per cent or thereabouts. After the first year rather more than one-half of the provisional cases appear to have been disposed of annually, the proportion of final awards increasing slowly meanwhile. A scrutiny of the figures year by year suggests that the rate at which cases are removed from the provisional category has been somewhat accelerated, but there is nothing to ustify an assumption that the reassessment process will in the future complete itself in less than five years, or that the proportion of life pensions then emerging will be greater or less than the 25 per cent suggested by the existing figures. This is a slender basis on which to found estimates of the future cost of the major benefit provided by the Act but, in the nature of things, it is the only one available. [STOP TIMING]

Put your reading time here........................

1. The cost of injury benefit—
    (a) Has remained steady from year to year.
    (b) Has varied greatly from year to year.
    (c) Has shown variation in occasional years.
2. The rates of awards for men are higher because—
    (a) The duration of benefit is greater for men.
    (b) Men are more prone to injury than women.
    (c) More old men are employed than old women.
    (d) More men work in dangerous jobs.
    (e) Women are more careful at their work.
3. The award of disablement benefit—
    (a) Is decided by a single medical examination.
    (b) Is decided by a medical examination and later re-examination.
    (c) Is decided by a medical examination and later re-examinations.
    (d) Is decided by a medical examination and regular re-examinations.
4. Estimates of the long-term liability have been difficult because—
    (a) Many of the claims are not permanently settled.
    (b) They do not know how many people will be injured in the future.
    (c) Another war would upset all calculations.
    (d) Local offices are too slow in dealing with cases.
5. The reassessment process should complete itself in—
    (a) About two years.
    (b) About five years.

    (*c*) About seven years.

    (*d*) About ten years.

6. What is the percentage of life pensions likely to be awarded?

    ....

You will find the correct answers at the foot of page 202.

This exercise has 1,200 words and you can work out your speed from this table.

Time	Speed	Time	Speed
2.00	600	3.00	400
2.10	554	3.10	378
2.20	513	3.20	360
2.30	480	3.30	343
2.40	450	3.40	327
2.50	423	3.50	313
3.00	400	4.00	300

Speed......................   Comprehension......................

USE YOUR GEARS

You must have variable speeds of reading, then, to cope with material of different levels of difficulty, but you must not make this an excuse for going back to your old inefficient ways. In this section you will find a series of exercises which become more difficult as you go on. You have a good idea now of how fast you are reading without reference to your watch, and I think that you should be able to read the first passage as fast as you have read any exercise in this book, the next at 50 to 100 words per minute less, and the third one at 50 to 100 words per minute less than that.

Here is the first one which you should be able to read very fast.

EXERCISE 38

To Singapore by Road in Six Months from Tim Slessor

[START TIMING] " No one has ever done it before so why don't we? " We looked at each other, gathered one winter evening over gas-ring coffee in Cambridge. " Well," someone repeated, " why don't we? " The expedition was born, its aim—to drive overland from London to Singapore. We made inquiries, we started preparations.

In the course of last summer we took our university examinations, obtained somewhat precarious degrees, fitted out our two Land Rovers—painting them dark and light blue for Oxford and Cambridge respectively, wrote the 1,500 letters necessary to get us on the move, organized an irrigation research programme as the expedition's other twin aim, gained the encouragement of the Royal Geographical Society, collected over fifty maps and worked out a route through Europe and Asia. Slowly we assembled our equipment—everything from sulpha drugs to sleeping-bags, had

Answers to Exercise 37—1 (a), 2 (d), 3 (c), 4 (a), 5 (b), 6 25%.

fourteen injections each, and then optimistically decided that we were ready. On 1st September, after five months of preparation, we moved the still-unpacked kit off the seats, climbed into the cars, said our good-byes and pulled away from Hyde Park Corner.

We drove to Paris. We were tired and not yet recovered from the last of our injections so in Paris we " rested " for three days. Then on through Germany, Austria, and Yugoslavia. In Belgrade the police momentarily mistook our red fire extinguishers for a more lethal weapon. After explanations, however, we exchanged the customary cigarettes and moved on with their good wishes.

Then through Greece to Turkey and into Istanbul. We motored through Aleppo and Tarsus and thought of Saint Paul, through Syria and Lebanon and saw the still-standing castles of the Crusaders. Our route ran across the Great Syrian Desert, alongside the 700-mile pipeline. The two cars drove many miles apart, but kept in indirect sight by the high dust plume that each threw up. In Bagdad we remained a week while the cars were overhauled and checked, then on northwards from the Tigris, over the mountains and into Persia. We had covered 5,000 miles and yet were not a third of the way to our destination.

From Tehran to the South-East was our longest single " stage " —to Karachi. For over two thousand miles we drove across the bare hills and brown desert of Southern Persia.

Across the Pakistan border, through the tribal territory of the Pathans and the old North-West Frontier town of Quetta and into Karachi. As we entered, past the international airport we noticed a huge hoarding exhorting one to " be in London in sixteen hours." We had taken two and a half months.

The expedition worked in the Thal Desert for six weeks and then crossed the border into India. Towards the end of this time one of the cars was driven up to Kathmandu, the remote capital of Nepal. This car was, in fact, one of the first to have ever made the journey into that kingdom " under its own steam." Previously the few cars that entered Nepal had to do so on the backs of coolies.

We returned from Nepal to the glare and heat of India. Our two Land Rovers took us past the Taj Mahal, through Bengal and finally to Calcutta. There we spent Christmas and prepared for our attempt to drive through Burma. London to Calcutta by " road " is 10,000 miles. But although it is a long way it has been done before. Eastwards from Calcutta, however, we were on our own; no one else had ever made the journey—though a few had tried.

Twelve days after leaving Calcutta we were on the frontier pass. Our Indian escorts bade us doubtful farewells, we waved until their jeeps had disappeared from the jungle clearing and then turned towards Burma. There was no sound but the rain. We climbed into our two Land Rovers, switched on the windscreen wipers, and started away down a forgotten road.

The road disappeared. But where once it had been there ran a narrow thinning in the undergrowth and this we followed. Slowly and in bottom gear we wound and twisted along.

On the evening of the fourth day, we drove into Myitkyina, the northern railhead of Burma. They asked us where we had come from.

Another week of driving through the paddy and the jungle and we were in Mandalay. From there the road ran eastwards, 400 miles over the Shan Hills and across the Salween, to Kengtung.

They were glad to see us in Kengtung—a lonely town set in the far corner of the Shan States near where the difficult frontiers of China, Laos, Siam and Burma come together. Hardly had we stepped from our cars when we were " signed up " by the ruling family for the annual cricket fixture. The expedition provided the highest scorers for either side, but the match is remembered for its social rather than its sporting success. While in Kengtung we also received the ruler's patronage for a unique society—the Kengtung Auto Club. World membership is exclusively confined to the expedition's two cars which now carry the Kengtung coat of arms fluttering from their wireless aerials.

From Kengtung to the Siamese border is a little over a hundred miles, but the road runs through the middle of an area much harassed by roaming bands of Chinese Nationalist irregulars. During the last few months these well-armed guerillas have attacked many convoys. Our reactions as we set out can best be imagined; there were four decrepit lorries, a pre-war bus, a motorcycle and ourselves—the escort consisted of one jeep and five policemen armed with rifles. The jeep alternatively raced ahead or broke down in the middle of one of the four known danger areas. Fortunately the Kuomintang must have been busy elsewhere for we eventually emerged two days later at the Siamese border.

We were in Bangkok long enough to read our letters, view some of the more contemporary " sights " and inquire at the Highways Department about the last part of our journey to the Malayan border. It seemed that only one more barrier remained—down in the Kra isthmus there was a 130-mile stretch where there was no road. But, then, that was what they had told us about Burma; with unfounded optimism, we set off southwards for the last 1,000 miles.

In fact there was no road; but we were lucky—a " service track " had just been grubbed out of the jungle in order to bring the bulldozers and earth-movers to the scene of intended operations. We thrashed along this track and upon emerging rather the worse for wear a day later followed the smooth and tarmacadamed highways of Malaya, the best roads since Germany—into Singapore. They gave us quite a welcome here, and opened the champagne. We were perhaps embarrassed but not the least ashamed, for it is a long way from London to Singapore—six months, sixteen countries, and nearly twenty thousand miles, in fact. [STOP TIMING]

Put your reading time here........................

1. The expedition was first discussed in ....
2. The vehicles used were ....
3. The secondary aim was a research into—
   (a) Population.
   (b) Irrigation.
   (c) Colonization.
   (d) Agriculture.
   (e) Road construction.
4. The expedition started on ....
5. In Yugoslavia the police thought that........................
   were weapons.
6. On the way the expedition saw—
   (a) The castles of southern England.
   (b) The castles of southern France.
   (c) The castles of northern Italy.
   (d) The castles of Greece.
   (e) The castles of the Crusaders.
7. The longest stage was—
   (a) 200 miles.

O

    (*b*) 1,000 miles.
    (*c*) 1,500 miles.
    (*d*) 2,000 miles.
    (*e*) 2,200 miles.

8. One of the cars was the first to enter—
    (*a*) Quetta.
    (*b*) Kathmandu.
    (*c*) Karachi.
    (*d*) Agra.
    (*e*) Tashkent.

9. Christmas was spent at...

10. The party took part in an annual.................................
    match.

11. The best roads since Germany were in...........................

You will find the correct answers at the foot of page 208.

This exercise has 1,160 words and you can work out your speed
from the table below.

Time	Speed	Time	Speed
1.30	773	2.30	464
1.40	696	2.40	435
1.50	632	2.50	409
2.00	580	3.00	383
2.10	532	3.10	366
2.20	497	3.20	348
2.30	464		

Now carry on with the next exercise which is slightly more
difficult and you may have to read a little more slowly.

EXERCISE 39

Oil Prices in Europe by Georg Tugendhat

[START TIMING] Much has been written lately on the price of
oil in Europe. The problem is not new. It was raised probably
for the first time during the war by British and American
Government Departments. Briefly, it is now alleged that the
eight major oil companies which control the output of the Middle
East oilfields, and who today supply the bulk of Europe's oil
requirements are keeping prices too high. Too high, that is, in

relation to the real cost of production of crude oil in the Middle East and of transportation to the consuming centres. Further, the price structure and organization of the industry is said to militate against the development of independent oil refineries, and thus to reduce the chances of competition.

Prices for finished products and crude oil in Europe are considered too high because they are not linked to the low cost of production of crude oil in the Middle East areas but to prices for comparative American crude oils and products as quoted in the Gulf of Mexico, United States.

The costs of crude oil production in the United States are much higher than in the Middle East. There, a few hundred thousand wells produced over 300 million tons in 1954. In the Middle East, with Iranian production running at a nominal figure, a few hundred wells yielded about 135 million tons. In the United States an annual expenditure of more than $2,000 millions is required on development drilling to maintain reserves at fifteen years' supply. In the Middle East even today estimated reserves amount to almost a hundred years' output at current rates. It is believed that oil reserves in Kuwait alone exceed the total oil reserves of the United States. For the last seven or eight years (that is, for the period which marks the emergence of crude oil production in the Middle East, outside Iran, from a few million tons per annum to more than 130 million tons) United States Gulf prices for American crudes of Middle East type have averaged about $2.75 a barrel f.o.b. or more than $20 a ton. Though Middle East crude prices have been based on American prices, they have not been identical but have been lower so as to allow for the greater distances from the centres of refining that they have to be transported. At present this " Freight differential " is such as to equalize prices with those of American crudes at the United States Eastern Seaboard. Over the last seven years Middle East crude oil prices averaged about $14 f.o.b. a ton. On a reasonable assumption of production costs in the Middle East, profits on crude oil before amortization but after deducting royalties, would appear to be of the order of $800 millions to $900 millions or £300 millions a year.

For the European refiner there are two main elements of cost for his crude oil: first, the f.o.b. cost at source of supply and, secondly, the freight cost of bringing it to the refinery. Similarly, the established price mechanism for finished products is made up of the f.o.b. price of those finished products in the Caribbean plus freight to carry the products to the particular centre of consumption. For this purpose it is immaterial whether the products are in fact imported or, as has increasingly become the case, whether they are being refined at the centres of consumption.

The freight item requires a little explanation. To begin with, it must be borne in mind that a great part of the movement of crude oil and oil products to Western Europe is made in fleets which belong to the major oil companies themselves. In the notional c.i.f. values, freights are costed by the oil companies on the basis of certain established " market " rates, which, up to the end of 1952, were certainly on balance much in excess of actual cost of fleet operation. More recently transport costs have been near the " market " rates.

While darkness shrouds the profitability of Middle East crude oil and shipping operations, some estimates are possible concerning the capital expenditure that has been required to expand Middle East production to its present level on which rests the new refining industry in Europe with its annual capacity of 100 million tons compared with 13 million tons before the war. Gross investment in the Middle East oil industry, which, according to United Nations estimates, had totalled $100 millions in 1925, $350 millions in 1935, $1,000 millions in 1945 and nearly $2,000 millions by the end of 1951, has been privately estimated at being well over $3,000 millions by the end of 1954.

This sum covers drilling, oilfield storage, gathering-lines, pipelines, terminal installations, and refineries erected in the Middle East. Post-war investment in European refineries, installations, etc., has by now probably exceeded the figure of $1,400 millions. To this must be added working capital required to finance crude oil, freight, refinery operation, and distribution, which may be estimated at about $1,000 millions, perhaps even more. According to available figures net participation of the United States and the public in these developments has been relatively small, perhaps of the order of $500 millions. In short,

---

Answers to Exercise 38—1 Cambridge, 2 Land Rovers, 3 (*b*),
  4 1st Sept., 5 The fire extinguishers, 6 (*e*), 7 (*d*), 8 (*b*),
  9 Calcutta, 10 Cricket, 11 Federated Malay States.

between 1945 and 1954 the oil industry has generated largely out of its own resources an investment of about $5,000 millions, which represents an industry delivery to the consumer of about 100 million tons of oil products a year. Large as this figure is, the consumption of petroleum per head in Europe is still only about one-tenth of that in the United States.

There is then a certain foundation for the assumption that between 1945-6 and 1954 Middle East oil operations have yielded the companies a profit of about £2,000 millions, most of which has been reinvested, not distributed. The European consumer can now call upon a virtually new industry capable of delivering about 100 millions tons of oil products per annum. The quality of these products conforms with few exceptions to American specifications, though the special premium brands of 96/98 octane are not yet available in Europe. To a large extent supplies from European refineries are meeting American military specifications. These refineries are thus an addition to the Allied war potential. By paying "American prices" for crude oil, the European consumer has at least made himself independent of Western Hemisphere sources of supply. What is more, he is buying a product which is competitive with other forms of energy: indeed so competitive that in many cases the Governments of countries concerned are able to apply substantial revenue-earning taxes.

Why did the oil companies adhere to a system of calculating product prices in consuming areas as if the products had emanated from the Gulf, when in fact the United States ceased to be physically the centre of export trade? Why has no serious attempt, apparently, as yet been made either by the industry or by national policies to base prices on the price at the supply point together with the appropriate manufacturing and profit margins? What would have been the consequences of such an action in the international field and upon national economies? Would private investors in Europe and elsewhere have provided the funds required for the development of the Middle East and the expansion of the industry in Europe? [STOP TIMING]

Put your reading time here......................

1. Oil prices in Europe are thought to be too....................
2. The prices for Middle East oil are based on—
   (a) The costs of production.

(b) American crude oil prices.

(c) Costs of production plus high royalties.

(d) American production costs.

(e) The highest price obtainable.

3. Where is crude oil produced at the lowest cost?............

4. Oil reserves in the Middle East are estimated at—

(a) Fifteen years.

(b) Thirty years.

(c) Seventy years.

(d) One hundred years.

(e) Two hundred years.

5. Profits on Middle East crude oil are estimated at—

(a) £100 million.

(b) £300 million.

(c) £600 million.

(d) £800 million.

(e) £900 million.

6. The two main elements of cost for the European importer of crude oil are—

(a)..................................... (b)...

7. Most of the tankers belong to......................................

8. Gross investment in the Middle East oil industry has been estimated at—

(a) 100 million dollars.

(b) 200 million dollars.

(c) 1,000 million dollars.

(d) 4,000 million dollars.

(e) 5,000 million dollars.

9. Most of this investment has been provided by........................

10. This expansion has resulted in the European consumer—

(a) Being overcharged for oil.

(b) Being independent of American supplies.

(c) Being able to buy the highest octane petrol.

(d) Being an investor in the oil companies.

(e) Buying oil at a low price.

You will find the correct answers at the foot of page 212.

This exercise has 1,240 words and you can work out your speed from the table on page 211.

Time	Speed	Time	Speed
2.00	620	3.00	413
2.10	573	3.10	392
2.20	532	3.20	373
2.30	496	3.30	354
2.40	466	3.40	339
2.50	438	3.50	324
3.00	413	4.00	310

Speed........................   Comprehension........................

The last exercise in this section is as difficult as any you have done in this book and you should be able to read it and get a good score on the comprehension test at the end if you read at about 150 words per minute slower than you read the first one.

EXERCISE 40

Cmd. 9372

[START TIMING]

HISTORY OF THE DISPUTE

The Original Claim of July, 1953

9. For a proper understanding of the events which led to our appointment as a Court of Inquiry it is necessary to go back to 3rd July, 1953, when the three Railway Unions presented a joint claim for an increase of 15 per cent in the rates of both the salaried and conciliation grades. This claim was based mainly upon the cost of living, comparison with rates in outside industries and recognition of increased efficiency and productivity. Negotiations on the claim failed to reach a settlement and the matter was ultimately referred to the Railway Staff National Tribunal, through the appropriate machinery.

The Agreement of December, 1953

10. On 3rd December, 1953, the Tribunal awarded an increase of 4s. in the weekly wage of all railwaymen, with proportionate increases for women and juniors. This Award (No. 15) was accepted by the Commission but was rejected by all three Unions, the A.S.L.E.F. and the N.U.R. threatening to withdraw the labour of their members as from 20th December unless in the

meantime the matter had been satisfactorily resolved. When subsequent meetings between the parties had failed to reach agreement you held further discussions with them and in the result an agreement was reached on 16th December, 1953, in the following terms—

" (1) The British Transport Commission have confirmed their acceptance of the award of the Railway Staff National Tribunal for an increase in rates of pay of salaried and conciliation staff. They are ready to implement it. In the light of the following, this position is accepted by the Trade Unions.

" (2) The British Transport Commission are prepared to examine with the Trade Unions their whole wage and salary structure. The British Transport Commission contemplate that this examination would be completely exhaustive, without conditions of any kind. Its purposes would be to correct anomalies and give added incentives (including differentials) in desirable cases; and to investigate all standard rates of pay.

" (3) At the same time the British Transport Commission and the Unions agree to confer in order to evolve ways of increasing the efficiency of the railway organization, not only by such adjustment of wages and salaries as may result from the above examination, but by all other appropriate means.

" (4) Recognizing that the comprehensive review of the whole wage and salary structure will necessarily take some considerable time and that the nature of the claim made by the Unions before the Railway Staff National Tribunal precluded the Tribunal from addressing itself to the question of the levels of the standard rates of pay, and after consultation with Her Majesty's Government, the British Transport Commission have given an assurance that, irrespective of other results emerging from the examination, within two months from the operative date of the award there will be a further improvement on a percentage basis of the standard rates in operation prior to the operation of the Railway Staff National Tribunal award No. 15."

Answers to Exercise 39—1 High, 2 (*b*), 3 The Middle East, 4 (*d*), 5 (*b*), 6 Cost at source, freight cost, 7 The big oil companies, 8 (*e*), 9 The oil companies, 10 (*b*).

Subsequent Negotiations

11. The further improvement of standard rates referred to in Clause (4) was implemented by an agreement dated 1st February, 1954, for a 6 per cent increase in wages and salaries to operate with effect from 24th January. This increase included the 4s. awarded by the Tribunal and implemented under Clause (1). Meanwhile, at a meeting held on 22nd December, 1953, to discuss the review of the whole structure referred to in Clause (2), the Commission had asked the Unions to submit proposals for a new wage structure for consideration. The three Unions submitted separate proposals which were discussed at a meeting on 12th January, when the Commission made it clear that it would first be necessary to agree upon the basic minimum wage (i.e. the wage payable to the adult male unskilled worker). There followed some months of negotiations on this point.

12. On 9th June, 1954, the Commission offered a basic minimum wage of 125s. rising to 127s. after 12 months' service (i.e. an increase of 6d. over the existing rate of 124s. 6d. and of 1s. 6d. for all those with one year's service or more)[1]. This offer was accepted by the N.U.R. as a basis for further discussions but it was not acceptable to the A.S.L.E.F. in respect of the grades in which they were interested. The A.S.L.E.F. therefore initiated separate negotiations in respect of locomotive grades, the N.U.R. later joining in on behalf of their own members in these grades. These negotiations were ultimately referred to the established conciliation machinery.

The Agreement of October, 1954

13. Meanwhile the discussions arising out of the Commission's offer of 9th June, so far as relating to conciliation grades other than locomotive staff, continued between the Commission and the N.U.R. Agreement was finally reached on proposals which, together with an interim settlement for salaried staff, were formally agreed on 8th October, 1954, at a meeting between representatives of the Commission and of all three Unions. The increases agreed for the conciliation grades ranged from the 6d. increase in the basic minimum wage already mentioned to 8s. 6d. and involved a few minor modifications in the wage structure of

---

[1] For employees in London the rates would be 3s. higher.

these grades. An agreed Note to which the new rates were appended set out the position in the following terms—

"Today's agreement is the culmination of negotiations arising out of the agreement made between the British Transport Commission and the Trade Unions at a meeting held, under the ægis of the Minister of Labour, on 16th December, 1953." (There followed a summary of that agreement, which is quoted in full in paragraph 10 above.)

"The improvements under clauses 1 and 4 of this Agreement were effective from 6th December, 1953, and 24th January, 1954, respectively, and those arising from today's Agreement will operate from Monday, 4th October, 1954.[3] Full details of the new rates of pay outside London are given in the accompanying statement. In London the adult rates are 3s. per week higher for wages grades and £10 per annum for salaried staff.

"In the case of Salaried Staff it is agreed that the settlement is an interim one and that there should be a thorough review of the salaries structure including the basis of classification.

"The A.S.L.E.F. raised no objection to the revision of the agreements affected by the above.

"(Footplate grades are excluded for the reason that the Unions' claims on their behalf are being referred to the Railway Staff National Tribunal.)"

The date of operation of the agreement (4th October) was ratified by the N.U.R. on 12th October, 1954, and the new rates of pay were thereupon implemented.

The N.U.R.'s Rejection of the Agreement

14. On 11th November, 1954, the N.U.R. wrote to the Commission informing them that the settlement of 8th October was unacceptable to the membership of the Union as regards conciliation grades and seeking a meeting with a view to reopening discussions on the basis of the original claim of July, 1953.

The Railway Staff National Tribunal's Award (No. 16) for Locomotive Grades

15. Four days later, i.e. on 15th November, the Railway Staff National Tribunal issued its Award (No. 16) in respect of locomotive grades, having heard the parties on 4th and 5th November.

---

[3] Subject to ratification of date of operation by the N.U.R.

The Tribunal recommended increases in wages for these grades ranging from 8·1 per cent to 22·6 per cent over the rates applicable prior to 6th December, 1953. The proposed basic minimum rate (that for an engine cleaner) was 127s. rising to 129s. after 12 months' service, i.e. an increase of 2s. 6d. rising to 4s. 6d. on the existing rate. This Award was accepted by all parties, including the N.U.R., on or about 24th November, 1954. A full statement of the pre-December, 1953, rates, the Commission's offer and the Tribunal's Award is set out in Appendix II.

Further Discussions

16. Meanwhile, faced with the rejection by the N.U.R. of the Agreement of 8th October, 1954, the British Transport Commission, at a meeting held between them and the Union on 18th November, indicated their view that there was a binding settlement so far as concerned the staff covered by that Agreement and that the Commission were not prepared to reopen discussions on the original claim of July, 1953. They therefore asked that the Agreement which had been ratified should be signed by the N.U.R. and accepted as a completion of the negotiations which had preceded it. If, however, the Union had any further submissions to make, they would be free to make them in any way they wished and the Commission would receive them without any commitments on their part as to their attitude to any such approach. At a further meeting on 24th November the N.U.R. stated their position as follows—

" (1) That the Memorandum of Agreement arrived at on 8th October, 1954, should not be signed on behalf of the Union at least until an indication was received from the Commission that something tangible in the form of increased wages for the staff covered by the discussions was forthcoming.

" (2) That on the question of the submission of a fresh application, as the original submission of the Union was for an increase of wages up to 15 per cent of the rates applying prior to 6th December, 1953, this should be maintained as the policy of the Union."

The Commission repeated the views expressed by them on 18th November and added that they would be prepared to receive and consider any further wage application as a fresh submission to be dealt with on its merits and that if the N.U.R. were not satisfied it would be open to them to pursue the matter through the normal negotiating machinery.

The N.U.R.'s Approach to the Minister of Transport and Civil Aviation

17. The N.U.R. Executive Committee next decided to approach the Minister of Transport and Civil Aviation. The Minister received a deputation from the Union on 13th December, 1954, and replied by letter on 20th December. He first quoted a statement by the Commission of their position which after outlining the recent course of events continued—

" In this situation the attitude of the Commission towards the claim now put forward by the N.U.R. is that they would be prepared to discuss through the appropriate machinery, and with all speed, any particular cases where anomaly is thought to have been created by comparison with the new level of wages for the footplate staff. However, the new N.U.R. claim goes much further than this and the Commission consider it to be essential that reference should be made to the R.S.N.T. on this claim on its merits in order that the conclusions of the body which produced a settlement for a part of the wages grades should also be available for the remainder. The Commission are convinced that a firm settlement for all the railway wages grades concerned can only be reached in this way.

" If the R.S.N.T. should conclude that the N.U.R. claim should be met in whole or in part the Commission propose to consult with the Minister of Transport and Civil Aviation on any consequences which acceptance of such a recommendation might entail in relation to their statutory duties under the Transport Act, 1947."

18. The Minister's letter then went on—

" The Government are concerned to secure an improvement in the position of British Railways. They believe that such an improvement can be expected from the combined effect of modernization of the Commission's plant and equipment, the greater freedom in charging provided for by the Transport Act, 1953, and the appropriate redeployment of labour on the railways. There is no reason to doubt that by a combination of these methods, and with the good will and co-operation of all concerned, the British Transport Commission will be able greatly to improve the prospects of their undertaking.

" After making full and careful examination both of the Commission's statement and of the views of the National Union of Railwaymen, the Government consider that, inasmuch as the normal processes of negotiation and arbitration have not been exhausted, they could not intervene without dealing a serious blow to the negotiating machinery in this industry and indirectly in the rest of industry as well. The Government could not properly substitute themselves for the British Transport Commission as parties to the wage negotiations. They are strongly of the opinion that the National Union of Railwaymen should take part in further discussions with the British Transport Commission in order to see whether agreement cannot be reached. They are convinced however that in the event of agreement not being reached, the right course for the National Union of Railwaymen is to take their claim to the Railway Staff National Tribunal in order that it may be considered, in the Commission's words ' on its merits '."

The Strike Decision

19. On 22nd December the General Secretary of the N.U.R. wrote to the Commission referring to the Minister's decision not to intervene and giving formal notice of his Executive's intention to instruct all members of the Unions to withdraw their labour as from midnight, 9th January, 1955, in accordance with the following decision—

" That having considered the reply from the Minister of Transport . . . it is clear we have exhausted all forms of negotiations on the above question.

" As we are determined to win the balance of 15 per cent on all Railway wages on pre-December, 1953, rates, we now decide to withdraw the labour of all N.U.R. members in the Railway industry as from 12 midnight on 9th January.

" We instruct the General Secretary to call special meetings of all our District Councils on Sunday, 2nd January, 1955, in order to perfect our strike machinery in all Regions."

This letter was acknowledged by the Commission without any comment or observation on its terms or the reasoning on which it was based.

20. It was in view of this decision that you held separate discussions on 23rd December with the Chairman of the Commission and representatives of the N.U.R. The Chairman confirmed the Commission's view that the claim of the N.U.R. should be referred to the Railway Staff National Tribunal on its merits. The N.U.R. representatives, however, did not consider that their case would be satisfactorily dealt with in this way. They further stated that they could only agree to resume negotiations with the Commission if the Commission were prepared to discuss their claim without regard to limitations placed on the Commission by their financial circumstances and with the prior assurance that their claim would be substantially met. It proved impossible to resolve this conflict of view, and it was in these circumstances that you decided to appoint us as a Court of Inquiry into the causes and circumstances of the dispute. [STOP TIMING]

Put your reading time here......................

1. The original claim in July, 1953, was for—
    (a) A new wage structure for railway workers.
    (b) A 15 per cent increase for all workers.
    (c) A 15 per cent increase for footplate staff.
    (d) A 15 per cent increase for conciliation staff.
    (e) A 15 per cent increase for salaried staff.
2. In December, 1953—
    (a) The Unions accepted the pay award.
    (b) The Union rejected the pay award.
    (c) The Transport Commission accepted the award.
    (d) The Union accepted the pay award conditionally.
    (e) The Transport Commission refused to give way.
3. The basic minimum wage was—
    (a) Not accepted by the Transport Commission.
    (b) Proposed by the Commission and accepted by all.
    (c) Proposed by the N.U.R. but rejected by the A.S.L.E.F.
    (d) Proposed by the Commission and accepted by the N.U.R.
    (e) Opposed by all parties.
4. Agreement was reached in October, 1954—
    (a) To raise the wages of all railway personnel.
    (b) To raise the wages of drivers and firemen only.
    (c) To raise the pay of all except drivers and firemen.

5. This agreement never came into force because—
   (*a*) The Union members refused to accept it.
   (*b*) The Ministry of Transport opposed it.
   (*c*) The Conciliation Board failed to reach agreement.
   (*d*) Of Communist propaganda.
   (*e*) It was unacceptable to all parties.

6. Whilst this was going on—
   (*a*) No agreement was reached about footplate staff.
   (*b*) Agreement was reached about footplate staff.
   (*c*) Nobody bothered about the footplate staff.
   (*d*) Footplate staff were concerned in the general negotiations.

7. The Union then approached—
   (*a*) The Prime Minister who supported them.
   (*b*) The Minister of Transport who did nothing.
   (*c*) The Minister of Transport who opposed them.
   (*d*) The Minister of Transport who supported them.
   (*e*) The Prime Minister who opposed them.

8. The Union then decided—
   (*a*) To take their claim to arbitration.
   (*b*) To ask for an independent tribunal to be set up.
   (*c*) To appeal to the general public.
   (*d*) To issue strike notices.
   (*e*) To drop their claim.

9. What percentage increase did the Unions ask for? ....
You will find the correct answers at the foot of page 220.

This passage has 2,300 words and you can find your speed from the following table.

Time	Speed	Time	Speed
3.50	600	5.30	417
4.00	570	5.40	405
4.10	552	5.50	394
4.20	534	6.00	380
4.30	511	6.10	375
4.40	492	6.20	363
4.50	475	6.30	354
5.00	460	6.40	345
5.10	445	6.50	336
5.20	431	7.00	328
5.30	417		

Speed........................ Comprehension........................

THE FINAL TEST

YOU have now completed the course and have for some time been reading material of much greater difficulty than that with which you started. The next exercise is the last, it is an extract from the same volume of Sir Arthur Conan Doyle's short stories as Exercise 2, and a comparison of the results will give you a good indication of the extent to which you have improved. You know the level of difficulty of this. You can read this at your maximum speed.

EXERCISE 41

Extract from " The Adventure of the Veiled Lodger "

by Sir Arthur Conan Doyle

[START TIMING] One forenoon—it was late in 1896—I received a hurried note from Holmes asking for my attendance. When I arrived, I found him seated in a smoke-laden atmosphere, with an elderly, motherly woman of the buxom landlady type in the corresponding chair in front of him.

" This is Mrs. Merrilow, of South Brixton," said my friend, with a wave of the hand. " Mrs. Merrilow does not object to tobacco, Watson, if you wish to indulge your filthy habits. Mrs. Merrilow has an interesting story to tell which may well lead to further developments in which your presence may be useful."

" Anything I can do——"

" You will understand, Mrs. Merrilow, that if I come to Mrs. Ronder I should prefer to have a witness. You will make her understand that before we arrive."

" Lord bless you, Mr. Holmes," said our visitor, " she is that anxious to see you that you might bring the whole parish at your heels! "

" Then we shall come early in the afternoon. Let us see that we have our facts correct before we start. If we go over them

---

Answers to Exercise 40—1 (*b*), 2 (*c*), 3 (*d*), 4 (*c*), 5 (*a*), 6 (*b*), 7 (*b*), 8 (*d*), 9 15%.

it will help Dr. Watson to understand the situation. You say that Mrs. Ronder has been your lodger for seven years and that you have only once seen her face."

" And I wish to God I had not! " said Mrs. Merrilow.

" It was, I understand, terribly mutilated."

" Well, Mr. Holmes, you would hardly say it was a face at all. That's how it looked. Our milkman got a glimpse of her once peeping out of the upper window, and he dropped his tin and the milk all over the front garden. That is the kind of face it is. When I saw her—I happened on her unawares—she covered up quick, and then she said, ' Now, Mrs. Merrilow, you know at last why it is that I never raise my veil.' "

" Do you know anything about her history? "

" Nothing at all."

" Did she give references when she came? "

" No, sir, but she gave hard cash and plenty of it. A quarter's rent right down on the table in advance and no arguing about terms. In these times a poor woman like me can't afford to turn down a chance like that."

" Did she give any reason for choosing your house? "

" Mine stands well back from the road and is more private than most. Then, again, I only take the one, and I have no family of my own. I reckon she had tried others and found that mine suited her best. It's privacy she is after, and she is ready to pay for it."

" You say that she never showed her face from first to last save on the one accidental occasion. Well, it is a very remarkable story, most remarkable, and I don't wonder that you want it examined."

" I don't, Mr. Holmes. I am quite satisfied so long as I get my rent. You could not have a quieter lodger, or one who gives less trouble."

" Then what has brought matters to a head? "

" Her health, Mr. Holmes. She seems to be wasting away. And there's something terrible on her mind. ' Murder! ' she cries. ' Murder! ' And once I heard her, ' You cruel beast! You monster! ' she cried. It was in the night, and it fair rang through the house and sent shivers through me. So I went to her in the morning. ' Mrs. Ronder,' I says, ' if you have anything that is troubling your soul, there's the clergy,' I says, ' and there's

P

the police. Between them you should get some help.' 'For God's sake, not the police! ' says she, ' and the clergy can't change what is past. And yet,' says she, ' it would ease my mind if someone knew the truth before I died.' ' Well,' says I, ' if you won't have the regulars, there is this detective man what we read about '—beggin' your pardon, Mr. Holmes. And she, she fair jumped at it. ' That's the man,' she says. ' I wonder I never thought of it before. Bring him here, Mrs. Merrilow, and if he won't come, tell him I am the wife of Ronder's wild beast show. Say that, and give him the name Abbas Parva.' Here it is as she wrote it, Abbas Parva. ' That will bring him, if he's the man I think he is.' "

"And it will, too," remarked Holmes. "Very good, Mrs. Merrilow. I should like to have a little chat with Dr. Watson. That will carry us till lunchtime. About three o'clock you may expect to see us at your house in Brixton."

Our visitor had no sooner waddled out of the room—no other verb can describe Mrs. Merrilow's method of progression—than Sherlock Holmes threw himself with fierce energy upon the pile of commonplace books in the corner. For a few minutes there was a constant swish of the leaves, and then with a grunt of satisfaction he came upon what he sought. So excited was he that he did not rise, but sat upon the floor like some strange Buddha, with crossed legs, the huge books all round him, and one open upon his knees.

"The case worried me at the time, Watson. Here are my marginal notes to prove it. I confess that I could make nothing of it, and yet I was convinced that the coroner was wrong. Have you no recollection of the Abbas Parva tragedy? "

"None, Holmes."

"And yet you were with me then. But certainly my own impression was very superficial, for there was nothing to go by, and none of the parties had engaged my services. Perhaps you would care to read the papers? "

"Could you not give me the points? "

"That is very easily done. It will probably come back to your memory as I talk. Ronder, of course, was a household word. He was the rival of Wombwell, and of Sanger, one of the greatest showmen of his day. There is evidence, however, that he took to drink, and that both he and his show were on the down grade at the time of the great tragedy. The caravan had halted for the night at Abbas Parva, which is a small village in Berkshire, when this horror occurred. They were on their way to Wimbledon, travelling by road, and they were simply camping, and not exhibiting, as the place is so small a one that it would not have paid them to open.

" They had among their exhibits a very fine North African lion. Sahara King was its name, and it was the habit, both of Ronder and his wife, to give exhibitions inside its cage. Here. you see, is a photograph of the performance, by which you will perceive that Ronder is a huge porcine person and that his wife was a very magnificent woman. It was deposed at the inquest that there had been some signs that the lion was dangerous, but, as usual, familiarity begat contempt, and no notice was taken of the fact.

" It was usual for either Ronder or his wife to feed the lion at night. Sometimes one went, sometimes both, but they never allowed anyone else to do it, for they believed that so long as they were the food-carriers he would regard them as benefactors, and would never molest them. On this particular night, seven years ago, they both went, and a very terrible happening followed, the details of which have never been made clear.

" It seems that the whole camp was roused near midnight by the roars of the animal and the screams of the woman. The different grooms and employés rushed from their tents, carrying lanterns, and by their light an awful sight was revealed. Ronder lay, with the back of his head crushed in and deep claw-marks across his scalp, some ten yards from the cage, which was open. Close to the door of the cage lay Mrs. Ronder, upon her back, with the creature squatting and snarling above her. It had torn her face in such a fashion that it was never thought that she could live. Several of the circus men, headed by Leonardo, the strong man, and Griggs, the clown, drove the creature off with poles, upon which it sprang back into the cage, and was at once locked in. How it had got loose was a mystery. It was conjectured that the pair intended to enter the cage, but that when the door was loosed the creature bounded out upon them. There was no other point of interest in the evidence, save that the woman in a delirium of agony kept screaming, ' Coward! Coward! ' as she was carried back to the van in which they lived. It was six months before she was fit to give evidence, but the inquest was duly held, with the obvious verdict of death from misadventure."

" What alternative could be conceived? " said I.

" You may well say so. And yet there were one or two points which worried young Edmunds, of the Berkshire Constabulary. A smart lad that! He was sent later to Allahabad. That was how I came into the matter, for he dropped in and smoked a pipe or two over it."

" A thin, yellow-haired man? "

" Exactly. I was sure you would pick up the trail presently."

" But what worried him? "

" Well, we were both worried. It was so deucedly difficult to reconstruct the affair. Look at it from the lion's point of view. He is liberated. What does he do? He takes half a dozen bounds forward, which brings him to Ronder. Ronder turns to fly—the claw-marks were on the back of his head—but the lion strikes him down. Then, instead of bounding on and escaping, he returns to the woman, who was close to the cage, and he knocks her over and chews her face up. Then, again, those cries of hers would seem to imply that her husband had in some way failed her. What could the poor devil have done to help her? You see the difficulty? "

" Quite."

" And then there was another thing. It comes back to me now as I think it over. There was some evidence that, just at the time the lion roared and the woman screamed, a man began shouting in terror."

" This man Ronder, no doubt."

" Well, if his skull was smashed in you would hardly expect to hear from him again. There were at least two witnesses who spoke of the cries of a man being mingled with those of a woman."

" I should think the whole camp was crying out by then. As to the other points, I think I could suggest a solution."

" I should be glad to consider it."

" The two were together, ten yards from the cage, when the lion got loose. The man turned and was struck down. The woman conceived the idea of getting into the cage and shutting the door. It was her only refuge. She made for it, and just as she reached it the beast bounded after her and knocked her over. She was angry with her husband for having encouraged the beast's rage by turning. If they had faced it, they might have cowed it. Hence her cries of ' Coward ! ' ''

" Brilliant, Watson! Only one flaw in your diamond."

" What is the flaw, Holmes? "

" If they were both ten paces from the cage, how came the beast to get loose? "

" Is it possible that they had some enemy who loosed it? "

" And why should it attack them savagely when it was in the habit of playing with them, and doing tricks with them inside the cage? "

" Possibly the same enemy had done something to enrage it."

Holmes looked thoughtful and remained in silence for some moments.

" Well, Watson, there is this to be said for your theory. Ronder was a man of many enemies. Edmunds told me that in his cups he was horrible. A huge bully of a man, he cursed and slashed at everyone who came in his way. I expect those cries about a monster, of which our visitor has spoken, were nocturnal reminiscences of the dear departed. However, our speculations are futile until we have all the facts. There is a cold partridge on the sideboard, Watson, and a bottle of Montrachet. Let us renew our energies before we make a fresh call upon them." [STOP TIMING]

Put your reading time here........................

1. The landlady was—
   (a) A tall, thin woman who lived in Hounslow.
   (b) A short, fat woman who lived in Kensington.
   (c) An elderly woman who lived in Brixham.
   (d) A middle-aged woman who lived in Brixton.
   (e) An elderly woman who lived in Brixton.
2. Mrs. Merrilow's lodger was remarkable because—
   (a) She never spoke to anybody.
   (b) She rarely showed her face.
   (c) She disliked everybody.
   (d) She was a foreigner.
   (e) She was a hideous dwarf.
3. She had chosen Mrs. Merrilow's house because—
   (a) It was lively and there was plenty of company.
   (b) It was quiet and she was alone.

(c) It was in a very pleasant situation.

(d) She liked to be near the sea.

(e) She was an old friend of the landlady.

4. Mrs. Merrilow had come to Holmes because—

(a) She was very worried.

(b) Mrs. Ronder was very worried.

(c) She suspected that Mrs. Ronder was a criminal.

(d) The police would take no action.

(e) She had known Holmes on another case.

5. When Mrs. Merrilow left, Holmes first—

(a) Had lunch.

(b) Talked over the case with Watson.

(c) Got in touch with Scotland Yard.

(d) Looked up the case in his files.

(e) Played his violin.

6. Ronder was—

(a) The strong man in a circus.

(b) The lion-tamer in the circus.

(c) A German acrobat in a circus.

(d) The owner of a number of sideshows.

(e) The owner of the circus.

7. At the time of the tragedy—

(a) The circus was not doing very well.

(b) The circus was doing reasonably well.

(c) Business was very good at the circus.

(d) They had stopped to give a show at Abbas Parva.

(e) They had not taken much money at their last show.

8. Ronder and his wife—

(a) Managed the circus together.

(b) Performed on a tight rope together.

(c) Did not appear together.

(d) Were two of the clowns.

(e) Were both in a lion-taming act.

9. Ronder and his wife fed the lion because—

(a) Everybody else was frightened of it.

(b) They thought it would get to like them.

(c) They did everything together.

(d) They had reared it from a cub.

(e) They were both fond of it.

10. When the alarm was raised—
    (a) The last show was just starting.
    (b) Everybody was having tea.
    (c) There was a rush for the fire buckets.
    (d) Everybody was in bed.
    (e) People were just getting up.

11. Ronder—
    (a) Had died of heart failure.
    (b) Was not dead when found.
    (c) Was dead with his scalp crushed.
    (d) Received such injuries that he died later.
    (e) Was savagely mauled about the arms and shoulders.

12. Mrs. Ronder—
    (a) Was severely injured about the face.
    (b) Was not seriously hurt.
    (c) Was dead.
    (d) Was inside the lion's cage.
    (e) Was saved by her husband.

13. Edmunds was—
    (a) A large, fat circus performer.
    (b) A thin, yellow-haired policeman.
    (c) The strong man of the circus.
    (d) A large and powerful police officer.
    (e) One of Watson's best friends.

14. Holmes could not understand—
    (a) Why the lion did not escape completely.
    (b) How the lion got out.
    (c) What the Ronders were doing there.
    (d) Why nobody came to their aid.
    (e) Why the police had done nothing.

15. The only things heard were—
    (a) The screams of Mrs. Ronder.
    (b) The screams of Mrs. Ronder and the roars of the lion.
    (c) The roars of the lion and a man's voice.
    (d) The screams of Mrs. Ronder, the roars of the lion and a
        man's voice.
    (e) The screams of Mrs. Ronder, the roars of the lion and
        two men's voices.

16. Watson thought—
    (a) That Mrs. Ronder had been running for help.

(b) That Mrs. Ronder was trying to get into the cage.
(c) That Mrs. Ronder was trying to get out of the cage.
(d) That Ronder lost his life defending his wife.
(e) That the lion had not killed Ronder.

17. Ronder was—
(a) A man of many enemies.
(b) Mild and inoffensive.
(c) Fairly popular.
(d) Well liked but a hard bargainer.
(e) Popular and talented.

18. What was the name of the lion ?..............................

You will find the correct answers at the foot of page 230.

This passage has 2,000 words and you can work out your speed from the following table.

Time	Speed	Time	Speed
2.30	800	3.50	521
2.40	750	4.00	500
2.50	705	4.10	480
3.00	666	4.20	461
3.10	631	4.30	444
3.20	600	4.40	427
3.30	571	4.50	413
3.40	545	5.00	400
3.50	521		

Speed........................   Comprehension........................

THE SUMMING UP

You have spent some time on reducing the bad habits of your old reading method, especially vocalization, but by now have established a direct path from the word to the brain without the sound barrier. You have increased your eye span and have moved your starting place. You have done well enough in the comprehension tests to prove to you that reading slowly and carefully is not the best method for adults. You know at what speeds you can read the different levels of material which you have met as you went through this book. You can vary your speed according to the difficulty of the material.

All this adds up to the fact that you have acquired a new reading habit which is greatly superior to the old in speed and at least as good for comprehension.

Where do you go from here?

This new technique has by now become almost automatic, but you must resist any tendency to go back to the old methods, especially Inner Speech. You can, if you wish, increase your speed still further if you make the effort.

Apply your new reading ability to all your reading, but don't try and read everything at the same high speed. Use your gears and as long as you read regularly you will never lose the ability to read quickly and accurately.

RE-TESTS

HERE are two long exercises to use as a check on your reading speed perhaps a month or two months after you have completed the rest.

Do not expect to be able to read them at your highest speed for you will find that they are in the middle range of difficulty, but do not be put off because they are long.

EXERCISE 42

Irish Impressions by D. W. Brogan

[START TIMING] You can come upon Dublin Castle quite suddenly, for it is not an acropolis like the castles of Edinburgh or Stirling, or even set off from the streets and byways of the city like the Castello Sforzesco in Milan. You go through an archway and there you are, inside the once hated walls of " The Castle." For Dublin Castle to-day is a specimen of a very rare thing, of a Bastille still existing, but in the hands of the people who stormed it. And there on the wall is a notice in Irish, a language never spoken in the past here except by servants and captive native princes like Red Hugh O'Donnell whose escape from Elizabeth's warding is as dramatic a story as the better known escape of the Duc de Beaufort from Vincennes. There, in the tricolour flag, in the chapel now Roman Catholic, in the Irish notice on the wall (duplicated in English as it has to be, for it deals with a serious matter, taxes) is the most visible proof, to the Irish in Ireland and to millions of Irish blood elsewhere, that a miracle has happened, that the prayer that

> Ireland long a province be
> A nation once again

Answers to Exercise 41—1 (*e*), 2 (*b*), 3 (*b*), 4 (*b*), 5 (*d*), 6 (*e*), 7 (*a*), 8 (*e*), 9 (*b*), 10 (*d*), 11 (*c*), 12 (*a*), 13 (*b*), 14 (*b*), 15 (*d*), 16 (*b*), 17 (*a*), 18 Sahara King.

has been heard and that Dublin, unlike Warsaw, its martyred sister, linked, it must be remembered in England, by European as well as Irish tradition, is the capital of an independent State. It is a more dramatic symbol than the rule of Mr. Nehru in New Delhi.

Everywhere in central Dublin there is this presence of history, embittering history. Here Lord Edward Fitzgerald was betrayed: there Wolfe Tone slew himself. Here the men of Easter Week were shot; there the victims of the Civil War. It is an atmosphere that London knows nothing of. But those little plaques have their equivalent in Paris. And as no knowledge of the rules of the French National Assembly will do you much good if you don't know why Paris streets bear names like " Rue Danielle Casanova," no careful assessment of the " realities " of the Irish situation will do you much good if you don't know why there is a Pearse Street or a Cahal Brugha Street in Dublin or why Pearse, son of an Englishman, taught his school, St. Edna's, in Irish, or why Charles Burgess called himself Cahal Brugha.

The Gaelic League

There is not merely a notice in Irish in Dublin Castle; there are notices in Irish everywhere. And if you believed your eyes only, you might think you were in a bilingual city like Montreal or Strasbourg or Brussels. You are not; you are in an English-speaking city where fewer people speak Gaelic than used to do so in the Glasgow of my childhood. But if it is a fiction that Irish is, in any real sense, the language or even a language of Dublin, it is a fiction with an impressive history behind it. For the attempt to " save Irish," begun nearly sixty years ago by the Gaelic League, forlorn hope as it was, was yet the beginning of modern Ireland. To a country exhausted by the great land war, dis-illusioned and disgraced by the Parnell split, on the verge of solving one problem, the domination of rural life by an alien aristocracy, the movement, whose greatest figure was the son of a Church of Ireland rector, gave to the Irish in Ireland a new aim and a new hope—the aim of preventing, as Douglas Hyde put it, " our ancient Irish nation " becoming " a West Britain." It was a refusal to accept as promotion admission to the world of Edward VII and H. G. Wells.

It is easy, it is tempting, it is necessary to debunk a great deal

of the nonsense written in Ireland about " the language." Indeed,
when people talk of " the Language," instead of " Irish " or
" Gaelic," they have taken off into the supersonic world of
rhetoric and emotion, as happens when people talk of " the
Movement " instead of the Labour party. But it was the zealots
defying progress, the progress that glowed so warmly in those
innocent Fabian days, who made modern Ireland. Because of
them the tricolour flies on Dublin Castle; there is the great
Shannon hydro-electric scheme; Professor Schrödinger is at the
Institute of Advanced Studies. They were fanatics; they believed
impossible dreams; they demanded much of themselves. " And
as we are shall Banba be." Some of their dreams came true and
a few years after Yeats wrote—

> Romantic Ireland's dead and gone,
> It's with O'Leary in the grave,

a handful of intellectuals rose in Easter Week and " a terrible
beauty was born."

Again, this has to be borne in mind. The labours of generations
of scholars, part of a general European movement, had restored
much of the old Irish learning. If the greatest of these scholars
was O'Grady, the names of others, Graves, Reeves, Petrie, suggest
the Gall more than the Gael, Newman, as Rector of the Catholic
University, had far more effective sympathy for these efforts than
had the Irish bishops of the school of Paul, Cardinal Cullen.
But the Gaelic League was another thing. It was no mere effort
of scholars; it was a " going to the people," paralleled elsewhere.
It matters little that Yeats knew little or no Irish; that Synge's
claims to represent the people have been contested; that Joyce
refused to bury himself in what he thought to be a backwater,
fed by too abundant springs of rhetoric. Modern Ireland was
made this way, not by speeches in Parliament, not by adjustments
to the European and still less to the English climate of opinion.
The Irish Republic was born in blood and faith. It is still scarred
by the forceps of its violent birth.

Trade and the Tongue

The English visitor, Broadbent, as Shaw called him, must, if
he is to make head or tail of what he sees and hears around him,
remember all this. He must remember that many, most things
that he thinks should be discussed in matter-of-fact terms, and

that, possibly, are being discussed in matter-of-fact terms, have
to be discussed also in terms of " the Language," of religion, of
culture. If the " fils de Camaret " prove as cunning as their
sisters and skim off the cream of the Irish lobster trade in the
West, it is especially ominous, for the West is the " Gaeltacht "
where people really speak Irish, not Dublin, where they say they
do. (Before embattled Gaels blow in on me I may say that I have
heard Irish spoken since birth and can tell when it is being
spoken.) If the Irish balance of trade is unsatisfactory the
remedies for it must be discussed in terms of language, culture,
and religion. Perhaps the balance could be righted, but possibly
at a cost intolerable to the " Irish-Irelander," that further
diminution of the number of people on the land, of that

> Bold peasantry a country's pride
> Which once destroyed can never be
> supplied.

And Ireland is a Catholic country, Dublin a Catholic city, and,
here, " Catholic " is not a vague, formal, easygoing acceptance
of the " Church as part of the furniture," as André Siegfried put
it of France. Dublin is Catholic in a way astonishing to one who
knows Glasgow or Boston, not to speak of Rome or Paris. You
may see as many priests and nuns about Bergamo, as many
churches and convents in Le Puy-en-Valey, see churches as well
filled in Mainz or Freiburg-im-Breisgau, be conscious of an
equally zealous and better organized Catholic life in Tilburg.
But none of these are like Dublin or Cork, for in all of these the
modern world is present, studied, resisted, compromised with.
Here it is denounced and ignored. The dance hall is cheek by
jowl with the church, the censored publicity for the films cheek
by jowl with " bondieuserie " that would startle the most backward shop in the Place Saint-Sulpice, with new churches of an
innocent ugliness that beats the worst Baptist horrors of the
Deep South. No matter. Here bishops don't argue: they tell
you. Here nationality and religion are one, one feeding or, possibly,
parasitic on the other. Here is a new Jerusalem besieged by the
modern Titus, the modern world, and officially confident that
God will know and save His own.

I learn from banner stories on the front pages of the two chief
Sunday papers published here that the citizens of Rome were

entertained by a fight between two rival Irish cycling teams. The
losers blamed both the British and the Italians. They, and they
alone, truly represented the United Cyclists of a divided Ireland.
This childish exhibition is a model exhibit of much that goes on
in contemporary Ireland. There is the search for scapegoats like
the British (what has happened to the good old word, English or
even Saxon?). There is the insult to the Italian hosts who, with
their own troubles, are called on to adjudicate between the
National Cycling Association and the Cumann Rothdidheachta
na hEireann. (To add to the troubles of the Italians, it is the
National Cycling Association who claim to be the true undivided
Gaels; Philip Clarke, M.P., is a member.) There is the effective
spanner thrown in the works of collaboration between North and
South, for the C.R.E. shared the Irish team with the North.
And what the cyclists have done on a small, squalid, and comic
scale more serious fighters for Irish unity have done on a greater.

In Ireland, as in other countries, there is a great difference
between public and private speech. If you believed all you read
in the papers, partition leads all other Irish problems in importance.
A priest, speaking on rural depopulation, obviously feels he is
being bold when he puts that problem ahead of partition " and
the language." Irish delegates to international conferences feel
they have not contributed anything till they have denounced
partition and its British creators. Open admission of the fact
that nobody over fifty is likely to see the end of partition is
impossible.

Behind the Tariff

But in private conversation one finds no such preoccupation
with partition, no belief that it is coming to an end, no sign that
there is any lively desire to end it. It is asserted, for example,
that the Protestants in the Republic want to end it. No one
seems to know. I have heard it asserted that the chief advantage
of a union with the North would be that Belfast business men
would descend on Dublin and drive out the Cork men. " Belfast
men have some heart. Cork men have none." Others speculate
on what would happen to various flourishing but highly protected
businesses in the Dublin area in a united Ireland. But these
speculations, like day-dreaming about what would make Bishop
So-and-so keep his mouth shut, have nothing to do with the

day-to-day life of the Republic. A generation has grown up that has never known an Ireland as united as it was under British rule, that can hardly conceive an Ireland with no border, with no smuggling. And no one can conceive what a united Ireland would be like, with a large Protestant working class, with a great international industry like shipbuilding, with a rich, confident minority resisting the creation of an Irish-speaking, Catholic-controlled, peasant State, " the world forgetting by the world forgot."

But this must not be said. So we have the odd spectacle of the complete absence of comment in the chief Dublin daily newspapers on the raid on Arborfield Camp. A weekly like the " Standard " may ask, " Are we at war with England? " and answer " No." But no daily comments on the activities of the Irish Republican Army. None of them express an opinion on the activities that sent Philip Clarke, M.P., to gaol. This is one of the many things that cannot be talked about openly. There are general warnings against violence, but no one dare mention the essential truth, that the obstacle to Irish unity is not the British Government or the British Army but the majority of the people of the Six Counties. It may be that not many people in the Republic know anything of the North. The few who do and say anything relevant, like Mr. Ernest Blythe, are sharply reminded of what they said in 1919 or did in 1925. That most things done in the Free State and in the Republic have made unity less palatable than ever before, simple truth as it is, is ignored. Instead, the British Army is blamed and the world is called to weep for the wrongs of Ireland, a world that has so many more serious things to worry about. These truths, we may suspect, are not concealed from Mr. Costello or Mr. de Valera or the Irish bishops or the editors of the Dublin papers. But there can be few countries where " toute vérité n'est pas bonne à dire " is more firmly believed in than Ireland.

The consequences are not, except in one way, very serious. Because some simple if disagreeable truths are not said, some well-meaning and brave young men are in gaol, further grounds of bitterness are created in Ulster, and collaboration, north and south, is made unnecessarily difficult, as Lord Brookeborough has sensibly pointed out. Ireland is a small island; some though not all of its problems are common: some though not nearly all of its sentiments are common. But " Ireland " is not a united nation. In the modern sense, there never has been a united Irish state, and in that sense " Ireland " is something to be made, not something that exists, but is hidden by a British smoke-screen.

The Fighters

The victims are often young men born into the extreme Nationalist tradition like Philip Clarke, M.P. There is nothing in a recently-published pamphlet to suggest that he has any serious (as apart from impassioned) thought about the present and future of Ireland. Since he has never been told differently, he can believe, naïvely, that only British bayonets maintain the authority of the Government of Northern Ireland and that all will be well when " the pikes will be in order at the rising of the moon." And fighting for Mr. Clarke is a powerful tradition— that of the fearless, representative minority who, by force of arms in every generation, have made Ireland's claim.

Easter Week was made by a minority. True that rebellion's leaders were in education and knowledge of the world, and in the situation of Ireland and England, very different from the leaders, whoever they may be, of the I.R.A. to-day. But how do you explain that to a young man of twenty-one in a country where truth about partition is so seldom spoken? There is, of course, less than no use in merely deprecating violence. Everybody in Ireland, north and south, knows that violence is the way to get the ear of England, in Ireland, Cyprus, Canada, or wherever else you like. But the truth that is concealed from Philip Clarke is that violence, if he is to succeed, will have to be used not against the English garrison but against Irishmen in Ulster. From that no unity can come.

Instead of serious study of modern Ulster (even the wide reading of the excellent B.B.C. pamphlet would help) there is an endless comedy of illusion. It may not be accidental that the organ of the highbrows, the " Leader," prints an able article defending the (alleged) refusal of the people of Goa to be united with Mother India in the same number as an article (in Irish) on Governor Harriman and partition. But the nationalist dailies, above all Mr. de Valera's organ, the " Irish Press," steadily befuddle the public mind. No visiting Congressman, anxious to please Irish-American voters or simply his hosts, can talk some vaguely promising nonsense about partition but he is given full publicity in the papers. The " Aurore," of all Paris papers, is quoted on the wrongs of Ireland—presumably because the editor of the " Irish Press " does not know that the " Aurore " is the perfect embodiment, in the French imperial context, of the Orange spirit. " Croppies lie down " might be its motto if for " Croppies " you read " Arabs."

The wrongs of Ireland (or the crimes of England, as Chesterton put it) were real enough. But the great surviving wrong done Ireland is the provision of a grievance to conceal real problems. The Irish Republic has plenty of them; the dwindling of the rural population, the balance of payments, the low birth rate, mass emigration, the stagnation of the economy, the state of the " Gaeltacht." But it is only too easy to ride off from them on the horse of partition, or to see the hand of England everywhere. If there is a campaign to end the export of horses for slaughter England is behind it, and what about Mau Mau? If the question of alleged excessive corporal punishment in the schools is debated, who is attacking the sacrosanct system of Irish education? The foreign enemy who forced teachers to beat the Irish language out of the children. (The current complaint is largely of the excess of zeal shown in beating the Irish language into them.) Some of those who most use the words Sinn Fein seem to have forgotten what they meant, an Irish version of Italia farò da se. Ireland will be united when an overwhelming majority of the Irish people want it, and that will only be when the Irish Republic has created so attractive a society that its young men (and still more its young women) want to stay there. Rhetoric about partition merely diverts attention from that task. [STOP TIMING]

Put your reading time here.......................

1. Dublin castle is now—
   (a) A symbol of oppression.
   (b) A quaint ruin.
   (c) An acropolis like Edinburgh.
   (d) A symbol of freedom.
   (e) Of no particular importance.
2. In Central Dublin—
   (a) People have forgotten the sad happenings of the past.
   (b) The past is always in mind.

(c) There has been a good deal of re-building.

(d) The atmosphere is rather like that of London.

(e) History is kept alive by street names and plaques.

3. In Dublin—

(a) Almost everybody is bilingual.

(b) About two-thirds of the people are bilingual.

(c) About half the people are bilingual.

(d) About a third of the people are bilingual.

(e) Hardly anybody is bilingual.

4. The Irish language was revived—

(a) Due to the rise of nationalism.

(b) Because English was not well known.

(c) Because it was falling into disuse.

(d) Because it was used in Glasgow.

(e) Due to the influence of English scholars.

5. Modern Ireland came into being because—

(a) The majority of the people wanted it.

(b) The English gave them self-government.

(c) Of the efforts of a small group of fanatics.

(d) Of the force of economic circumstances.

(e) Of the success of the Easter Rising.

6. The English visitor must remember—

(a) That Irish questions are settled on the facts.

(b) That the Irish are clear and constructive thinkers.

(c) That all Irish discussions are surcharged with emotion.

(d) That the Irish have few problems.

(e) That the Irish are incapable of clear thought.

7. In Ireland, the Church—

(a) Is less powerful than it is in England.

(b) Is more powerful than it is in Spain.

(c) Is less powerful than it is in France.

(d) Is not an integral part of the life of the people.

(e) Is an integral part of the life of the people.

8. A good example of Irish behaviour abroad was ....
....

9. Public speech in Ireland is entirely preoccupied with the
question of ....

10. Discussion of this question in private speech is—

(a) Full of the idea that it will soon end.

(b) Ill-informed and largely speculative.

(c) Rare and infrequent.
(d) Usually well informed and unemotional.
(e) Full of a strong desire to end it.

11. The real obstacle to Irish unity is—
    (a) The majority of the people of Ulster.
    (b) The presence of British troops in Ulster.
    (c) The disinterest of the Irish.
    (d) The religious question.
    (e) The Irish historical heritage.

12. The Irish refusal to face the facts—
    (a) Has no serious consequences.
    (b) Has caused trouble in England.
    (c) Has caused trouble with the United States.
    (d) Has caused a great deal of bitterness.
    (e) Is beginning to break down.

13. The young extreme Nationalists—
    (a) Have been convinced by rational argument.
    (b) Are the victims of a conspiracy of silence.
    (c) Have studied both sides of the question.
    (d) Are intelligent and well-informed.
    (e) Are inspired by the communists.

14. Irish newspapers—
    (a) Give a biased and irrational picture.
    (b) Are on the side of moderation.
    (c) Give an unbiased and impartial picture.
    (d) Give equal weight to all points of view.
    (e) Have had no influence on the people.

15. When will Ireland be re-united ?..

16. What is the effect of the Irish blaming all their ills on the
    English?..

This passage has 3,000 words and you can work out your speed
from the table at the end of the next exercise.

The correct answers to questions 1 to 14 are at the foot of page
240; the other two you must check yourself.

Speed........................   Comprehension........................

EXERCISE 43

Nepal Becomes Modern by Taya Zinkin

[START TIMING]   Nepal is Walt Disney Land.   Orchids orgy,

rhododendrons bleed regal red, blue pheasants flash along the steep slopes below the world's highest mountains. Amidst the jigsaw of the rice terraces of the valleys live men, barely five feet tall, perched like goats at dizzy heights; men whose women carry their infants like baby kangaroos, whose houses look like Neapolitan ice-cream (chocolate thatches, vanilla walls, strawberry foundations). There the Seven Dwarfs, two hundred of them, haul heavy steam-rollers over 8,000 ft passes to the pulse of a song. Unless they go by air there is no other way in. Wheels in Nepal are still religious—the prayer wheel and the Wheel of Life. The people of this fairy land, with its perpetual fragrance of wild narcissus and cultivated garlic, are sturdy, cheerful, and industrious, as only the cultivators of terraced rice can be. Long protected from progress by their high mountain walls, they have laughter and hard work as their daily bread. Their reactions are still as spontaneous as they are unpredictable. Only the day before a villager had decided to see whether he could run faster than the giant bird on wheels—my aeroplane—and the pilot saved his life by a touch of the joystick.

Landlocked

That Nepal can still be like this in a tarmacadam world because it is " land-locked " by its mountains is a bromide; but to believe with the more romantic ex-Gurka officers that it could remain insulated for ever is wishful thinking. Nepal is insulated neither from India nor China. Trade with China flourishes in the highlands. The Terai, where most of the population lives, is demographically and geographically part of the Indo-Gangetic plain. The handful of literates in the Valley of Kathmandu, who constitute Nepal's fermenting classes, read the Indian papers and listen to All-India Radio. Anyone who wants an education beyond matriculation must go to India. Nepal is tied to India by a live umbilical cord. Its political exiles lived peacefully in India, even under the British: nobody could tell them apart from the local politicians; they speak Hindi, they are Hindus. But Nepal is the India of a far older day than even the India of the

---

Answers to Exercise 42—1 (*d*), 2 (*e*), 3 (*e*), 4 (*a*), 5 (*c*), 6 (*c*), 7 (*e*), 8 The cycle teams, 9 Partition, 10 (*c*), 11 (*a*), 12 (*d*), 13 (*b*), 14 (*a*).

Princes. In Nepal royalty has a force no longer known elsewhere. Kings were once probably everywhere the incarnation of the gods; but only in Nepal it is still so. The King is God in the flesh, and his subjects will trek for days and weeks to get a glimpse of him from a balcony.

This Nepal has now had four full years of " democratic " government, with a constitutional monarch, a Cabinet, and a Supreme Court. It is not surprising that it does not quite work. Had Mr. Nehru been the only educated man in India, had India had no administration, army, politicians, or industries, even Mr. Nehru might have found it difficult to create a modern state. Mr. Koirala has found it impossible. Nepal before 1950 was a vacuum: economic, social, administrative. Since 1950, therefore, there has been political progress, but otherwise Nepal has on the whole gone backward from medievalism to chaos.

Before 1950 Nepal was governed by a ruthless autocracy, but the people knew where they were. Men were shot without trial merely for listening to speeches of Mahatma Gandhi; but they could be sure, at least, that the execution squad had loaded its rifles. To-day when people stay at home after dark in Kathmandu itself, for fear of robbers, the knowledge that the robbers may be tried—if caught—is small consolation.

Before 1950 the King, Vishnu incarnate, Colonel Tribhuvan Bir Bikram Shah Dev Sri Sri Sri Sri Sri Maharajadhiraja, known to his subjects as Sri Panch for short (Panch means five), and his son the Crown Prince, only 13 years his junior, were prisoners in their palace. The kings had been prisoners since 1846, when a rebel general made himself hereditary Prime Minister, with the title of Maharajah for himself and that of General for all his male descendants (legitimate or not); that is why there are so many generals in Nepal. Every office, from Ambassador to Bara Hakim (chief of a district), was held by a general, for every office was kept within the family. The King himself might have been dispensed with altogether had not his generals feared the people's religious devotion to the incarnation of Vishnu.

The Prime Minister's family were known as Ranas; their rule was of arbitrary iron. " Everything is forbidden until it has been permitted," explained the pleasant Law Secretary. The Rana Prime Minister ran government the old way, for his own benefit, not the people's welfare. Everything in Nepal was his property;

and each Prime Minister retired in turn when he had made £30 millions. The last Rana Prime Minister is said to have left after the revolution with three plane-loads of jewels. The money was not even invested in Nepal. There is Rana money in every Indian industry, every major Indian residential quarter, but in Nepal there are only a few mission schools, and the literacy rate, at under 3 per cent, is as low as anywhere in the world; and for communications this country as large as England and Wales has two roads, one ropeway, and thirty miles of railway. The Rana error was that they carried this principle into the army also. Nepal has the world's best infantrymen, the Gurkhas; but they were all exported. Nepal's own army had neither uniforms, nor pay, nor training, and the only policemen were posted at palace gates, dressed like French soldiers of the 1870s, in red-brimmed caps and blue trousers, regulating pedestrian traffic. Many of the revolutionaries were Calcutta gatekeepers and such; their only arms were rifles. They won because there was no resistance. The Ranas had neither loyalty nor force on which to rely.

Unrestrained

The Ranas' interests were French wines, Scotch whisky, women from anywhere, and the shooting of rhinoceros, elephant, and tiger in the Terai. Emissaries roamed the countryside buying up pretty little girls to be reared for Rana harems. Sex is indeed as much part of Nepal's life as snow. Religion is still tantrist, temples often pornographic, the people sometimes polyandrous, sometimes polygamous, sometimes both. Sex is not hushed up, Victorian fashion, as in India; it is clarioned from the rooftops. One of the princes goes out with his wife, her lover, and his Swiss " concubine," introduced as such. The Defence Minister's son keeps a corps de ballet of thirty girls. In Nepal, illegitimacy itself has been made almost legitimate. Ranas were classified into A, B or C classes according to whether their mother was the first, minor, or fancy wife of the Prime Minister. Only an A class Rana can become Prime Minister; but since all Ranas are born generals, the B and C class could always go into the army, the police, or the districts.

The most powerful Rana left is General Mahavir, once the financier of the revolution. His sophistication gives him a hold on the King, who had been so closely immured before 1950 that his first words, on reaching Delhi (when he fled), before even greeting Mr. Nehru, were " I want to go to a cinema." General Mahavir has done the King proud: there are now thirteen cinemas in Kathmandu, one for every ten thousand people, and he has even brought a night club to Kathmandu, a very private night club; Vishnu cannot be seen dancing rumbas.

The Nepalese Revolution happened in 1950-1. This was no accident. India became independent in 1947, and the Princes merged with India or Pakistan when paramountcy lapsed. The Chinese Revolution was followed by the " Liberation " of Tibet. Times were changing fast. The filling of the vacuum left by the British had begun: the race for spheres of influence had started. And in this filling of vacuums the Ranas had become a dangerous anachronism.

The democratic revolution of Nepal was financed from Calcutta by General Mahavir, who resented the fact that his C class origin debarred him from the fruits of higher office. He armed the Nepalese Congress, which was largely manned by gatekeepers and riff-raffs from Calcutta and was led by a handful of middle-class Nepalese who had played at politics in India during the 1942 Congress movement; one of them, Mr. B. P. Koirala, had even gone to gaol. General Mahavir secured an unofficial assurance of Indian support from the late Mr. Kidwai and, realizing the King's special position with his subjects, ensured his co-operation by helping him to flee to India. After some desultory fighting the Rana Prime Minister left for a comfortable retirement in Bangalore. The change-over was relatively smooth. The King was officially recognized both by Britain and by India as the Head of Nepal, and he set up a coalition of old-regime Ranas and Opposition politicians—a Cabinet with French stability. Behind the scenes the Indian Ambassador played a part so important that he roused all the suspicions of a people traditionally xenophobe, proud of their independence, and contemptuous of low-landers. Much of what he did was necessary; but he did not improve Indo-Nepalese relations. His successor suffered from the opposite defect—he was honest but too withdrawn, and he allowed Cabinet to tumble after Cabinet as the Koirala brothers entered into an almost fratricidal feud for power. (There are five Koirala brothers; fortunately only two thirst for power; the rest are content with minor offices or contracts). First Mr. B. P.

Koirala was in power, then his brother, " M. P.," then again
" B. P.," then " M. P.," and now both are out. Only now has
India in Mr. Bhagwan Sahay an Ambassador able to strike the
balance between too much and too little interference. Mr. Sahay
has both administrative experience—he was the Chief Secretary
of India's largest state, Uttar Pradesh—and diplomatic tact. He
handled the Princes and the zemindars to perfection at the time
of their merger into the United Provinces.

Nepal is too vital for India's defences—indeed, infinitely more
vital than ten Tibets—for India to permit Nepal to go under.
But the Nepalese resent all foreign interference, even Indian, so
much that even the Defence Minister (still to-day a Rana A class)
complained bitterly to me against the Indian guarantee to Nepal;
and that although China's 1954 maps include Nepal as part of
China. His complaint had echoes of Mr. Nehru on the South-
East Asia Treaty. " Who is the Prime Minister of India (he
asked) to talk about our borders without asking us first if we
want to be protected? We have had for centuries excellent
relations with China; we do not want to become involved." He
explained at length the benefits his country hopes to derive from
opening diplomatic relations with China—" through our Delhi
Embassy, of course, for we do not want more nosepoking by
outsiders, particularly by the Communists."

It is the newly emerged politicians who have been so much
helped by India who appreciate the protection India's guarantee
affords Nepal; and they are split into sixty-nine factions calling
themselves parties. " We left the Nepali Congress because we
believe in centralized democracy," one dissident leader explained,
and when I asked him to tell me what the Nepali Congress
believes in he answered firmly, " I do not know, but *we* believe
in centralized democracy." The truth is simple: only one man
can be Prime Minister at a time. " I am the only honest politician
in Nepal," one Minister said. Oddly enough all his colleagues
made the same claim but for themselves.

Lawlessness

" You have kept the Prime Minister waiting," said his personal
assistant. I had called on the Prime Minister at ten past four,
on the off-chance that he might be in. Apparently I had been
invited for tea at four; since the invitation never reached me my

turning up so near the appointed time was mere chance. Mr.
M. P. Koirala (who was still in office then) had changed since our
last meeting three years before. Features I remembered hollow
now sported the fleeting suspicion of a double chin. His hand
flashed a ruby over excellent cakes: "Lawlessness, spiralling
inflation, corruption, nepotism, lack of administration, communism, those are my problems and my colleagues sabotage my
efforts." He was right. The Nepalese rupee has lost half its
value; the Budget is in severe deficit; the tranquil valley of
Kathmandu has become the hunting ground of armed robbers.

There had been an important theft of gold coins and rhinoceros
horns (a potent aphrodisiac worth £4 an ounce) at the museum.
When I visited the museum, its reinforced police guard looked
so peculiar that I had refused to leave my camera with them at
the gate—although it was already too dark to take photographs.
I told Mr. Koirala that I would not be surprised if he discovered
that the police had done it. "How did you know?" My host
looked puzzled; he had just received a confidential report saying
the booty had been recovered from a police-sergeant. The Nepal
police is manned by the Calcutta riff-raffs of the revolution; they
were given the job, without pay, and even the police must live.
Yet the Prime Minister thought the whole thing was a plant by
his Cabinet colleagues in another of their efforts to discredit his
regime.

Nepalese courts are like the Nepalese police. Of the five judges
in Kathmandu two are matriculates; three only literates.
However, the law is administered with a maximum efficiency that
guarantees a minimum of 100 per cent arrests; indeed the
percentage often exceeds this creditable norm. On reporting a
theft the complainant is gaoled pending investigations which may
take anything beyond ten years. If the stolen property is recovered
from the accused he goes to gaol, but if the booty is not found
the complainant remains in gaol, and under no circumstance
does the police investigate. If, by pulling strings, the judgment
is reversed, then it is the judge who goes to gaol.

The Administration was selected not on merits but on favours;
it is as inefficient as it is underpaid. A secretary to Government,
with powers far wider than those of a Permanent Under-Secretary
of State (since he is the law and there are no questions in Parliament), gets £5 per week. Office hours are officially from ten to

three; in reality they are from twelve to three with a break for lunch, and as a seasoned business man explained, " What can you expect? If the man is honest he has to work on the side to make both ends meet; or else you have to pay him to make it worth his while to attend office."

Hopes too high

" The danger is not from Tibet but from India," Mr. Koirala said. His son had, together with the son of the Minister for Foreign Affairs, just been arrested for fellow-travelling pranks. He continued—" Every day the younger generation reads in the Indian press of the great achievements in China and in India; naturally they expect the same progress here. But nobody understands that for progress one must have a stable Government and a sound Administration: we have no Administration, and during the past four years my colleagues have all conspired against me in their selfish thirst for power. If democracy does not deliver the goods Nepal will go Communist; already there are many Communists in the Terai, and in the valley itself there are young school-going asses like my son who play at politics. We need help and sympathy and as much money for constructive work as we can get from our friends abroad."

Mr. Koirala was quite right in saying that the danger of Communism comes from India rather than from Tibet; in spite of the fact that the Boutia traders sell their goods for 50 per cent more to Tibet now that it has gone Communist. But the same xenophobia which makes invasion from India impossible protects Nepal from Tibetan or Chinese infiltrations, and the middle-classes who might be converted speak Hindi and English, not Chinese or Tibetan. But, if Nepal were to go Communist in frustration, then Dr. K. I. Singh—Nepal's ablest and most respected politician, now being trained in Peking together with a core of followers—might make a spectacular come-back and his trained cadres would be most useful.

But the danger is not immediate and time is not being altogether wasted; something is being done to create stability in Nepal. The Indian Government sent a working military mission to train Nepal's six thousand soldiers and in the last two years it has performed wonders by insisting on barracks, uniform, drill and pay: all previously unknown. The Indian Government is, moreover, spending some £6 millions on aid to Nepal. An all-weather airport is being built in Kathmandu, and a road fit for three-tonners between Kathmandu and the railhead in the plains. Scholarships are being lavished on Nepalese Government servants who go to train in the Indian Police Training College, in the Indian Administrative College, and in Indian universities. An advisory mission is trying to help the Government to organize itself. The part of adviser is, however, both thorny and wasteful. After two years of being advised to use files, the Secretariat still glues sheet after sheet into rolls.

America is helping too. The United States mission is spending $800,000, and about half that has to be added by the Nepal Government for the running of six community projects. The main difficulty in getting on with the work in Nepal is twofold: there is no real budgeting in Nepal and there is a dire lack of trainable people. Had there been more trainable talent available much more could have been achieved, for the villagers' response and willingness to improve their lot is remarkable; it is greater than in most of India.

The United Nations is also playing its part. W.H.O. has been carrying out a large-scale D.D.T. spraying against the malignant tertiary malaria, and it is providing training for nurses in Kathmandu. Experts are helping to set up dairy centres with hybrids between buffaloes and cows, and have set up a small pasteurization plant for the capital's milk supply. In fact, everybody is helping. The Ford Foundation has a cottage industry adviser; under the Colombo Plan a small hydro-electric scheme is being built to relieve Kathmandu's light that fails—with a predictability quite un-Nepalese. Some students are being trained in England. All these tit-bits add up. And from experience gained from them it appears that the best way to assist in Nepal's democratic birth-pangs is to concentrate as much as possible on those schemes which do not tax central administration for efficiency or finance, on working rather than on advisory missions, and on tact.

Hope lies in the closest of co-operation between the Crown Prince and the Government of India. The Crown Prince, whose vices are believed to be few and qualities many, has just been appointed Regent for his father. The Crown Prince has the same hold on the religious loyalty of his people as his divine father, and he has, if his first action on assuming responsibility is representative, much common sense. He announced that a political leader will be recognized as such only if he can show a list of twenty-five party members. In spite of their tall claims of support running into hundreds of thousands, the leaders are now canvassing their domestic servants for support. The next step for the Crown Prince to take would be to announce that there will be a transition period during which he will rule with a few advisers and then hold elections. The advisers ought to be lent by India at his request, and two would be adequate. Obviously, by letting Nepal remain medieval, the British left their job in the subcontinent incomplete. Now is the time for India to make up. The Crown Prince is new, little is needed beyond land reforms, a proper taxation system, some education. The people's habit of unquestioned obedience makes the task easy; but if India fails to strike the iron while it is hot Nepal will soon fall ripe from chaos into Communism. [STOP TIMING]

Put your reading time here........................

1. The people of Nepal are—
   (a) Small but hardy.
   (b) Tall and strong.
   (c) Tall and thin.
   (d) About the same size as English people.
   (e) Similar to the Indians.
2. Nepal is somewhat isolated because—
   (a) It is surrounded by dense jungle.
   (b) Deep rivers and torrents make communications difficult.
   (c) It is surrounded by high mountains.
   (d) It is a poor and backward country.
   (e) Foreigners are not allowed in.
3. The main crop in Nepal is—
   (a) Rice grown in the lowlands.
   (b) Cotton grown on the highlands.
   (c) Coffee grown on terraces.
   (d) Rice grown on terraces.
   (e) Cultivated garlic.
4. Nepal is linked with India because—
   (a) It is easy to reach India.
   (b) They used to be under the same government.

(*c*) India has helped Nepal with loans.

(*d*) All educated men have been taught in India.

(*e*) Of the former link with the British.

5. Nepal now has—

(*a*) A feudal type of government.

(*b*) A dictatorship.

(*c*) Minority rule by left wing groups.

(*d*) A constitutional monarchy which does not work.

(*e*) A socialist welfare state.

6. Before 1950 Nepal was ruled by—

(*a*) A ruthless autocracy.

(*b*) A despotic king.

(*c*) A Communist clique.

(*d*) The Congress party.

(*e*) Mr. Nehru.

7. The Rana Prime Ministers—

(*a*) Were kind hearted and just to the people.

(*b*) Were keenly interested in welfare.

(*c*) Were only concerned with amassing a fortune.

(*d*) Were disinterested and far-seeing.

(*e*) Were only interested in good relations with India.

8. The educational system of Nepal is—

(*a*) Adequate and comprehensive.

(*b*) Satisfactory as far as it goes.

(*c*) As good as that of India.

(*d*) Quite unsatisfactory.

(*e*) Fairly good.

9. The Ranas were easily overthrown because—

(*a*) Everybody hated them.

(*b*) The revolutionaries were powerful and well armed.

(*c*) Gurkha troops supported the revolution.

(*d*) The revolutionaries were helped by Indian troops.

(*e*) They had neglected the army.

10. The man who financed the revolution was—

(*a*) A rich Calcutta landowner.

(*b*) A former Prime Minister.

(*c*) A rich Rana.

(*d*) An emissary of a foreign power.

(*e*) A member of the Indian Congress.

11.   After the revolution, the King—
  (*a*) Went into retirement at Bangalore.
  (*b*) Came out of retirement at Kathmandu.
  (*c*) Took no further part in politics.
  (*d*) Has not been allowed out of the country.
  (*e*) Has become a prisoner in his own palace.
12.   India is interested in Nepal because—
  (*a*) There are many Nepalese in the Indian Army.
  (*b*) Pandit Nehru is interested in all small countries.
  (*c*) Of the long association under the British.
  (*d*) It is a buffer state between India and China.
  (*e*) Some of its leaders were former members of the Congress
      party.
13.   Since the revolution—
  (*a*) Nepal has settled down into a law-abiding state.
  (*b*) The value of the Nepalese rupee has doubled.
  (*c*) People in Nepal are wholeheartedly behind the govern-
      ment.
  (*d*) Nepal has never been in a better financial position.
  (*e*) Lawlessness and inflation have become menaces.
14.   The police and magistrates are—
  (*a*) Efficient and well trained.
  (*b*) Inefficient but well paid.
  (*c*) Well trained but badly paid.
  (*d*) Ill trained, inefficient and poorly paid.
  (*e*) Well trained, reasonably paid and reasonably efficient.
15.   The officials of the Nepal Government are—
  (*a*) Honest and incorruptible.
  (*b*) Fair and just.
  (*c*) Occasionally open to bribery.
  (*d*) Forced to accept bribes to live.
  (*e*) Caught up in a mass of red tape.
16.   The danger of Communism in Nepal—
  (*a*) Is mainly from Tibet which is Communist controlled.
  (*b*) Is mainly from the Communists of Nepal.
  (*c*) Is mainly from the Communists of India.
  (*d*) Is mainly from envoys from Moscow.
  (*e*) Is very slight and can be disregarded.
17.   The Government of India—
  (*a*) Is not helping Nepal with its problems.

(b) Has established an Indian base in Kathmandu.

(c) Is helping Nepal in many ways.

(d) Wishes to take over Nepal.

(e) Is interfering in the internal affairs of Nepal.

18. The United Nations—

(a) Has sent frontier observers to Nepal.

(b) Is trying to wipe out malaria in Nepal.

(c) Has built a new airport at Kathmandu.

(d) Has helped to re-organize the Nepalese army.

(e) Is building new roads for the Nepalese.

19. The Colombo Plan is assisting—

(a) Rice cultivation.

(b) The construction of schools.

(c) The training of teachers.

(d) Cottage industries.

(e) Hydro-electric development.

20. The main hope for Nepal's future is—

(a) The interest of the King in his people.

(b) The co-operation between the Prime Minister and India.

(c) The co-operation between the King and India.

(d) The co-operation between the Crown Prince and India.

(e) The maintenance of world peace.

The correct answers are on the next page.

This passage has 3,000 words and you can find your speed from the table below.

Time	Speed	Time	Speed
5.00	600	7.00	428
5.10	582	7.10	419
5.20	562	7.20	409
5.30	545	7.30	400
5.40	529	7.40	391
5.50	514	7.50	382
6.00	500	8.00	375
6.10	486	8.10	367
6.20	473	8.20	360
6.30	461	8.30	352
6.40	450	8.40	346
6.50	439	8.50	339
7.00	428	9.00	333

Speed........................   Comprehension........................

Answers to Exercise 43—1 (*a*), 2 (*c*), 3 (*d*), 4 (*d*), 5 (*d*), 6 (*a*), 7 (*c*), 8 (*d*), 9 (*e*), 10 (*c*), 11 (*b*), 12 (*d*), 13 (*e*), 14 (*d*), 15 (*d*), 16 (*c*), 17 (*c*), 18 (*b*), 19 (*e*), 20 (*d*).